Due

*American
Copper & Brass*

American
Copper & Brass

Henry J. Kauffman

Bonanza Books
New York

Copyright © MCMLXVIII by Henry J. Kauffman
All rights reserved.
This edition is published by Bonanza Books,
a division of Crown Publishers, Inc.,
by arrangement with Henry J. Kauffman.
a   b   c   d   e   f   g   h
BONANZA 1979 EDITION
Manufactured in the United States of America
Design by Harold Leach

Library of Congress Cataloging in Publication Data
Kauffman, Henry J   1908-
    American copper & brass.

    Reprint of the 1968 ed. published T. Nelson, Camden, N.J.
    Bibliography: p. 282
    Includes index.
    1. Copperwork—United States.   2. Coppersmiths—United States—Registers.   3. Brasswork—
United States.   4. Brass founders—United States—Registers.   I. Title.
[NK8112.K38 1979]   338.4'7'6733   79-20033
ISBN 0-517-30350-7

Contents

Acknowledgments

Everyone knows that researching and writing are lonely tasks. Authors can spend months without receiving encouragement, and often they doubt the value of their final product. But fortunately, there are pleasant moments too, particularly when friends and organizations contribute data and supply attractive illustrations.

Throughout the preparation of this book many such contributions have been made. For very substantial help, I would like especially to thank Mr. Herbert Anstatt, Mr. Charles Hummel, Mr. Frank Horton, Mr. Thompson Harlow, Dr. Henry Young, and the Henry Francis Dupont Winterthur Museum, The Historical Society of York County (Pennsylvania), and the Maryland Historical Society.

To all these kind and learned friends I am deeply indebted for what is good in this volume. Errors, found by perceptive and attentive readers, are mine and will be gratefully acknowledged and corrected.

Others who have helped in many ways are: Mr. William Ball; Miss Frances Backarck; Miss Dorothy Barck; Mr. Edwin Battison; Mr. Don Berkbile; Mr. Charles S. V. Borst; Mr. William Bowers; Mr. Eric deJong; Mr. John J. Evans, Jr.; Dr. Reginald French; Mr. Craddock Goins; Mr. John Graham, III; Mr. Donald Hutslar; Mr. Joe Kindig, Jr.; Mr. Benjamin Landis; Mrs. John Lockerman; Mrs. Margaret Mills; Mrs. Frank Mish, Jr.; Mrs. C. Brooks Reigle; Mr. John Rouse; American Philosophical Society; Chester County (Pa.) Historical Society; Colonial Williamsburg; Essex Institute; Historical Society of Pennsylvania; Lancaster County Historical Society; Library of Congress; Maryland Historical Society; Metropolitan Museum of Art; Old Salem, Inc.; Old Sturbridge Village; Smithsonian Institution; and William Penn Memorial Museum.

Preface

There was a time when casual buyers and collectors of Americana were chiefly concerned with the size of an object, of what substance it was made, and its value. The fact that most of such antiques offered for sale were local pieces made in America created little need for distinguishing the foreign from the native. Curators were more critical than individual collectors in selecting objects to be exhibited in museums, but the exacting identification desired today was not very important fifty years ago.

The tremendous number of copper and brass objects now being imported focuses attention on the importance of determining where they were made. The matter of identification is important in all areas; it is particularly important in metals, for unlike many other substances, the color and quality of metals are essentially the same throughout the world.

This desire for identification creates the need for a deeper and more thorough understanding of many facets which were thought unimportant years ago. The desire for it has led to the publishing of lists of craftsmen, both in Europe and America, and to a more critical appraisal of forms and styles of such objects as warming pans, saucepans, bells, and cannon.

This survey with its listing of makers' names is designed to help the reader to make reasonably positive identification or attribution of objects in his possession or of some he expects to buy, to enrich his knowledge of the way the objects were made and used, and to lead him to a fuller understanding of American copper and brassware.

*American
Copper & Brass*

I. The Metals, Copper and Brass

THIS survey of objects made of copper and brass, and the men who made them, is logically prefaced with information about the source of the raw material used in their fabrication and an examination of the mines and various mechanical devices used in the making of sheet copper and brass. There are no brass mines, for brass is an alloy of copper and zinc and is not mined, but manufactured.

As we are accustomed to surpluses, information about the processing of copper ore into sheets may appear of slight importance to the modern craftsman and consumer, but the fact that virtually every craftsman of the eighteenth century bought old copper and brass or took scrap metal in part payment for his products indicates that these metals were in short supply at that time. This method of payment was not only an example of payment by barter, common at that time, but was also a means by which the craftsman could acquire a supply of the commodity with which he worked. The extensive repairing of old objects was another common practice, for it was then more economical to repair than to discard and build anew.

This scarcity of sheet copper and brass did not arise entirely from a short supply of these items in England. Considerable quantities of these metals were available there and on the Continent; however, the mercantile policy of England before the Revolution regulated the flow of such items to America. It was the intent of the English to procure raw materials from the colonists, then sell them manufactured objects. Thus, the English looked with favor upon the search for mineral resources in the New World, but frowned upon the production of sheet metal and the fabrication of objects there.

This policy of encouraging the search for mineral resources and then forbidding their use placed the English in a difficult position, for when the colonists found copper ore they naturally wanted to refine it for their own use rather than send it to England. The search was brisk for all metal ores and, at one time or another, copper was found in most of the thirteen original colonies. Only a few finds developed into important productive mines; consideration will be given here only to the most important ones.

The Ontonagon Boulder from what is now Michigan shows that pure copper was occasionally found on the earth's surface. The first white man to visit the Ontonagon Boulder was Alexander Henry, an English trader at Mackinac, about 1766. In 1819, General Lewis Cass made the first explorations of the Lake Superior region for the U.S. Government and visited the Ontonagon River in order to see the boulder. Henry R. Schoolcraft, a member of the Cass expedition, describes it in his book, *Narrative Journal of Travels through the Northwestern Regions of the United States,* published in 1821. Attempts to move the boulder at that time were unsuccessful.

S. E. HAMLIN,

PEWTERER and BRAZIER,

Nearly **oppofite** the Epifcopal Church,

RESPECTFULLY informs the public, that he continues his bufinefs at the old ftand, where he offers at wholefale and retail, a handfome affortment of

Pewter-Ware,

of a quality and price as to render unnecef-fary the importation of foreign ware.

ALSO,

Block-Tin and other Tea-Pots
Ditto Tumblers and Soup Ladles
Tutania Table and Tea Spoons
Iron   do.   do.
Lead Weights of every fize in ufe
Deep Sea and Hand Leads
Window do.
And fundry articles of Brafs Ware.

LIKEWISE FOR SALE,

A fecond-hand Wheel with Frame and Crank, fuitable for a Block-Maker or Founder.

Orders from the neighboring towns or country faithfully attended to.

☞ Cafh paid for old Pewter, Brafs and Copper.

June 24.

Advertisement of Samuel Hamlin in a Providence, R.I., newspaper (Oct. 7, 1809) indicates he was eager to buy old pewter, brass, and copper. Hamlin is famous as a pewterer but his work in brass is not well known.

Kauffman Collection

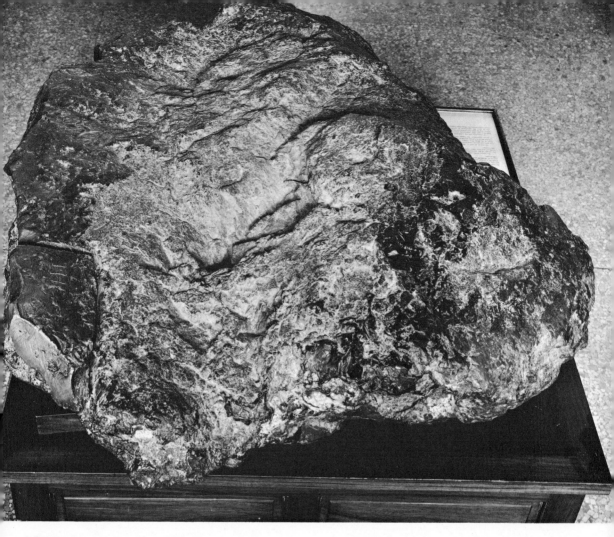

The Ontonagon Boulder. This pure copper boulder was found about 1766 in the Lake Superior region. It weighs about three tons.

In 1841, Julius Eldred, a hardware merchant of Detroit, purchased the boulder from the Chippewa Indians for $150. With great difficulty, Eldred moved it to Sault Sainte Marie. It was, however, claimed by the U.S. War Department, who moved it to Washington, D.C., in 1843. In 1860, it was deposited in the Smithsonian Institution, where it is now exhibited.

The boulder weighs about three tons and contains about $2,000 worth of copper. It has been described in the *Report of the U.S. National Museum for 1895* (1897), pages 1021-1030.

One of the earliest mines, and certainly one of the most famous, was located in Connecticut. It was reported in a town meeting of Simsbury in 1705 that deposits of silver or copper had been discovered within

Articles of Agreement made between the Undertakers of the Copper works to be Erected at Simsbury Aug[t]: 7: 1707 which undertakers are John Woodbridge Dudly Woodbridge Tim: Woodbridge Jun[r] and Hezekiah Willys & Elizur Brockett[?] of the Colony of New York

Imprimis Agreed that the undertakers will be at Equall Charge for the Carrying on the Copper works at Simsbury afores[d]:

2.ly And that they doe agree and oblige themselves Each to other, to perform the articles agreed upon on their part between the pro: prieto[rs] of the Copper Oar In the bounds of Simsbury and the said undertakers.

3.ly That the Copper belonging to the undertakers shall be disposed of in gross by him whome they shall appoint that then the product thereof shall be Equally devided Into four Equall parts to y[e] undertakers

4.ly That in Case any undertaker shall not carry on his part and is dis: posed to make Sale thereof he or they shall first make offer thereof to the rest of y[e] undertakers or if they or any one of them shall Refuse to purchase the Same he shall have Liberty to make Sale thereof to any other person that the majo[r] part of y[e] proprietors shall approve of

5.ly That In Case any of the undertakers shall fail in disbursing his part of the Charge In Erecting or carrying on of the Said Copper work the other undertakers or any of them that shall carry on his part that is thus deficient ~which Charge~ he or they shall be reimburst out of the Said deficient[s] part of Copper that is first Sold

6.ly That all Losses that arise from any failure of the Said Copperworks shall be Equally born by the Said undertakers

7.ly That if any of the afores[d]: Undertakers shall dye before the time agreed upon between the Said undertakers and the proprieto[rs] of the Said Copper Oar be Expired that then the Executo[rs] or administrato[rs] of the dec[d]: undertaker or undertakers ~they~ shall bare their Equall proportion of Charge, and have an Equall Right to the profits as is hereby agreed by the first undertakers

8.ly That the afores[d]: Timothy Woodbridge Jun[r]: and Hez: Willis shall ~Equall~ be allowed In Equall proportion by the undertakers for the carrying on Erecting and overseeing the Said Copper works three shillings and Six pence p[er] diem. In mondy

9.ly That any three of the Said undertakers shall have full power to procure and agree with and pay a masterworkman or workmen for Erecting and Improving the Said Copper works to be paid out of the Comon Stock or any one there Either men or Teams for the use of the Said works and also all perticular disbursments layd out by any of the S[d] undertakers that are nessary for the Said works shall be allowed by the undertakers being brought in by acccount

the town limits. By 1707, an association had been formed of all property owners in the town whereby they became joint owners of the mine, for it was located on unalloted ground. In 1709 the legislature authorized the association to proceed with mining copper.

The association only dug the ore, but illegally entered into a contract with three clergymen in Hartford to smelt it and make it fit for the market. The financial arrangement was to deduct one tenth of the profit for the town; after that, one third was allocated for the hiring of a competent teacher for the town school, another third was to be given to Yale College, and the final third was to be divided among the workers of the mine.

In 1714, the original association was dissolved and the mine was leased to three men, one of whom had been a member of the original association. German miners were used to mine the ore, but the mine was never successfully operated. The restrictive British Acts required that the ore be sent to England for smelting. It was hauled over poor roads to Hartford, and then sent by boat to New York. There it was reloaded onto ocean-going vessels and carried to England. Such oppressive regulations led the operators to run a bootleg smelter; unfortunately they lacked the technological knowledge to produce good copper. After deposits near the surface of the ground had been depleted, lengthy shafts and drifts were dug, but action finally ceased about 1745. In 1773 the State purchased the property and used parts of the underground area as a prison for the next 55 years.

In 1775, General George Washington assigned some men, who were considered flagrant and atrocious villains, to this prison. The operating committee had intended that these prisoners should dig ore and make their confinement a profitable enterprise for the state, but these dire offenders "inadvertently" dug in the wrong direction and escaped. Thereafter, prisoners were given other work to do.

In 1790, the State named the place "Newgate," and made it the State Prison. Despite breaks and riots, the prison continued to serve until 1827. The high cost of maintenance and growing criticism of its barbarous character finally forced the legislature to close it.

Articles of agreement concerning the operation of a copper mine at Simsbury, Conn.

The demand for domestic production of sheet copper led to another attempt to operate the mine, and in 1830 Newgate was reopened as a mining venture. The operators, however, were still unable to smelt the ore, and after shipping it to England for a number of years they finally closed the mine. Today the property is privately owned and is open to the public as a museum. Some of the old tools remain as part of the exhibit.

Another important deposit of copper ore was located near the site of Belleville, New Jersey. It is reported that, in about 1715, an old slave found a greenish stone in the area and showed it to his master. The master sent it to England and discovered that it was a rich specimen of copper ore.

The story goes that the master was so pleased with his servant's find that he told him he would grant three requests as a reward for his discovery. After considerable thought, the servant begged that he be allowed to spend the rest of his days with his master, that he might have a dressing gown with big brass buttons like the one his master wore, and that he might have all the tobacco he could smoke. The master, feeling that the recompense was inadequate for so important a discovery, asked the servant to make another request. The servant's final wish was for a little more tobacco!

The mine was owned by Colonel John Schuyler and is usually referred to as the Schuyler mine. This mine showed some prospect of rich and extensive resources, and its discovery rekindled interest in searching for metals in the New World. The ore was sent to England for processing, and mining it continued a profitable venture until the middle of the century. Then the flow of water, and subsequent drainage problems, made the mine a losing proposition.

Benjamin Franklin visited the mine in February 1750, and wrote to a friend about it:

> I know of but one valuable copper mine in this country, which is that of the Schuylers in the Jerseys. This yields good copper, and has turned out vast wealth to the owners. I was at it last fall, but they were not then at work. The water has grown too hard for

A letter concerning a proposal to lease the Schuyler copper mine in 1788. The conditions for the lease are outlined in the second paragraph of the letter.

Copy of a letter from Mr Arent J Schuyler Barbadoes Neck 27 Jany 1788

to Mr Nicholas Hoffman dated Barbadoes Neck 27 January 1788.

"

Dsantin

Mr Ogden handed me your proposals for leasing the mines, As they differ so widely from those I have mentioned to you I cannot think you and the gentlemen you represent are serious in your application — but it should be otherwise I shall repeat them —

1st I will lease the mines to you and Co, for twenty one years, on your delivering to me one tenth of all the ores, minerals &c cleaned in Cask in merchantable order at the works reserving to myself a small share in the undertaking

2

them, and they waited for a fire-engine (steam engine) from England to drain their pits. I suppose they will have that at work next spring; it costs them one thousand pounds sterling.

By 1750, steam engines were being widely used in England to drain mines, but this was an early instance of their use in America. The engine arrived in parts in New York in the summer or fall of 1753. With it came Jonathan Hornblower, a mechanic experienced with steam engines, who had to reassemble the engine and see that it performed properly. Little precise information is known about the shipping and arrival of the engine, for it was smuggled out of England. It is known, though, that Hornblower brought many duplicate parts for the engine with him, so that replacement would not become a problem or inconvenience, in case such additional parts could not be obtained from England.

Hornblower was faced with serious difficulties: the heavy parts had to be transported to the mine, a foundation had to be built, and the engine assembled by men who knew little about such devices.

The engine became a tourist attraction; travelers from home and abroad stopped to see it perform its miraculous function. Comments such as "astounding," "extravagantly costly," and "marvelously effective," were made about it. Unfortunately, in 1773, the engine was burned by some men who had been dismissed from employment at the mine.

In 1793, the New Jersey Copper Mine Association was formed. The steam engine was rebuilt and the works put into order again. German miners were employed. Again the project was unprofitable and soon the mine was idle again. Its final dismemberment came in the early part of the nineteenth century when the boiler was broken into pieces and carried to Philadelphia as scrap.

When the European traveler Jonathan D. Schoepf passed through New Jersey, he made copious notes about another mine, known as the Van Horn project. This one was located near Pluckamin, New Jersey, where a reasonably rich vein of copper ore was discovered. Schoepf reports that, in about 1774, a smelter was set up at the mine. From the start, the management was beset with financial troubles; they had difficulty in finding men who were technically competent to operate the smelting process; and they suffered from the unsatisfactory arrangement of sending ore or ingots to England for rolling. Finally, however, they brought from England an apparatus consisting of two smooth iron rollers, which operated horizontally. In a short time nearly four tons of copper sheet were ready for the American market. It was found that the new rolling mill could produce as much as two and a half tons of copper per week. The growing pride within the breasts of Americans, who were becoming industrially independent, is evident in Schoepf's comments about disposal of the copper in Philadelphia:

> The first specimens of this Jersey-made sheet-copper were brought to Philadelphia precisely at the time when Congress had passed the non-importation act of 1775; and there was so much pleasure taken in this successful and really fine product of the country that without any hesitation a price was offered of 6d in the pound higher than for English sheets, quoted as 3s.8d to 4s Pennsylvania Current.

Schoepf then reports that, despite this happy event, the outbreak of the Revolution and the demand for soldiers caused the mine to be closed, and finally the buildings were burned by American troops in an effort to extract the nails. When Schoepf visited the site in 1783, everything was in ruins and only a few insignificant samples of ore could be found.

The fourth mining area to be included in this survey was located in Maryland. Little is known about the first efforts to mine copper here; however, an Act of the Assembly of the Province of Maryland in 1742 records that John Digges was encouraged to construct a copperworks by making his workmen levy free for seven years and exempting them from working upon highroads or bridges and from attendance on musters, and so forth. The second effort to extract copper ore in Maryland was in around 1750 at the Mineral Hill mine between Finksburg and Sykesville where a small melting furnace was built.

A little later another facility, called the Fountain Copper Works, was reported in the *Maryland Gazette* of December 11, 1760; by 1780, Frederick County, Maryland, was a thriving mining community. A number of entrepreneurs were engaged in mining, refining, and rolling copper at that time. A newspaper advertisement, placed in the *Maryland* (Baltimore) *Journal*, February 2, 1780, by William Hammond, stated:

TO SILVERSMITHS, COPPERSMITHS, BRAZIERS, BUCKLEMAKERS, ETC.

William Hammond having purchased a quantity of copper from Dr. John Stevenson, is determined (If he meets with encouragement) to have melted into bars of two and three pounds each, if not he intends to ship it, in two months from the date hereof to France or Holland. Letters (Postpaid) will be duly attended to and answered. It is expected that a deposit will be made by the contractors.

This advertisement is of interest for a number of reasons. In the first place it is evidence that a mine and a refining apparatus were located in Maryland at that time. It confirms the fact that copper was cast into bars (or ingots) and later rolled into sheets, possibly at a long distance from the mine. Ingots were much easier to transport than thin sheets of copper. The intention to export the copper to France or Holland was obviously necessary for the colonies were then at war with the homeland, where most of the copper had previously been processed. Ore from the Schuyler mine was sent to Holland, but this is the first mention of any being shipped to France.

On July 18, 1780, Mr. Hammond announced that he had erected a furnace and had more copper for sale.

SHEET COPPER FOR SALE

Having erected a furnace and engaged Mr. Robert Wood's Rolling Mill, at Dr. John Stevenson's Copper Mine, in Frederick County, I am now making a quantity of sheet copper, fit for stills, or other work. It is not probable the quantity I may make will be sufficient for the demand. I am, therefore, determined to give every Purchaser an equal chance by completing the orders as they are sent in, agreeable to the time they are received, respectively. To prevent trouble, those who want their orders executed must send the money with them to the manager of the Copper Works, or to my house in Baltimore.

William Hammond.

Hammond must have been an ambitious person for, on November 28, 1780, he advertised in the *Maryland Journal* that he wanted to employ a man to erect a rolling mill for him:

> A person well qualified to erect a rolling mill, will meet with advantageous employment by applying to Mr. William Hammond. Merchant in Baltimore town or to the Manager of the Copper Works in Frederick County.

In 1782, Dr. John Stevenson, who previously had owned a copper mine, advertised that he had brought his rolling mill to perfection and that coppersmiths could be supplied with his product. He stated that Mr. Hazlit and Mr. Minshall of Baltimore approved of his copper, and that Major William Bailey of York Town (Pennsylvania) said that it was equal to any in the world. Dr. Stevenson also mentioned Mr. Wood's rolling mill in his advertisement and closed by saying that Mr. Richardson at Elk Ridge Landing "will have his mill in order in two weeks." On October 8, 1782, Dr. Stevenson advertised in *The Maryland Journal & Baltimore Advertiser* that he had a complete facility for making sheet copper, including a furnace, refinery, and rolling mill.

The impending end of the war and the prospect of importing sheet copper from England may have influenced Dr. Stevenson to advertise the sale of his copper mine in the *Maryland Journal & Baltimore Advertiser*, May 20, 1783. The heading of the advertisement was in very large letters.

FOR SALE
STEVENSON'S GRAND COPPER MINE
In Frederick County

The purchaser will have an opportunity of seeing an assay of the ore, and the exact Quantity of Copper it yields at the Air-Furnace and Refinery.—The Owner purposes to divide it into Twenty Shares.—A Gentleman minutely acquainted with the Works, will take either a Third or a Fourth Part, provided he approves of the other Partners—The ore sold from Forty-eight to Fifty Pounds Sterling per Ton, in London—The Drifts which contain Ore, may be entered on and worked immediately—The Blasting vein, from sixty to eighty Feet long, may be cleared in two weeks—The Level, a Work of ten Years labor, is complete.—There are two hundred Acres of Land, a good Dwelling House, and sundry Improvements. Many satisfactory Discoveries will be made by the Buyers.

John Stevenson

N. B. I have a large quantity of Copper now by me, forged out in the neatest manner, and warranted to roll; which I will sell as cheap as it can be imported.—I have likewise for Sale some curious Pieces of Ore, from One Hundred to Five Hundred Weight.

Ten years later, in spite of an obvious surplus of domestically produced copper, John M'Cauley, a coppersmith and merchant in Philadelphia, advertised in the *Pennsylvania Packet* (*Dunlap's Daily Advertiser*) of July 6, 1792, that he had for sale a sizeable amount of copper imported from England. The items were as follows:

TIN in boxes, English brass kettles in nests, finished or unfinished, 2000 pounds of sheet copper fit for building purposes, and 6000 pounds of sheathing copper ordered expressly for that purpose, at his Copper Store. No. 89 South Front Street.

Presumably copper continued to be produced in the various areas in which it was mined in America, although Benjamin Harbeson, an outstanding merchant in copper objects in Philadelphia, announced many times in the press that he was importing sheets of copper and brass. His advertisement in the *Pennsylvania Packet* (*Claypoole's American Daily Advertiser*) of August 11, 1796, carried the following information:

HARBESON, Benjamin & Son

Benjamin Harbeson & Son, At their Copper Warehouse, No. 75, north side of Market Street, opposite Strawberry alley, Have just received a compleat assortment of Copper in Sheets and bottoms, stills, cocks, rivets, borax, brass kettles in nests, and, as usual, stills from 30 gallons to 250, and which they are determined to sell on reasonable terms for cash or the usual Credit.

The fact that they were importing stills indicates that the European and American economies were competitive, and that Americans were still willing to buy European products after their bitter struggle with England in the Revolution. Most of Harbeson's imports came from England.

The importance of sheet copper in the new nation increased as her commerce and industry grew. Great quantities of sheet copper were critically needed for sheathing the hulls of ships. Copper was being imported for this important use, but America was a young and proud country, eager to produce enough copper to sheathe her own ships. Paul Revere, one of the great entrepreneurs of the new nation, decided that he could roll copper in the quantities needed. In 1798, Revere wrote to Benjamin Stoddert, then Secretary of the Navy, advising him of his interest in this matter:

> I understand you have advised the Committee for building the Frigate in Boston not to send abroad for anything they can get manufactured in this country; these Sentiments have induced me to trouble you with this letter. I can manufacture old or new Copper into Bolts, Spikes, Staples, Nails, etc., or anything that is wanted in Shipbuilding. . . . I supplied the *Constitution* Dove-tails, Staples, Nails, etc. etc. My greatest difficulty is to get Copper. Could I get a sufficient supply of Copper, I could undertake to roll Sheet Copper for sheathing ships, etc. . . . You will permit me to offer my Services to you in Manufacturing Brass Cannon, Bells, Copper Bolts, Spikes, etc.

Revere was sixty years old when he embarked on this important project of rolling copper. He built a rolling mill at Canton, Massachusetts, hired fifty workmen, and paid them two dollars a day when other workmen were earning only two dollars a week. He must have been eminently successful in his project for the log of the Frigate *Constitution* contained the following entry for June 26, 1803:

> The Carpenters gave nine cheers, which were answered by the seamen and the calkers because they had in fourteen days, coppered the ship with copper made in the United States.

In addition to the copper rolled for the *Constitution*, Revere is also known to have supplied sheets for the dome of the State House in Boston and for the dome of the City Hall in New York.

After Paul Revere, Sr., died in 1818, his son Joseph continued the dual business of casting bells and rolling sheets of copper. In the *Boston Business Directory* of 1821, he is listed as a bell founder and copper dealer. The same listing appears in the *Directory* of 1828. The business

BALTIMORE MANUFACTURED COPPER.

THE

BALTIMORE AND CUBA

SMELTING & MINING

COMPANY,

Having their new Rolling Mill at Whetstone Point in full operation, are prepared to furnish all kinds of rolled

COPPER,

Of approved quality, at a short notice. An assortment kept on hand of *Braziers Sheets*, 30 x 60 inches, various weights.

Sheathing Copper, 14 to 34 ounces, assorted.

Copper Bolt Rods ½ inch to 2 inches diameter, assorted.

Copper Nails, Tacks, &c. Also, *Refined Copper Ingots*, for Manufacturers' use,

FOR SALE BY THE AGENTS,

W. & H. McKIM,

No. 56 South Gay street.

N. B. *Pattern Sheets* made to order. OLD COPPER bought at the highest market prices.

Advertisement of the Baltimore and Cuba Smelting and Mining Company in a Baltimore *Business Directory of 1850.*

of rolling sheet copper was becoming highly competitive about this time because of the entry into the field of the Crocker Brothers of Taunton, Massachusetts, Levi Hollingsworth of Baltimore, Maryland, and the Swifts of New Bedford, Massachusetts.

In 1828, for the first time, outsiders were taken into the Revere business when James Davis and his son joined as partners. In 1848, the business was broadened by establishing a factory for refining copper ore at Point Shirley, Massachusetts. During the Civil War the company produced a gun a day for the Army; they also delivered fifty howitzers for the Navy in record time. In 1867, Joseph Revere died. The products of the later company have no interest to this survey, though Revere Copper and Brass Company continues in business today as one of the outstanding producers of copper objects in the world.

Although Paul Revere gained universal fame for his achievement in rolling copper to sheathe ships in the early nineteenth century, that aspect of the Revere business was relatively short in duration, for the development of the copper industry soon shifted to Baltimore. Baltimore was rapidly becoming one of the most important seaports in America and was producing some of the fastest sailing ships in the world. Because speed was abetted by the use of copper in sheathing the hulls, it was natural for a copper rolling industry to thrive there.

The production of sheet copper started in Baltimore in 1804 when Levi Hollingsworth set up the first rolling mill there. Some success in this venture led him to spend the year of 1811 in England where he worked in the industry, learning all he could about the various problems that needed to be solved in America. He returned to his homeland and, in 1814, erected the Gunpowder Copper Works. This plant cost $100,000 and was probably the best-equipped rolling mill in the country at the time. Hollingsworth directed the activity of the factory until his death in 1822; then Isaac McKim, with other members of his family became associated with the business. In 1837, the company was reorganized, and renamed Hollingsworth & Co. It was known as such until it ceased operations about the time of the Civil War.

The final and most fascinating part of the copper industry in Baltimore started in 1845 when the Baltimore and Cuba Smelting and Refining Company was organized. Haslett McKim, a relative of Isaac

McKim, was named its president. Furnaces were erected at Locust Point and Mariott Street and, in 1846, the plant was ready for operation.

It was the intent of the owners to obtain ore for the plant from Cuba where relatively rich mines of copper ore reputedly existed, but upon investigation it was found that the source was completely imaginary. No supplies were available to Baltimore from Cuba! Eventually ore was found in Chile, though the expense of shipping the ore around Cape Horn was greater than had been anticipated. However, the plant began to operate, and a rolling mill was added in 1849. Mounting losses doomed the venture and, in 1851, the plant was sold and demolition started.

Curiously, the apparent death of this company turned out to be its rebirth for, as the plant was dismantled, large deposits of impure copper were found remaining in the furnaces, left there by unskilled managers who thought them worthless. When this quantity of impure copper was sent to England to be refined, the return was so great that the company reorganized. In 1855, it purchased the plant of its biggest rival in Baltimore. By 1860, Baltimore was rapidly becoming one of the most important centers for producing copper in the world. The new Baltimore Copper and Smelting Company was the largest of its kind in America, and its furnaces were producing 6,000,000 pounds annually.

The problems of transportation from Chile during the Civil War, a rise in tariff on Chilean ore, and other financial troubles cast their shadow over the plant in the 1860s. In 1870, William Keyser was made president of the company, with instructions to liquidate the business. As liquidation was proceeding, small quantities of ore from Arizona and Montana arrived at Baltimore with the assurance that unlimited supplies were available. The company was immediately reorganized as Pope, Cole, and Company and, for the second time, was headed for prosperous days. The copper industry continued to thrive in Baltimore throughout the nineteenth century and into the twentieth.

Although the extraction of copper from its ore obviously confounded eighteenth-century technicians in America, the forming of brass was an even more perplexing problem. Brass was called a factitious (artificial) metal by the writers of the period; this essentially means that it was not an element but an alloy. The alloy is made of copper and zinc, so both these metals had to be produced before brass could be made. There is

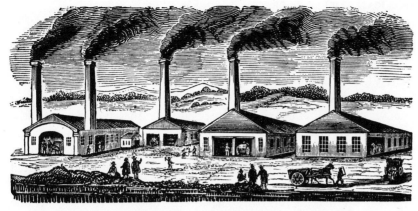

GUNPOWDER COPPER WORKS,
Established 1805.

GEORGE WILLIAMS,
AGENT OF THE GUNPOWDER COPPER WORKS,

Keeps constantly on hand an assortment of superior Copper of all descriptions, manufactured at the above establishment, comprising:

Bolt and Rivet Rods, Braziers Sheets, Boiler Plates, Raised Bottoms, Sheathing, Nails, Tacks, &c.

Pattern Sheets of all descriptions made to order.

All orders for Copper will be promptly and carefully executed at short notice, and on pleasing terms ; the article furnished warranted to be pure and of superior quality.

Warehouse No. 30 S. Frederick st.,
BALTIMORE.

Advertisement from Baltimore *Business Directory of 1850*.

no evidence that brass was made in America in the eighteenth century, but the numbers of brass founders working at that time suggests that they must have had some reasonably good source for this factitious metal.

The real problem in making brass arose because technicians did not know how to extract zinc from its ore. From the time brass was first made until 1781, the metal was made by combining copper with calamine, the ore of zinc. In 1781, the process of refining zinc was patented in England and the production of brass was simplified a great deal. The earlier process is described in *A Dictionary of Arts, Manufactures, and Mines*, by Andrew Ure.

BRASS. An alloy of copper and zinc. It was formerly manufactured by cementing granulated copper, called bean-shot, or copper clippings, with calcined calamine (native carbonate of zinc) and charcoal, in a crucible, and exposing them to bright ignition [great heat]. Three parts of copper were used for three of calamine and two of charcoal. The zinc reduced to the metallic state by the agency of the charcoal, combined with the copper, into an alloy which formed, on cooling, a lump at the bottom of the crucible. Several of these, being remelted and cast into moulds, constituted ingots of brass for the market. James Emerson obtained a patent, in 1781, for making brass by the direct fusion of its two metallic elements, and it is now usually manufactured in this way.

Primitive brass-casting procedure of the early nineteenth century.

courtesy Scovil Manufacturing Company

In the beginning, the ingots were hammered into sheets, just as other sheet metals were formed; however, the frequent mention of rolling mills in America in the eighteenth century suggests that these facilities for rolling iron and copper were soon adapted, or used, to roll brass into sheets. It is possible that the ingots were first hammered into a thick slab, which could then be more easily rolled into thin sheets. It is important to note that serious problems arose in the rolling of brass, for it work-hardens rapidly and must be annealed seven or eight times throughout the rolling procedure. In Europe, the problem of passing the slabs many times through the rollers was minimized by casting the brass into sheets of metal between two massive pieces of granite. The granite was five and a half feet long and three feet wide; it was bound with strips of iron, and bolted in the corners.

Information about casting and rolling brass in America can be found in *Brass Roots*, a book published by the Scovil Manufacturing Company in 1952 to commemorate their 150th anniversary. This book claims that brass was first cast in America in the workshop of Abel Porter & Company in Waterbury, Connecticut, sometime between 1806 and 1809. The heat for melting the constituents of the metal was supplied by a bellows powered either by water, man, or wind. The crucibles each held from five to ten pounds. When the metal was melted, it was poured into small molds made of cast iron with a cavity dimension of 7 1/2" x 1 1/2" x 5/16". The slab produced in this small mold weighed about one pound. Except for size, the molds used today are similar to those used in the 1806-1809 period.

There is a legend that the small castings were rolled on the site by iron rollers powered by horses; it is more likely that they carted the brass to the water-powered iron slitting and rolling mill operated by Frederick Wolcott and Company at Bantam Falls (then Bradleyville), near Litchfield. The twenty-mile trip required a day, and lucky drivers sometimes stayed overnight before returning with their load of precious metal. About 1815, the water power of Waterbury's Mad River was harnessed, and the trip to Bantam Falls was no longer necessary.

The production of narrow strips of brass, one and a half inches wide, was adequate for the manufacture of buttons and other small items, but to produce larger objects, it was necessary to roll wider strips of brass into sheets. In 1821, James Emerson, an Englishman with considerable experience in the working of metals, was induced to join the growing brass industry of Leavenworth, Hayden, & Scovil in Waterbury. Later he was sent back to England to pirate as much information as possible about the rolling of brass there, and to influence skilled workmen to return with him to America. In 1836, an observer reported that the company was casting brass in a size approximately fifteen inches long, four to six inches wide, and one half to three fourths inch thick. Another major improvement occurred in 1852, when the Scovil Company installed their first steam engine to power their plant. At last the company was on the way to the mass production of metal, which was destined to make brass a common commodity for all Americans.

II. The Trades

YEARS of research and extensive examination of objects made of sheet brass and copper confirm the fact that numerous craftsmen worked in these metals in America in the eighteenth and nineteenth centuries. Many facets of their trades and their products will be examined in this survey.

A. THE COPPERSMITH

The first characteristic one notices is a fluidity in the use of the term "coppersmith." It would seem that a man who made objects of copper would have been called a coppersmith, and a man who formed objects of sheet brass would have been termed a brazier; such logical reasoning was not followed. Regardless of where, when, and what was made, whether the products were formed of sheet copper or brass, the craftsmen were called coppersmiths, or braziers, or a combination of both. Coppersmith was the most frequently used and, since most of the objects under discussion here were made of copper, the term "coppersmith" should cause no confusion.

The situation is lucidly explained by Rev. Dionysius Lardner in *The Cabinet Cyclopedia:*

> The business of the coppersmith is as extensive and as diversified as the purposes to which the metal is applied on a large scale are considerable. The appellation of brazier, although in strictness applied to an artificer in brass, as contradistinguished from one who works in copper, has long since sunk into a synonym with the

33

first-mentioned term; and it is likely even in times and countries very remote from our own, both metals might be fashioned into domestic or other utensils by the same class of workmen.

The next step in this survey of the trade of the coppersmith is to discover what this craftsman made. This can easily be done by examining a large number of newspaper advertisements and business ledgers, and then compiling a list from the entries found. Such a procedure will clearly show that most tradesmen made objects for the house, such as teakettles, chocolate pots, and fish kettles. Men who worked in a seaport made special items for use of ships, while those who worked in inland cities concentrated on household utensils and possibly kettles for hatters, dyers, brewers, and others. In addition, many individual pieces were made, such as master measures for sealers of weights and measures, butter churns, weathervanes, and decorative headers for rain spouts.

The following advertisement of George Orr lists products typical of those made by a coppersmith in Philadelphia, Pennsylvania, about 1750. It appeared in the *Pennsylvania Gazette* on February 13, 1753.

GEORGE ORR

Is removed from Front-Street, to the house where Mr. Peacock Bigger lately dwelt, in Market-Street, opposite the Presbyterian Meeting House; where he continues to serve the publick with all sorts of copper work, viz.

STILLS, furnaces and kettles of all sizes, Dutch ovens, stewing pans, frying pans, kettle-pots, ship-kettles, tea-kettles, sauce-pans, coffee-pots, chocolate-pots, dripping-pans, etc., brass kettles of all sizes, beams and scales, lead weights. Also mends and tins all sorts of braziers work. Those who are pleased to favor him with their custom may depend on being served in the best manner, and on the most reasonable terms.

N. B. He gives the highest price for old copper, brass, and pewter; and has a parcel of wool-cards, which he will sell for ready money.

In 1791, William Billings, a pewterer, coppersmith, and brazier, advertised the following wares in Providence, Rhode Island:

WILLIAM BILLINGS

MAKES and sells all kinds of PEWTER WARE, warranted good as any made in this Town, or State.——Also, all sorts of Braziery, viz.——Brass kettles, Coffee pots, Sauce-pans, Skillets, Skimmers, Ladles, Warming-pans, Stew Pans, etc.——He makes Stills and Worms of all sizes, and on the newest and most approved Construction; Dyers' Copper Kettles, Sugarhouse Ladles and Skimmers; all kinds of Ship Work, such as leading Hawse-Holes, Scuppers, etc., in the neatest Manner and with Dispatch.——He also makes Lead Weights, from 1 oz. to 14 lbs., or larger, if wanted.

An unusual variety of objects was offered in New Bedford, Massachusetts, by A. D. Richmond & Co. in 1859. The list not only indicates that the company supplied ships with critical products, but also suggests that the day was not too distant when the coppersmith would engage in plumbing. Their advertisement appeared in the *New Bedford Directory and City Register* for 1859.

A. D. RICHMOND
Brass Founders and Coppersmiths
No 103 N. Water Street
New Bedford

Have constantly on hand, Composition Bolts, Spikes, Nails, Fore-locks, Eye-Bolts, Copper Balls, Coolers, Cooler and Hose Cocks, Brass Stop Cocks, Brass Signal Lanterns. (Plate glass)

Manufactured to order, Richmonds' Patent Composition Lead and Brass tipped Candle Molds. Also Rudder-joints and Block Sheaves, and all the various copper and composition articles in general use. Plumbing in all its various branches attended to. Water Closets, Shower-Baths, Bath Tubs, etc. made to order and fitted up in a workmanship-like manner.

This advertisement by A. D. Richmond is significant. In the first place, his location in a seaport, like that of Billings in Providence, Rhode Island, would suggest he catered to the sea trade. The noncorrosive quality of copper and brass favored marine work, and there must have been many craftsmen on the eastern seaboard who produced objects like those of Billings and Richmond.

The Richmond business is unusual, however, because it combined coppersmithing and brass founding. This combination might logically have been followed by many of the earlier craftsmen, although none has been discovered; most of them worked only in forming objects of sheet metal or by casting them. Richmond's combination of the two trades foreshadowed a new industrial trend, in which many materials and procedures were to be used by one man or company to produce the object best suited for its intended use. Finally, the trend toward the establishment of the modern plumbing business is evident; it was only a short time before the trade of the coppersmith disappeared from the industrial scene in America. The casting of brass was a highly specialized business conducted in a brass foundry from colonial times until the present. Although modern brass foundries are partially mechanized and automated, many retain some of the features used when A. D. Richmond was in business.

It should also be noted that many of the tradesmen who worked in sheet copper and brass also did other work. William Billings, as noted, made lead weights. E. Brotherton of Lancaster, Pennsylvania, included tinwork with his coppersmithing and advertised a sideline of patent medicines. James M'Calmond of York, Pennsylvania, had a dry-goods store in addition to his work in coppersmithing. The most frequent combination was with tinsmithing.

The following list itemizes the objects made by most of the coppersmiths from 1738 until the time of the American Civil War. Most of the products would have been called hollow ware. A minimum number of tools was required to make them, and the forms were reasonably simple. Little, if any, repoussé work was used to decorate them. As a matter of fact, only a very few were decorated at all. Their simple forms were graceful, functional, and well suited to shipboard environment or home decor. Their attractiveness today is proof of the competence and discrimination of the craftsmen who made them.

Examination of old objects made of sheet copper and brass reveals that they were made by able craftsmen. Rarely does one find ill-fitting joints, thin spots, or careless shaping. The explanation of this condition lies in the method by which craftsmen were trained and the standards of workmanship they were taught to uphold.

Bakepans	Dutch ovens	Ship kettles
Brass kettles	Dyers' kettles	Skillets
Brewers' kettles	Fish kettles	Stewpans
Chocolate pots	Fullers' kettles	Stills
Cider kettles	Hatters' kettles	Sugarhouse ladles
Coffeepots	Ladles	Teakettles
Copper pots	Planking kettles	Warming pans
Dripping pans	Saucepans	Washbasins

These early tradesmen were trained under the apprenticeship system. An experienced or master craftsman would take one, two, or possibly three apprentices and teach them his trade. The apprenticeship period began when the apprentice was about fourteen years of age and terminated when he was about twenty-one years old. An agreement called an indenture, signed by both parties at the start of the boy's career, outlined the specific responsibilities of both master and apprentice.

In the eighteenth century indentures were long and explicit, so that no detail of the relationship was left in doubt. Two identical documents were witnessed by the proper persons, stamped with the seal of a notary, and recorded in the Court House of the community in which the master lived. One copy was held by each of the parties concerned, and when the apprenticeship was satisfactorily completed, the apprentice was given both copies, his possession of the two being evidence that he had completed his apprenticeship.

When first executed, the two copies of the indenture were held together and irregular identical cuts, or tears, were made across the top edge of both copies (indented). This was designed to minimize the opportunity for fraud in the forging of a second copy by an unscrupulous apprentice before his experience was complete. The cutting soon became only a formality, for the edges of many indentures are so simple they could be duplicated with ease.

The execution of an indenture was an important matter, but it obviously did not guarantee the implementation of its conditions. Many apprentices ran away from their masters, possibly to engage again in the work under a more sympathetic teacher, or, after having worked at coppersmithing for some time, to take on another trade or occupation

THIS INDENTURE, Made the

Twenty first Day of *July* in the Year of
our Lord, One Thousand ~~Seven~~ *eight* Hundred and *Three* BETWEEN
Lewis Rush, Henry Sparks & Wm Sheed
John Adolph, John R McMullin, John
Hewson, Fredrich Shinkle Junr Jo. Worrell
Managers of the House of Employment, of the one Part, and *Edward Gill*
of Philadelphia Brass founder of the other
Part, WITNESSETH, that the said Managers, by and with the Consent of
two of the Aldermen of the City of
Philadelphia, whose Hands and Seals are hereunto put, according to the Form of the Act of
Assembly, for the Relief of the Poor, have put *Edward Preistley aged*
fifteen Years an Apprentice, to dwell with and serve the said
Edward Gill his Executors, Administrators,
or Assigns, from the Day of the Date hereof, for and during the full End and Term of
Six Years next ensuing, in all lawful and
reasonable service: And the said *Edward Gill his* Executors, Administrators, or Assigns, during the said Term, shall find and provide for the said Apprentice,
sufficient Meat, Drink, Apparel, Washing, and Lodging; and shall teach or cause *him*
to be taught *the Art & Mystery of a Brass founder and*
Caster, to have six quarters half day schooling
When free to have two Suits of Cloaths, one to
be New, & Thirty Dollars in Cash

This Indenture not to be assigned without the Consent of the Managers for the time being.

IN WITNESS WHEREOF, the said Parties to these Presents, have inter-
changeably set their Hands and Seals, the Day and Year above written.

Edwd Gill

Mr Hillegas

John Barker

Lewis Rush

Henry Sparks jun

Wm Sheed

John Booth

John R McMullin

John Hewson

Fredk Shinkle jun

which looked more attractive. The lack of communication in colonial times made it difficult for the master to take action against such runaways, but he frequently advertised in the local newspaper (if one existed) and offered a reward to any person who assisted him in the return of his apprentice.

On the other hand, many apprentices stayed with their masters, and the whole agreement was satisfactory to both parties. Unless the apprentice was the son of the master, he left his home and lived under his master's roof. This frequently occasioned a fine arrangement for orphans or illegitimate children, whose living conditions otherwise might have been extremely difficult. The plan of apprenticeship also provided an opportunity for a poor lad to upgrade his lot in life by learning a profitable trade.

The major responsibility of the master was to teach the boy the secrets of his trade; he also had to feed and clothe him, teach him the rudiments of reading, writing, and arithmetic, and familiarize him with the Bible. Sometimes the German language was specified, particularly if the craftsman lived in rural Pennsylvania. At the end of the apprenticeship, it was customary for the master to give the boy a set of hand tools, and often a new suit of clothing. Sometimes the apprentice married the master's daughter, became a partner in the business, and inherited it after the master's death or retirement. However, few partnerships existed in the eighteenth century; although there was some legal arrangement if more than one person owned a business, it was usually conducted under the name of one man. On some occasions, widows owned and operated businesses under the names of their deceased husbands, or even under their own names. For example, the widow Hamsher advertised in the *Pittsburgh Gazette* on July 20, 1810, for two journeymen coppersmiths to work for her.

The major obligations of the apprentice were to serve his master faithfully in all his commands, to keep secret the information the master imparted to him, and not to waste the goods of his master. He was

Indenture of Edward Priestley, apprenticed to Edward Gill, brass founder of Philadelphia on July 21, 1803. The conditions of indenture varied from time to time and from place to place. In 1803, the conditions of indenture for a brass founder and for a coppersmith were essentially the same.

not allowed to play cards, dice, or tables, nor was he permitted to marry or haunt taverns and playhouses. He could not buy or sell merchandise in competition with his master.

The most interesting survival of the agreements within the indenture is the one concerned with keeping the secrets of the trade. This mandate, included in most indentures, was, for some mysterious reason, held to more rigidly and for a longer time by coppersmiths than by other tradesmen. Only one book in the English language is known to have been published which explains the techniques of the trade in any detailed fashion. After an extensive and unrewarding search for such a book, John Fuller, a master coppersmith, finally supplied the need himself. His book, entitled *The Art of Coppersmithing,* appeared in 1893. This book was written in defiance of all advice given him, for in the introduction he states, "One of the most imperative injunctions received by the writer from his father was to faithfully guard his patrimony from the scrutiny of prying eyes, it having descended to him through a long line of ancestors for many generations, who had plied their craft with various degrees of proficiency, thus maintaining their respectability and independence to an honorable old age, in evidence of which in Canterbury, England, four years ago one of his kinfolk could be yet seen working at the brazier's bench at the advanced age of 87 years." Secrecy concerning the processes of the trade continues today and may explain the scarcity of information and written material about it. Most information about trade secrets has been gleaned from John Fuller's writings. He was one old coppersmith, with experience and wisdom, who finally ceased to feel bound by the injunctions of his ancestors. Scattered sources available in books and magazines add to his information.

Comments might be made about the quaint language of the indenture, the gradual change of conditions in the nineteenth century, such as allowing apprentices to work in the hayfields in the short period of haymaking, and the shortening of the apprenticeship period when manufactured parts became available. The indenture was an important legal document; its impact on the quality of the products of the times must be considered with awe and respect. It has been said that the conditions enumerated and the precise language used made either a slave or a fine artisan of the apprentice. The document certainly conveyed an image of high ideals and the importance of fine workmanship; it was a valuable contribution to a well-regulated society.

Many persons assume that the dull and battered objects of copper and brass found today were not carefully made, but such a conclusion cannot be truthfully drawn. Although objects made of these metals had a low status at various times, it must be recognized that the master coppersmith was a craftsman in his own right. He served an apprenticeship as long, as well-organized, and as rigid as did the men engaged in most trades. There is virtually no evidence of slipshod forming or fitting, and it is clear that some creativity was called for in fitting old metals to new uses. The coppersmith was a respected citizen in his community, although his status frequently suffered because later craftsmen changed or repaired his product with less skill and imagination than he had originally employed. An objective appraisal of his products should lead to a fuller appreciation of their quality.

The trade techniques of coppersmithing look so forbidding today that one despairs of an apprentice's ever learning how to make a teakettle or a still. Many of the master craftsmen were wise teachers and by taking the apprentice gradually from simple operations to more difficult ones, they ultimately taught the boy his trade. The first chores of the apprentice consisted of cleaning the shop, polishing stakes and hammers, starting the forge fire, filing sharp edges on utensils, and polishing small items such as ladles, skimmers, and chocolate pots. Later he learned to trace patterns on sheet copper and cut them out, to thin edges by hammering them, to solder joints, and to insert rivets where solder could not be successfully used. Finally, he was allowed to cut out, form, and assemble complete objects, such as fish kettles and saucepans.

It was important for the apprentice to know how to proceed with the making of objects if he were to become skillful in his trade. The same knowledge is also pertinent to an understanding of the old objects of copper and brass which are found in antique shops and museums today.

Many of the products of the trade were kettles, cylinders that are either straight-sided or flaring inward or outward. Two methods to form cylinders were used. The one most frequently employed by coppersmiths was to make a cramped joint resembling the dovetail joint

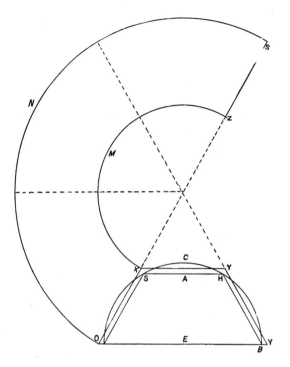

Method of Describing Pattern for Half Ball

Showing Pattern Doubled Up

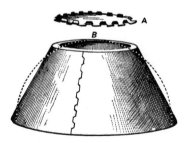

Pattern Formed with Seam Brazed and Lag Raised

Raising Down the Lag for Bottom

Sketches showing the development of the pattern for a flaring object such as a basin or funnel. The bottom is inserted with a cramped joint; the same joint is used on the side seam.

from *The Art of Coppersmithing*

used in furniture-making. To make this joint, tabs were cut into one of the vertical edges of the curved sheet, every other one of which was bent outward at right angles to the surface of the sheet. The uncut edge was then brought against the base of the raised tabs, which were then hammered flat on the sheet. Thus, half of the tabs were on the outside of the cylinder and half on the inside. After being swabbed with flux, the overlapping joint was heated to a low red heat and spelter (solder) flowed throughout it. After soldering, the double thickness at the joint was reduced by hammering to the original thickness of the sheet copper. The cylinder was usually made as large as the biggest diameter; then by wrinkling and hammering, portions were reduced to specified diameters. This method required that a separate bottom be inserted with a cramped (dovetail) joint similar to that used on the side of the object. Stills, teakettles, saucepans, measures, chocolate pots, and similar articles were made in this manner.

Hammering the wrinkles out of a vessel in the raising process.

from *The Art of Coppersmithing*

Floor Block with Stakes and Head for Forming Half Balls

The second method of forming cylinders is known as "raising," one of the skills every coppersmith had to learn. When this process was used, the entire main body of the object was made of one piece of metal. No bottom was inserted. The bottom of the proposed object was usually left flat while the extended sides were wrinkled, thus raising them and reducing the diameter. The raised wrinkles were then reduced to their smallest diameter with a hammer on a stake. Sometimes this operation had to be repeated to bring the sides into the desired vertical position. Most warming pans were made in this manner.

After a copper object was given its desired form by shaping and joining, the surface of the metal was distorted and rough. The final process, except for tinning and polishing, was called "planishing." This technique was used on most hollow ware made of copper, iron, silver,

A patented device used to planish objects with a variety of contours without removing them from the stake.

from U.S. Patent Office Specifications

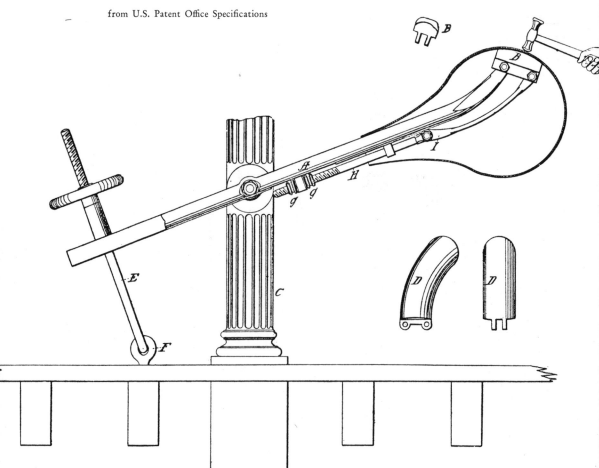

and brass which was fabricated by hand methods. It was also used on objects made of pewter in the eighteenth and early nineteenth centuries, for these pieces were cast of a relatively soft metal which could be made more attractive and rigid by planishing.

The flagrant abuse of the planished texture by modern reproducers of metalware demands that the function of planishing be explained here. The following definition is taken from the *Oxford English Dictionary*, published by the Oxford University Press, London, 1955.

> PLANISH. To make level or smooth; to level. To flatten (sheet-metal or metalware) on an anvil with a smooth-faced hammer, etc.; to flatten and reduce (coining-metal) to the required thickness by passing between rollers; to polish (paper, etc.) by means of a roller 1688. Hence *Planisher,* a person who planishes; a tool or instrument used for planishing . . . as *p. hammer,* a hammer with polished slightly convex faces, used for planishing sheet-metal.

The explanations in this definition suggest that planishing had two important functions—to reduce the thickness of metal and to make the surface smooth. The reduction in the thickness of metals is not significant at this point of the discussion, but making the surface smooth is to be considered.

Many modern reproductions have a very rough surface which appears to have been created by hammering with the round end of a ball-peen hammer. This hammered appearance is intended to resemble the surface texture of metalware created by hand methods and to suggest that these marks are in some way connected with the making of the reproduction. Neither of these premises is correct. It was the purpose of planishing to make the surface smooth, and the dictionary definition definitely excludes the concept of fabrication by planishing. As a matter of fact, the marks left by a planishing hammer were so delicate and shallow that most of them have disappeared after a hundred years of use and polishing.

Although different hammers were needed to planish the surface of a still or a saucepan, the greatest flexibility was needed in the variety of stakes (coppersmith's anvils) necessary to support the objects being planished. The radius on the surface of the stake had to be suited to the contour of the object being planished, and a number of stakes were needed. The demands on the stake were exacting, for it had to fit the restricted interior shapes of the copper objects. Hammers had more flexibility in striking the outside surface of the objects. Both the stake and the hammer had to be free of all foreign materials and highly polished at all times.

The apprentice was taught many other standard practices which the connoisseur of wares made of copper and brass should understand. Edges were wired to make them smooth and rigid; spouts were formed by adding an extra piece of metal or by stretching the side of a vessel; handles and lids were made for saucepans and teakettles.

After forming and planishing of the vessels, the procedure was to cover the inside with a thin coating of tin. A recent statement concerning the need for tinning the inside surfaces of copper vessels designed for the preparation of food is found in *Corrosion Resistance of Copper and Copper Alloys,* published by the American Brass Company. Their statement follows:

> Copper and its alloys are resistant to corrosion by most foods and beverages. However, consideration must be given to the possibility that such products handled in equipment made of copper or its alloys may dissolve traces of copper in amounts sufficient to discolor the product or alter its taste.

An older and more threatening version of the need for tinning is found in *The Domestic Encyclopedia,* by A. F. M. Willich, M.D.

> With respect to the poisonous qualities of copper, when introduced into the stomach, it is less dangerous than arsenic; as the former is more easily dissolved.—And though the editors of *Encyclopedia Britannica* have declared that they have not met with any well-authenticated instances of a person who has died in consequence of having swallowed even verdigris itself, yet so many examples have lately occurred, that there is not the least doubt of the deleterious properties of copper. Of the many cases that might be adduced, we shall select one, which is authenticated by Dr. Pergival of Manchester. A young lady had eaten about three or four ounces of pickled samphire, strongly impregnated with copper, and had drunk afterwards the 5th part of a pint of vinegar, on an empty stomach. [Yipes!] She had not applied for medical aid for two days, and in the course of ten, she died.

Dr. Willich's article also mentioned that the Chinese were known to have invented a process for making white copper, which, presumably, would not have the deleterious effects of red copper. This substance is known as paktong.

The actual tinning of the interior of a copper object was a reasonably simple procedure. The entire surface was perfectly cleaned and covered with a flux called sal-ammoniac. Then a quantity of tin was placed within the vessel and heated until the tin was melted. By swirling the liquid tin around inside the vessel and swabbing it with a brush, the entire surface was covered with tin. The excess was poured out while still fluid.

Although tinning was a simple process, it was in many cases inadequate; the layer applied by this method was usually very thin, and constant use for a long period of time eroded most of the tin. The vessel then had to be taken to a coppersmith, who cleaned the object and retinned it. In 1738, Peacock Bigger advertised in the July 6 issue of the *Pennsylvania Gazette* that he "tins and mends old Copper Work."

Various attempts were made to produce a longer lasting coating on the inside of copper vessels. Enameling was tried, but the brittle surface chipped easily and, after a few chips cracked off, the rest of the coating was of little value. A method highly regarded by Dr. Willich was to create a rough surface on the inside of the copper vessel so that it would have better holding power and more tin would stick to it. Sometimes a second tinning was done with a mixture of tin and zinc. The second coating became quite hard and, by smoothing the entire surface by hammering, it became solid, smooth, compact, and beautiful. Most small culinary vessels made in the eighteenth and early nineteenth centuries were tinned when they were made, but little of the coating remains on them today. If any does remain, it will be found in corners and other obscure places.

Most of the coppersmith's operations culminated in an object which he finished and sold, but one unusual facet of the trade, followed by some craftsmen, was the making of plates for copper-plate engravers. *The Handmaid to the Arts*, printed for J. Nourse, London, 1764, defines copper-plate engraving thus:

> By engraving is to be understood only that kind which relates to printing. In this sense, it is the making, correspondently to some

delineated figure or design, such as concave lines on a smooth surface of copper or wood, either by cutting or corrosion, as to render it capable, when charged properly with any colored fluid, of imparting by compression an exact representation of the figure or design to any fit ground of paper or parchment.

The actual engraving procedure—that is, the preparation of the plate and the creating of the design on the plate—will not be a part of this discussion. Making the plate, however, was part of the trade of coppersmithing and the various operations involved in the work will be discussed here.

It has been said that redness of the copper signifies it is of good quality for engraving, but this asset alone was not sufficient. The metal had to be malleable so that it could be spread with a hammer or easily rolled into the smallest or largest sheets needed by the engraver. The surface had to be flawless, that is, it could not have any veins, specks, nicks, or scratches which would be reproduced when an impression was made. Particular care was necessary to reject pieces of copper which had previously been used as part of a vessel, such as a still.

Spring hammer for planishing objects made of sheet copper. These were used in the nineteenth century and lessened the labor of the coppersmith considerably.

from *The Art of Coppersmithing*

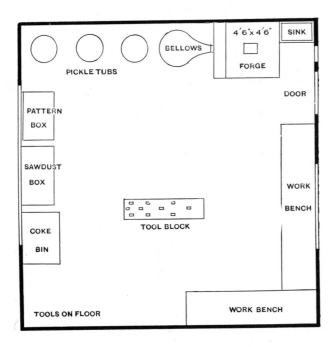

Floor plan of a coppersmith's shop. This layout was probably the standard as long as coppersmithing was a hand art.

from *The Art of Coppersmithing*

After the metal was selected and cut to the approximate size desired, it had to be forged and planished by the coppersmith. The operation had to be done while the metal was cold for the object of the procedure was to compact the molecular structure of the copper.

Finally, some attention should be given to the workshop and the tools of the coppersmith. *The Art of Coppersmithing* by Fuller pictures a workshop with the following equipment installed in it: pickle tubs, bellows, forge, sink, coke bin, sawdust box, pattern box, tool block, and workbenches. The various facilities were advantageously arranged so that maximum use could be made of them at all times. In addition, there were special facilities for making copper rain-spouting and marine work. The bellows were mounted next to the forge and, of course, there was a chimney to carry away the smoke from the forge fire.

The hand tools consisted of a great variety of hammers and stakes. Stakes were round or flat, ridged or smooth, broad or narrow, straight

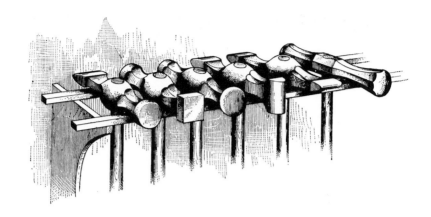

Rack of hammers used by a coppersmith. All the surfaces had to be kept bright and free of dents and nicks.

from *The Art of Coppersmithing*

Layout of the forge and scouring sink in a coppersmith's shop.

from *The Art of Coppersmithing*

or offset. Many varieties of offset forms were needed to extend into the multiplicity of shapes created by the versatile craftsman. The face of the stakes was highly polished so that a mirror-like surface was created on the inside of a vessel when the outside was struck with the polished end of a hammer. Other tools, such as files, clamps, squares, and soldering irons, were properly placed on racks where they were accessible when needed. A number of vises were mounted on the workbench; one type was called a leg vise because a portion extended downward and was attached to or tenoned into the floor. In the nineteenth century some of the craftsmen probably had lathes, drop hammers, drill presses, and other mechanical devices to help them perform their work.

The art of coppersmithing was pursued by American craftsmen from about the middle of the seventeenth century, when most of them must have been repairmen, until the middle of the nineteenth century. One of the earliest records of such a craftsman is the daybook of Shem Drowne of Boston, now preserved in the library of the American Antiquarian Society in Worcester, Massachusetts. His earliest entries were made in the 1720s and his most famous product is the grasshopper weathervane for Faneuil Hall in Boston. When this weathervane was

Benches and stake holder. The variety of stakes, or anvils, show the wide range needed by the coppersmith.

from *The Art of Coppersmithing*

Stamp of John Getz, Lancaster coppersmith.
Kauffman Collection; courtesy *The Magazine Antiques*

removed and examined, a scrap of paper was found in it, inscribed, "Shem Drowne made it. May 25, 1742."

Fortunately, the matter of identification was handled in a more lasting manner by many other American coppersmiths. Documents similar to this one are located in the archives of historical societies; however, identification of a maker can frequently be made by finding an imprint of his name on the product. The practice of imprinting their names on their products was one of the most attractive procedures of American coppersmiths; European coppersmiths followed the custom less frequently than American, and their marks are not as pleasing as the ones used here.

In the eighteenth and early nineteenth centuries the data was usually imprinted with an intaglio die, which compares favorably with those used by the silversmiths of the period. It usually consisted of the first initial and the last name and, on some occasions, the place of residence. The letters were raised within a recessed panel, often bordered with a design of escallops, or dots, or both. Years of polishing have frequently rubbed these raised letters into obscurity and they cannot now be read. Indiscreet application of a modern mechanical polisher produces the same unfortunate result in a much shorter time.

The men who had intaglio dies in the eighteenth century continued to use them in the nineteenth century, but the newcomers, who were not trained in the old traditions of the craft, used individual block letters for imprinting the desired information. The data included their names, often the place of their residence, sometimes the year in which the object was made, and, in rare cases, the capacity of the object. A coppersmith named Kidd, who worked in Reading, Pennsylvania, engraved his name on some of his products.

Records and signed surviving examples of objects indicate that hundreds, possibly thousands, of craftsmen formed objects of sheet copper and brass. Although most of the emphasis has been given to men who worked on the eastern seaboard, the following excerpt from the *History of Saint Louis City and County* by J. T. Scharf, Philadelphia, 1883, indicates that much activity in shaping these metals occurred west of the Mississippi River at a time much earlier than is generally suspected.

In 1816, John Dowling commenced the business of a copper and tin manufacturer in St. Louis, in a shop in the rear of Mr. Robidoux's store, and near Matthew Kerr's store. Copper and tinware were made and repaired. In 1817 Reuben Neal commenced the manufacturing of copper and tinware in the house lately owned and occupied by Mr. Joseph Brazeau, opposite Mr. Hempstead's in Church Street, St. Louis, where he made stills, fullers',

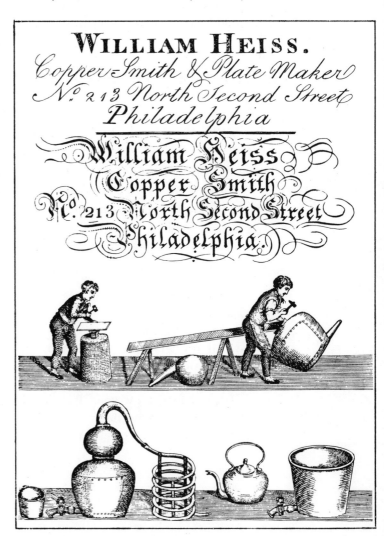

Trade card of William Heiss, coppersmith of Philadelphia. He was also a copper plate maker. Few men advertised this trade as an adjunct to their coppersmithing.

Kauffman Collection

Hatters', wash-, stew-, and teakettles, and copper-sheet-iron ware of all descriptions. In 1820, Neal and Liggett carried on a copper and tin-shop on South Main Street, opposite Antoine Danglin, Block 36. According to the census of 1880, the number of manufacturers engaged in the production of tin, copper, and sheet-iron ware was one hundred and twenty.

Viewed in perspective, it is evident that American craftsmen were prolific producers of objects made of sheet copper and brass, and the quality of their products compared favorably with those made by their competitors across the sea. They devised a number of new forms, one of which was the distinctive American copper teakettle. Without doubt they made many other individual objects which have not survived and are not known of today. The inherent charm of American copper and brass ware is widely recognized today and subsequent discussions in this survey will describe the craftsmen's products in detail.

B. THE BRASS FOUNDER

Literature on the subject of brass founding and consideration of the surviving products of the craftsman engaged in such work indicate that he was an important artisan in the economy of early America. It is also clear that he was confronted with many problems. John Taylor, an early brass founder in Richmond, Virginia, discussed some of them in a letter to Henry Lee, Esq., Governor of Virginia. His letter dated May 27, 1793, is recorded in *The Virginia Calendar of State Papers, 1793*, pp. 381-382. Taylor's comments are self-explanatory:

> I am compelled from the peculiar situation in which I am at this time placed, to address your Excellency & Council; humbly hoping that your well-known lenity and indulgence will, after a true recital of my affairs, be extended to me in as full a manner as the strict duties of your office will permit, and the emergency of my situation require.
>
> I was honored by your Excellency and Honbl. board in being permitted to become the purchaser of a damaged brass Gunn, then lying at Taylor's Ferry, in Hanover county; which purchase I

made in January 1792, and at considerable loss of time, labor, and expense, I brought it to this place—for which said gunn your assistant clerk, Mr. Samuel Coleman, called on me for my Bond, which I chearfully granted your Excellency for the sume of £75 6 8, payable on demand. Not long since, I received a notice from John Pendelton, Esq., auditor, informing me that unless payment of the said Bond be made by the 9th day of June next, a Judgment will be obtained against me for the said sum of £75 6 8; which said notice and requisition is not in my power to comply with at this time, without considerable derangement of planns equally beneficial to the community at large, as to myself. I have to observe your Excellency, and I trust the observation will have its due weight with you, that the establishing a Foundry—either brass or iron—is attended with many difficulties, even in a country where every material can with ease and convenience be procured; how much more difficult must it be in this country, where every useful article must be brought from Philadelphia, and many from Europe? I have laid out upwards of three hundred Guineas in the Business, and altho' every exertion has been made on my part, the business but Just now begins to wear the appearrence of success. I should not ground a single hope for success in this my petition, was I not so well assured of the strenuous exertions made by every person in authority throughout the United States to promote and advance the interests of every foreign mechanick resorting to this country for employment. The erecting a Brass Foundery and the compleating it so far as to execute work in a masterly manner, take time & is attended with great expense and labour; the short time I have been employed, the situation of my foundery at present, together with samples of my work already executed, must I trust convence any person acquainted with the business, that my exertions have been great. My knowledge of the business perfect in all its various branches, and unless checked in its present Infant state, there cannot exist a doubt of its answering the desired effect, the procuring myself & family ease and convenience, and the community at large, great and essential service—two instances occur to prove my last assertion, i.e. my selling 20 pr.c. lower than imported Goods, and giving a price for old metal, which till I came to this place or within twelve months past, was in many parts of the country doomed useless. I can tho' not without having a good many inconveniencys to encounter, pay by the time prescribed, one-half of the debt, and beg indulgence 12 months for the balance & Interest . . .

I trust your Excellency will look on the circumstances here
stated with a favourable eye, and remedy the evil attendant only to
the individual and of little service to the Commonwealth.

I have the honor to be with every sentiment of respect & Esteem,
Your Excellency's most H'ble Petitioner.

The brass founder learned his trade by the apprentice plan, as the
coppersmith did, after which he was permitted to engage in a business
of his own, and train apprentices if he were able to get them to work for
him. The trade of brass founding was not one of the most desirable
ones in colonial times; it was a dirty, laborious business, not likely to
attract as many young men as did the silversmithing or tailoring trades.
The use of various metals demanded a reasonably thorough knowledge
of metallurgy. In addition, in the eighteenth century, the brass founder
must also have had to have been a pattern maker, for no such single
trade has been found in records of the era.

The work of the founder is described in the *Encyclopedia; or, a
Dictionary of Arts and Sciences*, printed by Thomas Dobson, Philadelphia, 1798:

> *FOUNDER*, also implies an artist who casts metals in various
> forms, for different uses, as guns, bells, statues, printing-charac-
> ters, candlesticks, buckles, etc. Whence they are denominated gun-
> founders, bell-founders, figure-founders, founders of small works,
> etc.

The same source describes a foundry as follows:

> Foundery, or foundry, the art of casting all sorts of metals into
> different forms. It likewise signifies the work-house or smelting-
> hut, wherein the operations are performed.

While the above definition of the trade of the founder is reasonably
precise, the description of his premises is vague. The use of the term
"smelting-hut" suggests that some foundries were perhaps only tempo-
rary buildings or, at best, not very substantial ones. The reason for this
poor facility may have been the constant danger from the great heat
generated in the furnaces—fireproofing was not then a well-established
art.

Other than a roof and walls to protect the founder in inclement weather, the most important part of his equipment was the furnace for melting metals. The furnace is described in the *Cyclopedia or, an Universal Dictionary of Arts and Sciences,* by E. Chambers, London, 1751:

> The furnace wherein the fusion is made, is much like the smith's forge; having, like that, a chimney, to carry off the smoke, a pair of bellows, to blow up the fire; and a hearth, where the fire is made, and the crucible is placed. It is the use of this hearth that chiefly distinguishes the furnace from the forge.
>
> In the middle thereof there is a small cavity, ten or twelve inches wide, which goes to the very bottom: it is divided into two, by an iron grate; the upper part serves to hold the crucible, and the fuel; and the lower to receive the ashes.
>
> When the fuel, which is to be of dry wood, is pretty well lighted, they put the crucible full of metal in the middle, and cover it with an earthen lid; and, to increase the force of the fire, besides blowing it up with a bellows, they lay a tile over part of the aperture or the cavity of the furnace.

To understand the trade and products of the brass founder it is essential to have some knowledge of the place where he worked, the techniques he used, and the metals he cast into the various objects he made. The bell- and gun-founder used metals other than brass and the men who made andirons and door knockers also used metal other than pure brass. Andirons often have a reddish "cast" which indicates that either the founder or the purchaser was not sensitive to a departure from the use of yellow brass. These bronze alloys may have also been used because bronze was an agreeable metal to form by the casting process.

Before the metal was placed in the crucible for melting, considerable work had to be done in the craft known as pattern making. And pattern making itself was preceded by the creation of a design for the object to be made. The creation of a design always has been of great importance. In the eighteenth century, designing a product was the work of the producer, for no separate trade of designers is known to have existed. It was, no doubt, his special knowledge of design that separated the true artisan from the craftsman. Both coppersmithing and brass founding were invariably called arts rather than crafts, and with some justifica-

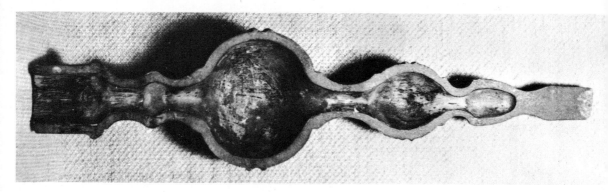

A half pattern for the top section of a hollowed andiron.
Kauffman Collection

tion. It was this unusual combination of artists-craftsmen who produced the objects of metal which are proudly called American today.

After a design was agreed upon it was given to a man who would today be called a pattern maker. Since there is no evidence that a separate trade of pattern making existed in the eighteenth century, and the procedure of pattern making is rarely mentioned, it is presumed that this work was regarded as an integral part of brass founding. Pattern making does appear as a trade in a few business directories of the early nineteenth century, and by mid-century many pattern makers were working at their lathes and benches.

For a fuller understanding of the examples of brass casting which have survived, two facets of the work of the early pattern maker should be emphasized. First, there was a distinct advantage in making an object round. It was easier to make a round pattern on a lathe than to carve it by hand tools; also round castings could be more easily cleaned and polished on a lathe than by time-consuming hand methods. Secondly, many of the patterns were only half patterns. After the exterior shape of an andiron was shaped on a lathe, the pattern was parted in the middle and the interior was removed so that only a shell of the outer design remained.

This procedure was followed for two reasons. Scooping out the inside area of the pattern effected a substantial saving in the amount of metal needed to cast such objects as andirons, as they could be made very thin. Light weight is one of the criteria often used to determine whether or not an andiron is really old. The second reason for halving the pattern was that coring was very poorly understood at that time, and by casting two hollow shells and brazing them together, the making of a core was eliminated. Today, cores are made of baked sand; and after the molten metal flows around the core and is cooled, the core is easily removed by shaking or tapping the part. Treatises about foundry work in the eighteenth century do not mention cores, but in the nineteenth century their use was a common procedure.

After the pattern was made, the founder was ready to produce the part. For reasons of safety and convenience, large objects, such as bells, were cast outside the foundry, usually in a hole in the ground. Founders of small works cast their objects on the foundry floor in boxes called "flasks." Flasks were made of wood, they separated in the middle, and had neither a top nor a bottom. They varied in depth, length, and width, depending on the size of the casting to be made.

The first step was to place the pattern on a board in the center of the bottom half of the flask, which was called a "drag." The drag was filled with moistened sand and tamped solid so the pattern would stay wedged in the drag, though there would be some porosity for escaping gases. The drag was then turned upside down, bringing the pattern on top. The top half of the flask, called a "cope," was then placed on the drag. The sand and pattern were dusted with a parting powder, the cope filled with sand and tamped, as was done to the drag. A vertical hole, called a "sprue," was cut to the middle of the flask, which was later connected to the pattern cavity by a channel called a "gate." The cope was then removed, the pattern removed from the sand, the gate cut to the sprue, and the flask reassembled. Reassembling could be perfect, for the mating parts in each half always fitted exactly together.

To pour the molten metal into the flask, either the crucible was lifted from the furnace with a pair of tongs designed for that purpose, or the metal was dipped into a ladle and carried to the desired location. After the metal cooled, it was removed from the sand and was ready for the finishing procedure.

Much has been written about the casting of metals by the brass founder; however, almost nothing is mentioned about the final shaping and polishing of the castings. The parts which were round were mounted

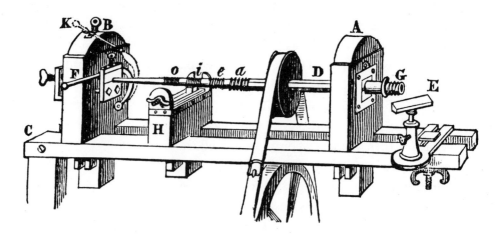

Brass turner's lathe and tools. The various parts of brass were mounted on the lathe and cut to shape by tools held in the operator's hands. Tools for cutting brass today are rigidly held in a tool holder.

from *The Cabinet Cyclopedia*

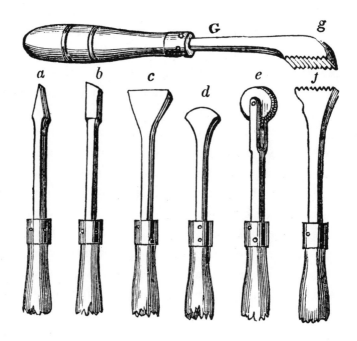

on a lathe and cut to their final form with tools resembling those used by wood turners today.

The accompanying figure is a sketch of a brass turner's lathe as shown in *The Cabinet Cyclopedia*, by Rev. Dionysius Lardner. The lathe consists of two upright puppets (called a "headstock" and a "tailstock" today) mounted on a frame and held in place by two tapered wedges forced between the puppets on which cylindrical objects could be turned; on one end a threaded stud extends to which various chucks could be attached. The power could be supplied by a kick treadle, by a reel, or by water power.

The cutting tools shown in the accompanying figure were held by hand and applied to the metal so that more perfect detail in design could be made than foundry procedure permitted. After the tool work was finished, fine sand and oil was applied to a stick and held against the brass, the final polishing being done with rottenstone and oil.

There is considerable confusion among antiquarians about the burnishing of objects of metal. Today, most people think that buffing with a cloth wheel charged with an abrasive is identical to burnishing. This assumption is not correct. A burnisher is defined by the *Cyclopedia or, an Universal Dictionary of Arts and Sciences* by E. Chambers as:

> Burnisher, a round polished piece of steel, serving to smooth and give lustre to metal. Of these there are various kinds, of various figures; strait, crooked, etc.—Half burnishers are used to solder silver, as well as to give lustre.

Thus, burnishing is simply "the act or art of smoothing and polishing a metallic body, by briskly rubbing it with a burnisher."

The work of the brass founder was both extensive and important. Possibly the best listing of objects made by him is provided by the advertisement of Daniel King which appeared in the *Pennsylvania Chronicle*, April 20, 1767. In it he lists the following products:

Firedogs

Brass fenders of all sorts

Fire shovels and tongs

Candlesticks

Sconces

Brasses for gristmills, windmills and sawmills

Brass cocks

Founder's work for gunsmiths and coppersmiths

Chandeliers   Cylinders for pumps
Bells of all sizes   Brass for West India sugar mills
House bells   Buckles
Horse bells   Brass door knockers
Criers' bells

And to keep him busy in his spare time, "He also rivets broken China, in the neatest manner"!

III. Products of the Coppersmith

THE subject of kettles does not seem one to arouse indecision or controversy; yet in the late eighteenth century a close distinction was made between a pot and a kettle. The *Encyclopedia Perthensis* defines a kettle as: "A vessel in which liquor is boiled. In the kitchen the name *pot* is given to the boiler that grows narrower towards the top, and of *kettle* to that which grows wider."

A. KETTLES

Despite vague differences between pots and kettles, it is evident that the coppersmith made a great many kettles, but few pots. Ten of the twenty-four items enumerated in his products are called kettles, and they will be so regarded in this survey even though some grow narrower toward the top, and some grow wider. The list includes brass kettles, brewers', cider, dyers', fish, hatters', planking, and ship kettles, and teakettles.

Teakettles

It is difficult to determine now which objects on the list were in greatest demand in the eighteenth and nineteenth centuries. But as more teakettles have survived than any other form, they will be considered first in this survey of kettles. There are several other reasons for making them the first object to be examined. A researcher is naturally interested in the material of which an object is made, and it is to be noted that, though European craftsmen frequently used brass for mak-

Teakettle made of brass about 1850 for James W. Adams of the U.S. Navy.
courtesy James Knowles

ing teakettles, only one brass teakettle has been recognized as the product of an American craftsman. The billhead of Benjamin Harbeson, dated 1794, pictures a teakettle which closely resembles some made of brass by Dutch craftsmen; but no examples of this type and material have been found bearing the name of an American craftsman. Some researchers consider that this lack of brass teakettles resulted because brass was scarcer than copper or that it was more difficult to make one

The handle on this copper teakettle
by F. Steinman has been slightly
shortened; otherwise, it is a
typical product of a Pennsylvania
coppersmith. The maker's name is
stamped on the handle. The
engraving is of the maker, one
of the early owners of the Steinman
Hardware Store in Lancaster, Pa.
When the store closed in 1965,
it was the oldest hardware store in
continuous operation in America.

Kauffman Collection

of brass than copper. Both conclusions are correct, but they still do not explain why only one skilled American craftsman produced a teakettle made of brass.

Copper teakettle made by G. Reid of Winchester, Va. The form of the pot, the shape of the handle, and the intaglio imprint of his name are attractive features of this kettle. courtesy Colonial Williamsburg and *The Magazine Antiques*

Two copper teakettles by Pennsylvania craftsmen showing the range of sizes in which teakettles were made. The large one is signed by Getz, the small one is unsigned.

McMurtrie Collection; courtesy *The Magazine Antiques*

A second major difference between European and American teakettles is that many of those made in America were signed by the men who made them. This does not imply that kettles made in Europe were never signed, but that signing them was a much more common practice here than in Europe. It might also be noted that a larger proportion of teakettles were signed in America than were other products of the coppersmith. It is difficult to account for this practice, but one might suppose that, because the teakettle was difficult to make, the craftsman wanted to be identified with his product. The flaring portion of the body was no more difficult to form than any other piece with a similar flare, but to draw the sides into the horizontal position of the top required much skill and patience. The spout with its interesting contour

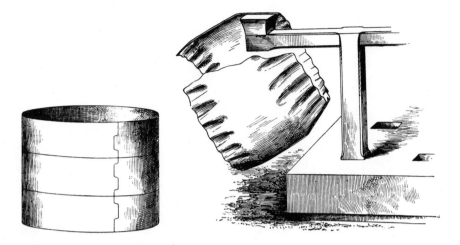

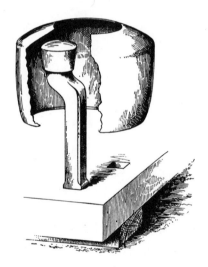
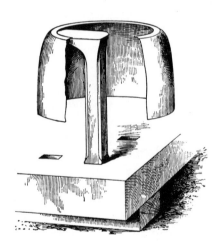

Body of Gallon Glue Pot or Teakettle   *Forming Teakettle Body*

Razing Down Top on Bullet Stake   *Turning Lag on Bottom Stake*

Techniques used in making a copper teakettle. The Bullet Stake and the Bottom Stake
are specialized in the making of teakettles.

from *The Art of Coppersmithing*

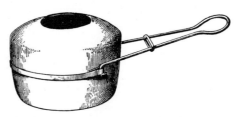

Clamp for Holding Teakettle while Being Tinned

Putting in Bottom

Charger

Tow-Wisp Used in Tinning

Planishing Teakettle Side

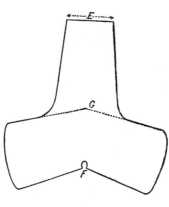

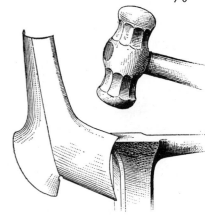

Dimensions of the Teakettle Spout   *Pattern for the Spout*   *Working the Throat Down*

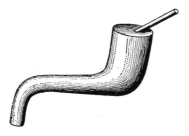

End of Spout Bent

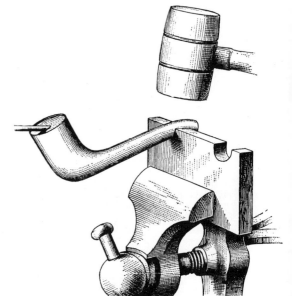

Improved Way of Bending   *Bending Spout over Lead Piece*

The pattern for and the shaping of a spout for a copper teakettle. The spout was filled with lead so it would not wrinkle when it was bent.

from *The Art of Coppersmithing*

and reverse bends was also a challenge to the craftsman, whose attempts must have sometimes ended in failure.

That no two copper teakettles are identical may have some bearing on the great number of them that were signed. Most likely they were regarded as an art form by the coppersmiths who made them and, in the tradition of men who create unique objects, they signed them proudly. Then, too, the broad, flat handle was an excellent place for the craftsman to imprint his name, particularly when this area is compared with the forbidding round surfaces found on such objects as stills and funnels. Whatever the reason, the fact remains that more copper teakettles are signed than any of the other products of the American coppersmith, and the reason for this practice can only be conjectured.

A study of early teakettles indicates that, although the form varied, depending upon place and period of manufacture, the greatest variation was in size. Unfortunately the smallest kettles attributed to Ameri-

Copper teakettle of the late nineteenth or early twentieth century. Although it was probably fabricated by hand tools, it lacks the charm of earlier kettles.

Snyder Collection

can craftsmen are not signed, but must be identified by their distinctive style. A few of these small ones, with a diameter of less than six inches, have been found unsigned; a number in the six-inch diameter range bear the names of American craftsmen and are unquestionably indigenous to America. By all odds, the greatest number of signed teakettles are within the eight- to eleven-inch range, while a few very large ones are in the twelve-inch size. A signed one with a diameter larger than twelve inches must be regarded as a rarity.

Teakettles were made in America over a long period of time. The following advertisement of Peacock Bigger in the August 3, 1738, issue of the *Pennsylvania Gazette* includes teakettles among a variety of other products.

PEACOCK BIGGER, BRAZIER

in Market-Street, near the sign of the Indian King: Makes and Sells all Sorts of Copper Work, Viz., Tea Kettles, Coffee Pots, Warming Pans, Copper Pots, Sauce Pans, Kettle Pots, Dutch Ovens, and Stew Pans, Brass Kettles, and other sorts of Copper Work when bespoke: He tins and mends old Copper Work and sells Tinwork at reasonable prices, and gives ready money for old Copper and Brass.

The utility and attractiveness of the American copper teakettle is evidenced by the fact that it was one of the common products of the coppersmith for more than a hundred years.

The popularity of the teakettle is apparent from its consistent use in the literature relating to the trade. The trade cards of Philip Apple, Benjamin Harbeson, and William Heiss show teakettles as one of their products. William Bailey used a "cut" of a teakettle on the top of his advertisement in the July 7, 1772, issue of the *Pennsylvania Staatsbote*. In many newspaper advertisements it was one of the first-mentioned products which the coppersmith had for sale. Copper teakettles were perhaps more popular in Pennsylvania than in New England; at least, there are many more signed ones from Pennsylvania than from New England. A few signed ones are known which were made by craftsmen who worked in New York, city and state, and in Virginia; at least one was made in Ohio.

The style of the eighteenth century survived long into the nine-

Typical copper teakettle from Scandinavia. Only the handle has a shape similar to the handles of American copper teakettles; the spout, body, and lid are very different.
Machmer Collection

teenth century with little change. Eventually the shape was changed so that a portion of the bottom extended into the round openings of cast-iron cookstoves, and the meticulously shaped joint, resembling a dovetail, was discarded for a seamed joint which could be quickly and easily made by a craftsman with only limited experience. The gooseneck spout was dropped for a straight flaring spout, also joined by a seam, that was much less attractive but equally as functional as the original shape. Handles were made of thin metal with edges reinforced with wire to make them rigid. After 1850, few craftsmen imprinted their names on the handles and their product can only be identified as "a late copper teakettle."

Perhaps the most significant observation to be made of the early fine teakettles is that American craftsmen created a new style. There was ample precedent for them to copy European kettles, and occasionally certain European features were imitated here. However, the teakettle created in America was a far-distant cousin to that made in Europe. No American teakettles seem to have the covered spouts of those made in Scandinavia, the bulbous bodies of those from Holland, nor the cast handle used so frequently on kettles made in England. Most American examples are well made, many are signed by their makers; and all of them are attractive examples of American design.

Cooking Kettles

Although coppersmiths made many kettles, there is such scarcity of data about them that there is considerable uncertainty now about their various shapes, sizes, and functions. This condition relates particularly to cooking kettles which were not mentioned in the advertisements, were never illustrated, and were generally disregarded in what little literature is available about the products of the coppersmith. This obscurity presents another mystery for, despite the lack of information about them, they are, next to teakettles, the most common objects available today. They are made of both copper and brass, and several have been found bearing the names of American coppersmiths.

Most of the copper kettles were made of three pieces of sheet copper —two sides and a bottom. The slightly flaring sides were joined from top to bottom with the cramped joint used in the making of teakettles and other objects of copper. A similar joint was used to insert the bottom, usually a convex shape on the outside. A reasonably heavy piece of wire was inserted in the top edge and completely enclosed by the copper to make the joint attractive and to protect the iron wire from deteriorating influences. Just under the wired edge, two ears were attached with rivets and a forged bail of iron was looped through the opening in the ears. The ears were made of copper, iron, or brass. Almost none of these copper cooking kettles were tinned on the inside.

Although most of the copper cooking kettles were made as described above, some were made by the raising process and have no joints. Both methods included careful planishing which not only made the metal smooth, but also made the vessel round and rigid.

Copper kettle on an iron tripod, used to cook apple butter.

courtesy Pennsylvania State Museum

The convex shape of the bottom dictated that the kettle be used on a tripod or suspended from a crane in a fireplace. The function of the smaller ones (two to three gallons) is not known today but a large one (ten to fifty gallons) was definitely used to prepare the Pennsylvania delicacy called apple butter. In the late nineteenth and early twentieth centuries, most of the farmers (at least in eastern Pennsylvania) had one or two of these kettles which were normally stored in the attic; but on apple-butter making days they were brought down, scrubbed, and used in stewing down apples to make a product similar to jam, which was eaten on bread.

The outside of the kettle was never cleaned for it was exposed to direct fire, which created a thick, tough coat of oxidation on the copper. The kettle was placed on a tripod of iron, just the right height, so a fire could be conveniently burned under it for a number of hours. The ingredients were placed within the kettle and, as the product thickened, a rotary device was operated which kept the butter in constant motion so it would not burn and stick to the sides of the kettle. This rotary apparatus was made of wood; it was attached by a saddle over the

Extremely rare type of brass kettle, made of one piece of brass, without joints. The forming was done completely by hammer. Signed "W. Heyser/Chambersburg" (Pa.).
Horst Collection

ears of the kettle; and the crank on its top was hand turned by a stick long enough so the operator could stand back from the heat of the fire.

The following recipe for apple butter is taken from *A Dictionary of Every Day Wants,* by A. E. Youman, published by Frank M. Reed, New York, 1872.

Apple Butter (Pennsylvania method)

Boil new cider down to one half. Pare, cut and core, equal quantities of sweet and sour apples. Put the sweet apples in a large kettle to soften a little first, as they are the hardest. Add enough boiled cider to cook them. After boiling half an hour, stirring often, put in the sour apples, and add more boiled cider with molasses enough to sweeten moderately. Boil until tender, stirring to prevent burning. Pack in firkins or pots for winter use.

Another use of copper kettles was in preserving pickles so that they would stay green and appear more appetizing than ones with faded color. The above publication mentions this practice with disapproval:

> All vegetables, when subjected to the influence of heat lose a considerable portion of their natural coloring matter, or undergo some chemical change, which renders the color faded and sometimes withered in appearance; if therefore, pickles must be bright green, they must be colored, and the most common way in which that was done was by letting them be in a copper vessel. The vinegar with which they are covered absorbed some portion of the copper, and gave a green tinge (which, however, was highly poisonous) to the pickle. So many accidents occurred from the use of these pickles that the fashion declined, and makers who advertise pickles ceased to mention their green color as one of their recommendations.

Copper kettles are attractive and popular today, though in quantity they take second place to brass kettles. The plentiful supply of brass kettles occurs because, throughout the second half of the nineteenth century, they were spun on a machine. Not all brass kettles, of course, were spun; some had cramped joints like the copper kettles and some were raised from one piece of sheet brass, but machine-spun composed the greater part. In making spun kettles, a lathe was used to supply the power and tools were manipulated by hand to create the shape. They can be identified by the many concentric circles on the surface of the kettle, the result of the spinning technique.

Spinning metal was first done in America by pewterers when they realized that their dull, fragile product was losing ground to china and glass in the manufacture of eating utensils. A new metal, called Britannia, was invented in England in the late eighteenth century and, by 1825, the pewterers of the Connecticut River Valley were busy spinning objects of this bright new metal. The process was fast, reasonably easy, and Britannia metal was well suited to it. Brass was harder, more difficult to spin, and had to be softened occasionally throughout the spinning process. Considerable skill and patience was required to utilize the method in forming sheet brass, and in 1851, Hiram Hayden of Waterbury, Connecticut, patented a machine for spinning brass kettles.

Although Hayden's name and patent date are stamped on the bottom of the kettles he spun, he really did not make an invention, rather he

Spun brass basin by Hiram Hayden of Waterbury, Conn. This must have been one of his earliest products since it bears the patent date 1851.

Kauffman Collection

adapted a fabricating technique to a metal not previously formed by this method. The following data is taken from the files of the United States Patent Office.

Hiram W. Hayden of Waterbury, Connecticut.
Machinery for Making Kettles and Articles of Like Character
from Disks of Metal.
Specification forming part of Letters Patent No.
8,389, dated December 16, 1851

To all whom it may concern:

Be it known that I, Hiram W. Hayden, of Waterbury, New Haven County, State of Connecticut, machinist, have invented, made and applied to use certain new and useful improvements in the application of mechanical means for forming brass kettles or similar metallic vessels by stretching or distention of a flat disk of metal on a proper form or forms by the compression of a proper tool operating on a disk of metal while rotating with and against the form; and I hereby declare that the following is a full, clear, and exact description of the construction and operation of the same, reference being had to the annexed drawings, making part of the specification wherein—

Subsequent patents were taken out for similar machinery by J. J. Marcy of West Meriden, Connecticut, in 1869, and by C. F. Spaulding of Saint Johnsbury, Vermont, in 1866 and 1867; however, their products are extremely rare. The only product, other than kettles, known to have been made by Hayden are basins. Only a few of them have survived but thousands of kettles can be found in the marketplace.

Brewing Kettles

Brewing kettles can be only of academic interest to the reader and householder today, but brewing was an important matter for many people in the eighteenth and nineteenth centuries. William Penn erected a brewhouse on his estate at Pennsbury and, in 1739, the following advertisement appeared in the *Boston News Post*.

To be Let, by Thomas Foster, Brazier in Marlborouth-Street
A very good Copper, fit for making soap, or
brewing, that will boil off two full barrels.

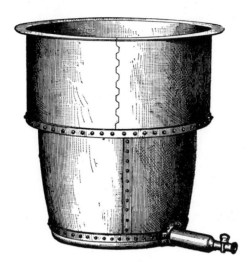

Brewer's kettle. This is
the only example found in this survey.
from *The Art of Coppersmithing*

The size of this kettle suggests that it was used on a commercial scale. Such kettles are known to have had capacities varying from 50 gallons to 36,000 gallons, the latter being the largest one built in England in the nineteenth century.

The brewing kettle illustrated was designed to hold 50 gallons. Regular brewing kettles consisted of only the lower portion. Most of them had open tops; the bottoms were depressed inward so that all of the fluid would drain to the edge and flow out of the drain tube. The sides were slightly bowed outward, and the joints were riveted. The second portion on the top of the one illustrated was made of lighter copper, both for the sake of economy and because it would not be directly exposed to the deteriorating heat of the fire. In rural areas of Pennsylvania, these kettles were used in a separate brew- or still-house; though brewing could be done within a residence, if necessary.

In his *Dictionary of Every Day Wants*, A. E. Youman discusses a brewing boiler or kettle. Apparently he had the amateur brewer in mind rather than the professional.

The Boiler
The material of which this is made requires attention. An iron boiler will be found suitable, but it is much less desirable than one of copper. A copper boiler, although at first more expensive, is to

be preferred, as it can be kept cleaner, is more readily heated, will last longer, and as old metal will be worth about half its original cost. A boiler which can contain about 45 gallons will be found most convenient for domestic use. It is large enough to produce a hogshead of strong ale, and the same quantity of table beer, which for many families will be found sufficient quantity. A pipe of about an inch and three quarters in diameter should project from the bottom of the boiler, and beyond the brickwork with which it is built up, and the pipe ought to be situated so as completely to drain off all the liquid from the boiler, but this it cannot do unless the internal orifice of the pipe be on a level with the lowest part of the boiler.

Dyers' Kettles

Little information is available about the form and function of dyers' kettles. Most coppersmiths advertised them, and their importance is attested in that directions for making one are included in *The Art of Coppersmithing*. The following excerpt from that book indicates Fuller's thinking about the making of such a kettle.

> Dyers' coppers, as compared with some others, are not a difficult job, which will be readily seen by referring to Fig. 466. A dyers' copper is made with a cylindrical body and a segment of a sphere for a bottom. The sides are usually made of two pieces, and the bottom in one. These coppers may be made with a broad or narrow brim, similar to that of a tallow copper; or they may be supplied with a lead apron to catch and convey the drip and slopping, which is always a contingent circumstance in the dyers' art. Let us make a dyers' copper to hold 150 gallons American standard. Now, we have learned from experience that the easiest way to build this vessel is to make the bottom one-fourth the depth and the sides three fourths, without the brim, although this, like all others, may be made any style or shape to suit the taste or convenience of the purchaser.

The description gives minute details about computing capacity, forming the various parts, joining them with rivets, smoothing the inside, and planishing the entire piece. The reasons copper was used to make a dyer's kettle were probably the same as those advanced for using copper to make a brewer's kettle. The inside could be kept scrupu-

Copper dyers' kettle used in the textile industry. Diameter 42 in. at the top edge; 46 in. at the bulge. The ears and handle are of cast iron. Records indicate that this kettle was made by Howard and Rodgers in Pittsburgh, Pa., in 1837.

courtesy Old Economy at Ambridge, Pa.

lously clean; it was easily heated; it lasted longer than iron; and as scrap metal it was worth half its original cost. Their high resale value as scrap metal may explain why so few have survived.

Fish Kettles

Round kettles were not easy to make, but generally speaking, they were easier to make than kettles of other shapes. Fish kettles were oblong, with circular ends and straight sides. They were made of reasonably light metal; the sides were about five and a half inches high; and the top edge was wired to make it smooth and attractive. There were handles on each end or a single handle spanned the whole kettle, with a notch in the center to hang it over the fire on a crane or other support. The lid had a recess around the edge so it could be kept comfortably on the kettle; it, also, had a handle of strap copper. Within the kettle a perforated fish plate was fitted with a handle on each end to facilitate removal of the fish without breaking it. The entire plate and the interior of the kettle were tinned, including the bottom surface of the lid.

Copper fish kettle with the names of two Philadelphia coppersmiths imprinted on the handle of the lid, "G. & F. Harley."
courtesy Bucks County Historical Society

Only one signed fish kettle by an American craftsman is known, though European examples can be found in a number of important collections. Fish kettles are an unusually attractive form of copperware, and one which is signed by an American craftsman must be regarded as a rarity.

Hatters' Kettles

No data has been available about the shape and function of hatters' kettles made in America; however, an excellent illustration and description of an English one is available. That information is included here on the premise that the technique of hat-making was fairly similar on both sides of the ocean.

After the hair used in making hats was bowed into a flat mass, a piece of leather was pressed over the fleecy surface to make it more compact. This pressing process produced triangular sheets of compacted hair, after which the edges were joined and made into a cone. A piece of paper was placed inside the cone to prevent the inner surfaces from sticking to each other. This cone was then taken to the hatter's kettle.

The kettle was a large cauldron, heated by a fire underneath, and the top edge provided with six or eight sloping boards which served as

Men working at a hatter's kettle, showing several stages of hatmaking.

from *The Pictorial Gallery of the Arts*

workbenches. At these workbenches the hat was wetted, rolled, pressed, ruffed, and blocked. At the beginning of this procedure the distance from the apex of the cone to its edge was about twenty inches. After two hours of dipping it into the hot acid liquor in the kettle, and subjecting it to the various ordeals mentioned, the fibers or hairs were perfectly intermixed, or "felted." During these operations the cone would shrink to about fifteen inches. It was then processed in various ways until a fine felt hat was produced.

Other Kettles

Unfortunately, all the various forms and functions of kettles made by coppersmiths are not known. No ships' kettles have been identified, and soap and wash kettles are not illustrated in the literature concerned with the subject of coppersmithing. Some kettles for making apple butter were signed by the Schaums who worked in Lancaster, Pennsylvania, in the eighteenth and nineteenth centuries, but signed examples of any other copper kettles are extremely rare.

B. PANS AND POTS

Warming Pans

Like many elements of American culture, the use and manufacture of warming pans seem to be a practice imported from England. Warming pans were highly regarded objects in the seventeenth century, often singled out in wills to be passed on to a favorite relative or friend. Some elegant English warming pans were made of silver. "Born with a silver warming pan in his bed" was as commonplace an expression then as "born with a silver spoon in his mouth" is now. English dictionaries and encyclopedias of the eighteenth century always seem to refer to a warming pan as "made of brass"; one must conclude, therefore, that although a few were made of silver, most early English examples were of brass.

It is dangerous to generalize about objects made a long time ago; however, the newspaper advertisements of American coppersmiths indicate that most of the warming pans were made in the eighteenth

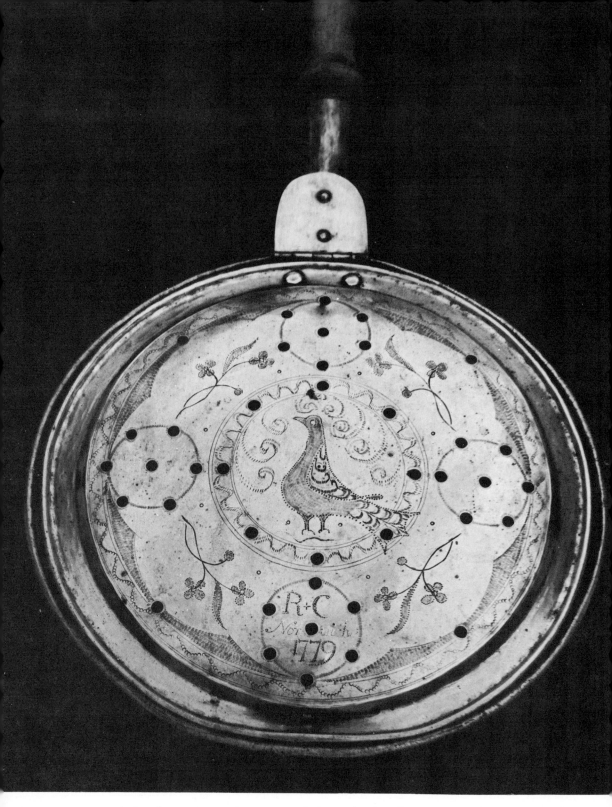

A signed copper warming pan, made by Richard Collier of Norwich, Conn., in 1779.

courtesy Mr. & Mrs. Frederick P. Albertine

century, and more were made in big cities than in small towns. Peacock Bigger made them in Philadelphia in 1738, Richard Collier made them in Providence in 1763, and Caleb Allen made them in Boston in 1774. A footnote, found in *The History of Norwich* (Connecticut) by Frances Manwaring Caulkins, about Collier, who lived there for a time between his stays in Boston and Providence, tells that "warming-pans were at that time a conspicuous article in the assortment of a brazier, and a row of them adorned the front of Collier's shop." It must have been an attractive display. A present-day resident of Norwich now owns a warming pan signed by Collier, one of the most prized pieces of American metalware extant.

Advertisement of Richard Collier in the *Providence Gazette*, Aug. 6, 1763.

The importance of warming pans in times past and the popularity of the object today invite some comment on the probable origin of the thousands that have been on the market in the past, and now are part of collections all over America. Extremely few of them were signed by the makers, and of the few signed ones, only a small percentage have been identified as the products of American craftsmen. We do know that Collier placed his initials, a date, and the town name of Norwich on at least one of his products. Quite likely he marked others which have not yet been discovered. Although this pan has a very attractive folk-art motif engraved or chased on the lid, it could not positively be said from the design that it was the product of an American craftsman. The signature was its only means of positive attribution.

At least one other American coppersmith is known to have signed his warming pans—William C. Hunneman of Boston. Two are now known with his name on them. Since he signed a number of his other products, it is possible that a larger number of Hunneman pans are extant. Two pans are known with an intaglio stamp "I.W." on the hinge, which could stand for Joshua Witherle, a coppersmith living in Boston in the late eighteenth century. The few other surviving signed pans have not been identified as the products of American or English craftsmen. The odds are in favor of finding additional signed pans made in the Boston area, for it seemed a more usual practice to sign pans in that region than elsewhere.

If the making of a copper teakettle was the supreme test of a coppersmith's skill, the making of a warming pan was close behind it. The earliest pans were reasonably easy to make. They consisted of a slightly flaring pan with an iron band attached to the top edge to make it rigid, to which was attached a handle made of iron. The handle was a slender flat or round shape, often tapering toward the end away from the pan and terminating in a hook which was used to hang the pan on the wall near the fireplace. The lid was domed and attached to the handle with a hinge which permitted the lid to be opened and closed. On the lid was lavished the art of the coppersmith in a profuse display of design and workmanship. In addition to holes, which were both ornamental and useful, as a means for allowing the smoke to escape, motifs were applied by engraving, chasing, or repoussé processes. The high lights of the design sparkled in the glow of the fire in the fireplace, and it is easy to understand why it was a cherished possession.

The type of warming pan made in the eighteenth century was somewhat different in shape from earlier ones; in particular, the side flare was carried into an offset or brim about one inch wide near the top edge. The sides in all models had to be wrinkled to raise them, and the offset was an additional problem for the coppersmith. This brim was made rigid by enclosing a piece of wire in its edge. The lid, attached by a hinge as on the earlier models, fitted within the wired edge.

Copper warming pan stamped with the initials "I.W." on the hinge. The design is not unusual but the initials on the hinge are rarely seen.

Kauffman Collection

The lid on the later models was domed, but it also had an offset, or brim, to make it more rigid than lids on earlier pans. There were holes for the smoke to escape and the designs were chased, engraved, or repousséed. Animals and geometric designs were the most common patterns used on the lids. For some reason, human figures are never seen

Dish Wrinkled for Razing

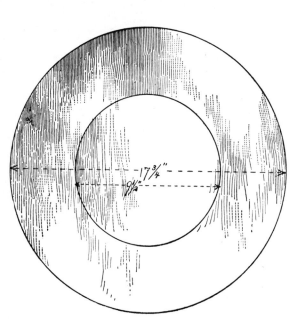

Disk Marked for Bottom

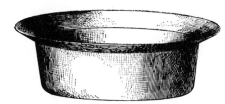

Wrinkles Worked Out of Pan

Brim Worked Out on Pan

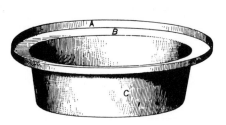

Body of Warming Pan

Manner of Wiring Pan and Cover

Socket for Handle   *Cover Joint*

Edge Turned on Pan to Receive Cover

The Finished Warming Pan

Steps in the making of a warming pan.

from *The Art of Coppersmithing*

on them. (Why didn't some coppersmith think to place a uniformed
soldier of the Revolution on the lid of one of his pans!) A variety of
birds are found on lids, some of strange anatomy. The pans are made of
all copper, all brass, with a lid of brass on a base of copper, and with a
copper lid on a brass base. The combination types might have been
marriages of odd lids and bottoms.

The handles of the pans made in the eighteenth century, particularly
the last half, were usually made of wood. They were attached to the pan
by a socket arrangement with a hole in the bottom for a nail or a screw.
The wooden handle was beautifully turned on the lathe into an extrav-

Hot-water copper warming pan; signed
"A. D. Richmond/New Bedford" (Mass.). This is
probably a unique example.

owned by The Henry Ford Museum, Dearborn, Michigan

agant display of curved areas which coincided stylistically with the rest of the pan. Maple was most commonly used, probably because it was easily available and was well suited to turning. A handle of cherry or walnut is found on rare occasions.

The art of making warming pans deteriorated greatly in the nineteenth century. The earlier form was continued, but the ornamentation of the lid usually consisted only of holes for the smoke to escape. The wooden handles lacked the graceful curves of earlier models and almost resemble a modern broom handle. The late examples were usually made of copper.

Apparently there were two schools of thought about the correct way to use the warming pan. One group insisted that the pan be used with the bed closed, the other argued that the bed should be opened. The latter group contended that the smoke would soil the bed linen and, therefore, the bed should be open when the warming pan was used. This argument was probably never resolved to anyone's satisfaction, but there was a warming pan invented which should have pleased both sides.

This new warming pan was made of two domed discs of copper, joined around the edge to make the vessel watertight. When the handle was removed, an opening was created to fill the pan with hot water; replacing the handle made the pan watertight again. This smooth, compact pan did not tear the linen nor smoke the interior of the bed, and was reasonably easy to make. One such pan is signed by A. D. Richmond, a coppersmith working in New Bedford, Massachusetts. Obviously this type was not as decorative as the earlier type, with its engraved designs and apertures.

Saucepans

Saucepans are a scarce item today, though they were plentiful enough in the eighteenth century when almost every coppersmith advertised them among his wares. Fortunately, at least two signed ones have survived and are proof of the shape and size made in America.

The saucepan had a flat bottom with a bellied side section receding into a smaller diameter toward the top edge and sometimes had a lip for pouring. The shape was developed from a straight-sided cylinder.

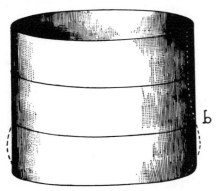

Manner of Razing Top Part of Body

Lag Drawn in for Bottom

Lipped Saucepan

Slack Left for Forming Lip

Oval Pudding Pot

Some steps in the making of a saucepan. The dotted lines on the figure at top left indicate the final shape of the object.

from *The Art of Coppersmithing*

Large copper saucepan; diameter 10 in.; depth 5 in. Made by J. Bentley Sons, Philadelphia; the name is imprinted on the tubular handle. Although Bentley worked about the middle of the nineteenth century, his products were made in the old traditions of coppersmithing.

Kauffman Collection

Copper saucepan with lid. On the handle is imprinted "Crabb and Minshall," the names of two craftsmen in Baltimore in the late eighteenth century.

courtesy Dauphin County Historical Society

The top edge was usually reinforced with a piece of wire to make it rigid and smooth. A short, tapered cylindrical handle was attached near the top edge; into this a wooden handle was placed for comfortable lifting of the pan. The inside surface of all the pans was tinned. Most of them had lids, and the name of the maker was sometimes imprinted on the handle of the lid, it being wide and flat like the handle of a teakettle.

Stewpans

American coppersmiths advertised stewpans, but none signed by American craftsmen was located in this survey. A large number of examples on the market today are coming from Europe, and many have the marks of European craftsmen on them.

The body of the stewpan was a straight-sided cylinder with one cramped joint on the side, with the bottom joined in similar fashion. A few late examples do not have the cramped joints and are obviously machine made. A handle of iron or heavy copper was attached near the top edge, without provision for attaching a piece of wood, as in a sauce pan. A hole at the end of the handle was used for hanging the pan on a hook. The name indicates they were used for cooking and, because they were relatively easy to make, great quantities of them were made and are available today. It is not uncommon to find sets of them ranging from six to ten inches in diameter.

Styles were made which are generally described as shallow, medium, and deep. The shallow ones are one half their diameter in depth; the medium ones, two thirds their diameter in depth; and the deep ones have the same dimension for their diameter and depth.

The lids are flat with an offset edge which centers them to the pan. A strap handle, similar to the one on the pan, is attached to the lid and

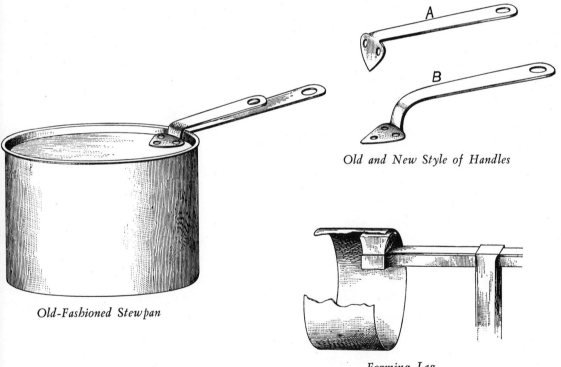

Old and New Style of Handles

Old-Fashioned Stewpan

Forming Lag

The production of a stewpan. Both handles were attached by rivets.

from *The Art of Coppersmithing*

Copper dipper or pan used in the candy industry. The maker's mark cannot be distinguished but the place "New York, New York" is clear. Probably dated late nineteenth century. The inside has never been tinned.

Kauffman Collection

extends out over the edge of the lid so that both handles can be grasped at the same time. Both handles are usually the same shape, though the one on the lid is often shorter than the one on the pan.

The interior surface of the pan is tinned in the usual manner, so the vessel can be safely used for cooking food.

Frying Pans

Frying pans were easy to make and it is very probable that many apprentice coppersmiths first learned the process of wrinkling and hammering while making one. A disc of copper was cut to size with provision for decreasing the diameter by wrinkling the edge and hammering out the wrinkles. Only a few tools were involved in making such a pan and the small chance for spoiling the metal must have made it a popular object for apprentices to gain experience.

They were made in diameters ranging from nine to fifteen inches and from two to three inches deep. The ratio of the flare was usually two to one. If the side were two inches deep, then the diameter of the

Hollowing Hammer

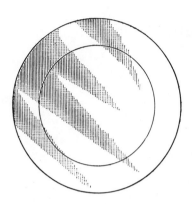

Pattern of Frying-Pan

Disk Wrinkled

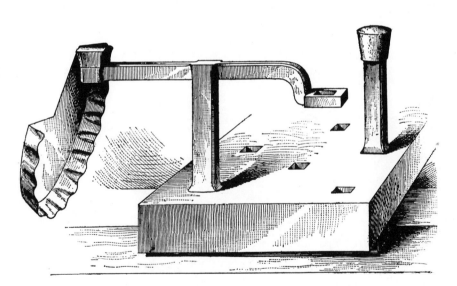

Razing Pattern on Tea-kettle Shank

Steps and tools used in making copper frying pans.

from *The Art of Coppersmithing*

Copper frying pan made in Philadelphia by a coppersmith whose name cannot be distinguished. The handle is of cast iron and is fastened with copper rivets.

Kauffman Collection; courtesy *The Spinning Wheel*

pan would be twelve inches at the top and ten inches at the bottom. Some were made with socket handles into which wood was fitted, while others have handles of cast iron. A few marked examples by American craftsmen are known to exist.

Coffee Pots

Coffee pots were also advertised by American coppersmiths, but none are known signed by American craftsmen. English examples are narrow, tapering cylinders, usually about two and a half times the top diameter in height. They have flared spouts and a socket at right angle with the spout for inserting a wooden handle. They have hinged lids with a finial on the top which is both decorative and functional. The interior surface is tinned.

Coffee Pot

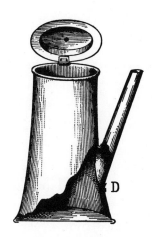

Joining Spout to Coffee Pot

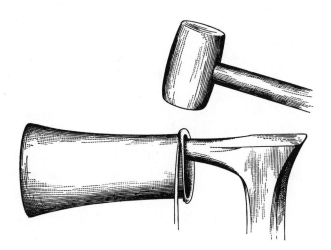

Wiring Body of Coffee Pot

Steps involved in making a copper coffee pot.

from *The Art of Coppersmithing*

C. STILLS

There is much evidence that the still for distilling alcohol was one of the most important products of the coppersmith. The value of this device in this survey can be readily recognized by the facts that alcoholic beverages have delighted society for thousands of years, that alcohol has important uses in the commercial world, and that copper is the best medium for making stills.

To understand the form and function of a still in the eighteenth century, a knowledge of the distilling process is helpful. Two distinct operations are involved in the production of alcohol. The first is the conversion of vegetable matters into alcohol, the second is the separation of alcohol from other substances with which it is necessarily blended in its production.

The use of vegetable matter is essential to the formation of alcohol from sugar. This process is quite direct when molasses and similar products are subjected to immediate fermentation. The same results are indirectly obtained by subjecting grains to processes in which the starch they contain is first converted into sugar, and the sugar later turned into alcohol. For the latter procedure, the various grains are subjected to bruising or mashing operations, then homogenized under constant agitation in a proper quantity of water in the mash-tun. The mash is then run into fermenting vats. Mixed there with a small quantity of yeast, the mash is allowed to ferment from six to twelve days, the time depending on the quantity of liquid and the temperature of the atmosphere. As fermentation continues, the mash, or wash, becomes thinner. When the desired consistency is reached, the wash is drawn off and subjected to heat. It is in the application of heat and the subsequent distillation of the wash that the still plays a major role.

Although great quantities of stills were made in the eighteenth and nineteenth centuries by coppersmiths, only a few remain to verify their size and shape. The shape was reasonably constant over the span of years, but their capacities ranged from a gallon or two to about one hundred gallons. Two stills have been carefully examined for this survey: one made by Francis Sanderson, a coppersmith who worked in

Eighteenth-century copper still. The parts are riveted together in the traditional manner. The condensing coil is missing.

courtesy Bucks County Historical Society

Copper still made and signed by
Francis Sanderson of Lancaster, Pa.,
and Baltimore, Md. This one is unusual
in that it is joined by cramped joints
rather than by being riveted.
courtesy Colonial Williamsburg

Lancaster, Pennsylvania, and Baltimore, Maryland, the other by Eisen-
hut of Philadelphia. Both examples are essentially the same size and
almost identical in design.

Stills consisted of three important parts. One was a large bulbous
body in which the wash was placed to be heated. Another part was the
still-head, a smaller bulbous part with a flange on the bottom edge
which fitted tightly into the body of the still. To the still-head, a taper-

ing tube was permanently attached, the smaller end being the same diameter as the pipe which lead into the worm. The third part was the worm, or coil, a piece of pipe shaped into a spiral and placed in a tub of water to condense the volatile liquid into an impure combination of water, alcohol, and fusil oil.

Distilling, which appears a simple operation, was actually a complicated one. The body of the still was set on a tripod or an enclosure of bricks to retain the heat and direct it to the still. After the wash was placed in the body of the still, heat was gently applied by a fire under the still until the vaporizing point of alcohol was reached. The alco-

Water-color rendering of a still submitted to the U.S. Patent Office by J. Weitzel in 1834.
courtesy Mr. & Mrs. Harry Illgenfritz

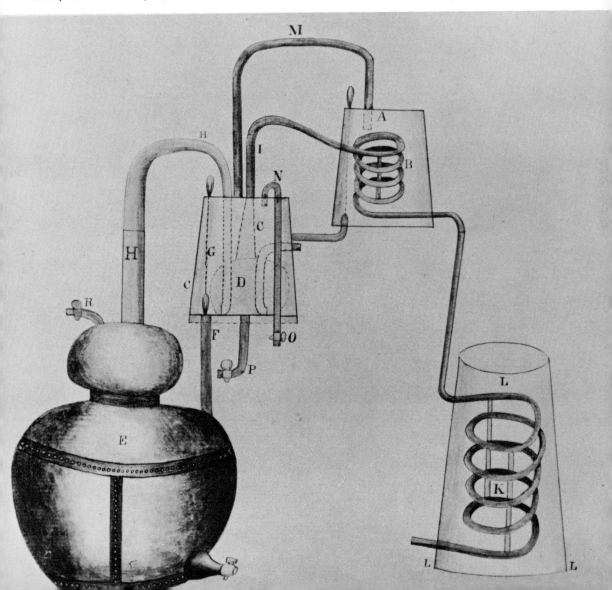

Index of patents issued from the United States Patent Office from 1790 to 1873, inclusive—Continued.

Invention.	Inventor.	Residence.	Date.	No.
Still and condensing tub	J. Wheatley	Fauquier County, Va	Nov. 13, 1813	
Still and evaporator, Perpetual	R. Gillespie	Seneca County, N. Y	Apr. 2, 1810	
Still and rotary steam-engine	S. Adams		Nov. 21, 1808	
Still and water-boiler, Perpetual steam	P. M. Hackley	Herkimer County, N. Y.	Jan. 11, 1811	
Still and water-boiler, Steam	P. Bernard	Whitestown, N. Y	Nov. 17, 1810	
Still-attachment to prevent fraud	W. J. Walker	Baltimore, Md	Dec. 4, 1866	60,294
Still-attachment to prevent fraud in the revenue	W. J. Walker	Baltimore, Md	Nov. 13, 1866	59,688
Still-attachment to test the proof of spirits	W. James	Richmond, Va	Jan. 8, 1867	61,072
Still, Beer, &c	C. B. Jarvis and J. W. Goff	Cincinnati, Ohio	Aug. 8, 1871	117,890
Still boiler and worm	T. Weston	Peacham, Vt	Feb. 13, 1815	
Still-casing	J. Merrill	Boston, Mass	July 30, 1861	32,951
Still, Coal-oil	S. G. Clark	Cleveland, Ohio	Apr. 1, 1862	34,816
Still-condenser	P. Coats	Cincinnati, Ohio	May 12, 1868	77,718
Still, Copper	J. Wright and D. Polley	New York	Apr. 4, 1833	
Still, Double perpetual	J. J. Giraud	Baltimore, Md	Dec. 22, 1810	
Still, Double steam-bath	J. J. Giraud		Apr. 18, 1804	
Still for alcoholic and other liquids, Cold-cap	J. B. Mason	Chapel Hill, N. C	May 17, 1870	103,064
Still for alcoholic spirits	W. and G. W. Robson	Cincinnati, Ohio	July 13, 1869	92,477
Still for alcoholic spirits	C. E. Werner	Brookfield, Mo	Dec. 16, 1873	145,704
Still for continuous distillation, Tubular	P. H. Vander Weyde	Philadelphia, Pa	Feb. 12, 1867	62,006
Still for distilling fatty bodies	S. Childs	New York, N. Y	June 13, 1854	11,059
Still for refining and distilling oil	S. Gibbons	Binghamton, N. Y	Sept. 17, 1867	68,974
Still for refining and distilling oil	S. Gibbons	Binghamton, N. Y	Jan. 12, 1869	85,810
Still, Fruit and alcohol	J. A. Campbell	Rockingham County, Va	July 19, 1870	105,547
Still furnace, Coal-oil	J. Reese	Pittsburgh, Pa	July 8, 1862	35,838
Still-head and condenser	E. Richardson		Dec. 16, 1803	
Still head, Wooden	C. Jenks	East Windsor, Conn	Apr. 25, 1812	
Still heads, Quilted clothing for copper	C. Jenks	East Windsor, Conn	Apr. 25, 1812	
Still, Hydrocarbon	J. B. Edwards	North Greenbush, N. Y	Mar. 15, 1870	100,874
Still, Hydrocarbon, &c	J. Gracie	Pittsburgh, Pa	Jan. 25, 1870	99,081
Still, Hydrocarbon	J. Gracie	Pittsburgh, Pa	May 16, 1871	114,802
Still, Hydrocarbon	S. A. Hill and C. F. Thuman	Oil City, Pa	Mar. 29, 1870	101,364
Still, Hydrocarbon	S. A. Hill and C. F. Thuman	Oil City, Pa	Mar. 29, 1870	101,365
Still, Hydrocarbon	C. Lockart and J. Gracie	Pittsburgh, Pa	July 28, 1868	80,204
Still, Hydrocarbon	C. W. Requa	Albany, N. Y	Apr. 21, 1868	77,094
Still-indicators, Oil and other	W. Hart	Philadelphia, Pa	May 28, 1867	65,078
Still, Naphtha and petroleum	A. H. Tait	Jersey City, N. J	Nov. 16, 1869	96,997
Still, Oil	J. Gracie	Pittsburgh, Pa	May 16, 1871	114,803
Still, Oil	J. Gracie	Pittsburgh, Pa	July 25, 1871	117,405
Still, Oil	J. Gracie	Pittsburgh, Pa	July 25, 1871	117,406
Still, Oil, &c	C. A. Hardy	Pittsburgh, Pa	Oct. 6, 1863	40,168
Still, Oil	C. A. Hardy	Pittsburgh, Pa	Mar. 21, 1865	46,899
Still, Oil	C. A. Hardy	Pittsburgh, Pa	Nov. 21, 1865	51,042
Still, Oil	J. Hofferberth	Baltimore, Md	July 26, 1870	105,683
Still, Oil	J. Reese	Pittsburgh, Pa	May 19, 1863	38,602
Still, Oil	E. Schalk	New York, N. Y	Feb. 18, 1873	136,008
Still, Oil	J. D. Smedley	Chicago, Ill	Feb. 17, 1863	37,709
Still, Oil	W. B. Snow	Brooklyn, N. Y	Apr. 1, 1873	137,496
Still, Oil	J. L. Stewart and J. B. Dubler	Philadelphia, Pa	Mar. 4, 1873	136,557
Still, Oil	D. Symonds	Lowell, Mass	May 28, 1867	65,136
Still, Oil, &c	W. G. Warden and T. K. Petty	Pittsburgh, Pa	Dec. 23, 1862	37,263
Still, Oil, &c	J. Warren	Flushing, N. Y	Dec. 14, 1869	97,998
Still or boiler	L. Beatty		Jan. 19, 1804	
Still, Perpetual	S. Emery	Philadelphia, Pa	Apr. 9, 1833	
Still, Perpetual proof	B. J. Kallenback	Philadelphia, Pa	Aug. 6, 1821	
Still, Perpetual steam	J. J. Giraud	Baltimore, Md	Mar. 24, 1814	
Still, Perpetual steam	J. J. Jirand	Baltimore, Md	May 15, 1811	
Still, Petroleum	J. Bibby and A. Tapham	Brooklyn, N. Y	July 25, 1865	48,896
Still, Petroleum	E. G. Kelley	New York, N. Y	Aug. 20, 1867	67,988
Still, Petroleum	E. G. Kelley	New York, N. Y	Nov. 17, 1868	84,195
Still, Petroleum, &c	A. Lapham	Brooklyn, N. Y	Oct. 30, 1866	59,317
Still, Petroleum	C. Lockhart and J. Gracie	Pittsburgh, Pa	Nov. 17, 1863	40,632
Still, Petroleum	J. Rogers	New York, N. Y	Oct. 3, 1865	50,276
Still, Petroleum	J. S. Shapter	New York, N. Y	Jan. 22, 1867	61,474
Still, Petroleum	J. L. Stewart and J. P. Logan	Philadelphia, Pa	Apr. 18, 1871	113,811
Still, Petroleum, &c	A. H. Tait and G. W. Avis	JerseyCity, N. J.,and Matteawan, N. Y.	Feb. 11, 1873	135,673
Still, Petroleum	P. H. Vander Weyde	Philadelphia, Pa	Mar. 6, 1866	53,062
Still, Petroleum, &c	S. Van Syckel	Titusville, Pa	Dec. 27, 1870	110,516
Still, Petroleum	J. Warren	Flushing, N. Y	Apr. 19, 1870	102,186
Still, Petroleum	W. C. Welles	Parkersburgh, W. Va	Jan. 15, 1867	61,291
Still, Petroleum double	P. H. Vander Weyde	Philadelphia, Pa	Oct. 2, 1866	58,512
Still, Portable	L. A. De Lime	Saint Louis, Mo	Nov. 23, 1869	97,058
Still, Rosin	F. Bowman	Somerville, Mass	May 15, 1855	12,852
Still, Salt-water	N. W. Wheeler	Brooklyn, N. Y	Feb. 6, 1866	52,176
Still-slop, Making spirituous liquors from	D. White	Fredonia, N. Y	June 17, 1828	
Still, Spirit	A. Booze	Buchanan, Va	Nov. 7, 1871	120,701
Still, Spirit	E. Herring	Walton-upon-Thames, England.	Sept. 1, 1857	18,094
Still, Spirit	G. Kaiser	New York, N. Y	June 2, 1868	78,596
Still, Spirit, &c	W. Makely	Alexandria, Va	June 6, 1871	115,751
Still, Spirit	E. Metton	Flemingsburgh, Ky	June28, 1870	104,752
Still, Spirit	J. E. Morris	Baltimore, Md	July 25, 1871	117,445
Still, Spirit	J. C. Thompson	Brooklyn, N. Y	Aug. 6, 1872	130,336
Still, Steam	A. Anderson		Sept. 2, 1794	
Still, Steam	S. Bacon	Lanesborough, Mass	Feb. 9, 1811	
Still, Steam	J. G. Foley	Harrisburgh, Pa	Feb. 23, 1826	
Still, steam, and water baths, Pharmaceutical	R. P. Buckland, jr., and G. A. Gessner.	Fremont, Ohio	Aug. 8, 1871	117,738
Still, Steam or stove	J. Stone, jr	Worthington, Mass	Dec. 8, 1814	
Still-tub	I. Bennitt	Newtown, Conn	Dec. 12, 1808	
Still, Turpentine, &c	R. W. Lamb	Wilmington, N. C	Apr. 20, 1869	89,051
Still, Turpentine	A. K. Lee	Galveston, Tex	May 6, 1873	138,508
Still, Turpentine	J. E. Winants and J. F. Griffen	New York, N. Y	Sept. 15, 1868	82,263
Still, Vacuum	H. Grogan	Flatbush, N. Y	Sept. 14, 1869	94,884
Still, Vacuum, &c	C. G. C. Simpson	Montreal, Canada	May 28, 1872	127,197
Still, Vinegar	R. L. Vance	Saint Louis, Mo	Feb. 4, 1868	74,174
Still, Whisky, &c	H. G. Dayton	Dayton, Ohio	Jan. 18, 1870	98,853

holic vapor rose to the top of the still where it was directed into the
worm and condensed into an impure solution of alcohol.

This operation required skill and patience; the fire might become
hot enough to vaporize other substances in the still, considered unde-
sirable parts of the condensed liquid; or the heat might become so great
that the semiliquid wash in the bottom of the still would be scorched
or burnt, and if not detected quickly, a large portion of the distillate
would be spoiled. The remaining wash would also be spoiled so that it
could not be fed to cattle and hogs.

The first distillation of substances, in addition to the alcohol, was a
liquid that proverbially would "grow whiskers on billiard balls." A
process called rectification necessarily followed. This involved mixing
the distilled product with water and repeating the distilling procedure.
A number of rectifications, depending on the condition of the distillate,
finally produced virtually pure alcohol without a distinctive taste.
Brandy is distilled from wine; rum is produced from products of sugar-
cane; and whiskey is produced from grain. It was necessary for the
rectifier to know what impurities should remain with the alcohol so
that each drink had its appropriate flavor.

Although a knowledge of distilling might not seem necessary to
understand the construction of stills, such knowledge does lead to an understanding of the changes made in stills by American craftsmen, particularly in the nineteenth century. Many coppersmiths became in-
ventors in their attempts to improve the functions of stills. It was an
obvious disadvantage that the still had to be cooled and dismantled for
recharging; this problem was partially remedied by building larger
stills. But there was a limit to the size of stills one could build. A man
named Anderson solved the need by inventing a method for filling stills
while they were operating. A sketch of his still and the report of its
advantages appears in *The Domestic Encyclopedia*, Vol. II, by A. F. M.

Partial listing of inventions made in stills in the nineteenth century. Many, of course,
were not used for distilling alcohol.

courtesy U.S. Patent Office

Willich, M.D. Following is an explanation of the annexed engraving of Anderson's Patent Condensing Tub.

1. Still to contain 110 gallons, exclusively of the head, as near this shape as possible.
2. Half globe made of copper 30 lb. to the sheet, bottom of copper a thimble on the center of the top, 24 inches in the bottom, 16 high.
3. Tub for holding the charge of wash, 36 inches wide in the bottom, 33 at top, and 34 deep, made of 1 ¼ cedar or white pine.
4. Small brass cock to be opened when the charge is let into the still from the tub.
5. Stuffing box made of copper, to prevent the steam escaping by the spindle; the box stuffed with tow, and screwed down fast.
6. Pipe from head of the still, 4½" wide.
7. Pipe: the lower end fitting into the pipe F, and receiving the pipe H, and large enough to slip up on pipe H, so as to leave the head free to be taken off.
8. Pipe: the lower end fits into pipe C, and passes through the bottom, 4 inches, to prevent the condensed steam returning into the still, and fastened firmly in the bottom of the half globe.
9. Pipe to convey off condensed steam into the worm, fitted even in the bottom of the half globe; the other end fits into the mouth of the worm.
10. Iron spindle, with its handle to stir the still, with the cross piece and chains.
11. Charging pipe, 3 inches wide, with a large cock screwed into the bottom of the tub, and the lower end fitting into the pipe M, in the breast of the still.
12. Stuffing box made of wood.
13. Spindles when used by water.

The problem of rectification also received the attention of coppersmiths who tried to reduce the time required for this procedure. A variety of apparatus was devised and incorporated into the distilling mechanism, usually between the still and the worm. One plan was to insert a number of baffle plates above the still so that the ascending vapor struck them and was condensed. The temperature of these plates was controlled so that the vaporized alcohol passed over them but the water and the various oils dropped back into the still. This procedure

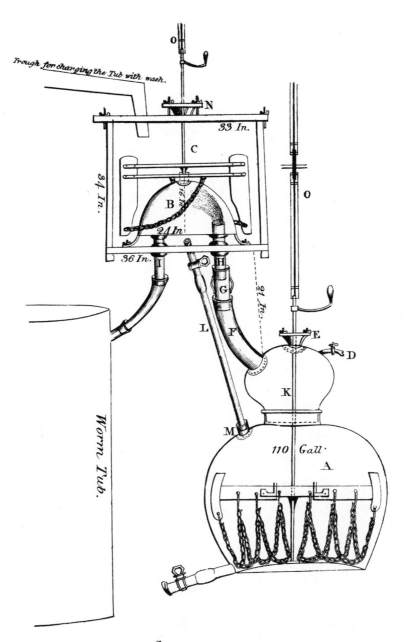

Trough for changing the Tub with wash.

O

N

33 In.

C

34 In.

B

16 In.

24 In.

36 In.

O

H

G

L   F

E

D

K

M

21 In.

110 Gall·

A

Worm Tub.

$\mathscr{ANDERSON'S}$

Patent Condensing Tub.

Date	Description		
November 8th 1821	Michael Barnitz, To a brew kettle weighing 531¼ pound at 45 cents per pound	240	69
November 13th 1821	Jacob Stambach To mending an old Still	2	50
September 4th 1822	Do To mending an old Still and makeing a new collar to an old head	7	00
November 15th 1821	Conrad Maul To mending a Still and worm	5	00
November 24th 1821	Ditto To mending a Still	1	12½
November 28th 1821	John Hoffman To sundris	3	50
December 1th 1821	Do To repearing three worms	1	50
September 2th 1822	Do to a piece to a worm	1	25
December 8th 1821	John Bauersacks To a new still cock and new pipe	9	50
December 31th 1821	Do To puting a piece to a worm	1	50
February 21th 1822	Ditto to a new brest and bottom case	11	00
December 10th 1821	Fretheric Bauchman To puting a new piece to an old worm	2	00
	Do To takeing off a cock and puting onn another one on	1	50
April 9th 1822	Ditto To mending an old Still	3	50
January 29th 1822	Frideric Bauchman Junr To a new Still head and worm weighing 214 pounds at 43 cents per pound	92	2
April 19th 1823	Ditto to a washkettle	16	50

July 2th 1822 Received in Cash —————— 240 | 69

October 14th 1823 Received one half bushel of chesnuts at 00 | 37½

December 5th 1823 Received in Cash —————— 10 | 12½

November 22th 1821 Received one Cord of oak wood at | 2 | 12½

January 17th 1822 Received in Cash —————— 4 | 00

December 1th 1821 Received one bushel of rye at | 00 | 55
and one bushel of buckweet at | 00 | 50
40 bundles of Straw at 5 cents per bundle | 2 | 00

December 8th 1821 Received one cord of oak wood | 1 | 00
December 29th 1821 Received 10 pounds of old copper at 16 cents per pound —————— | 1 | 60
Do one cord of oak wood —————— | 2 | 00
august 5th 1822 Received in Cash —————— | 5 | 00
February 21th 1824 received in Cash | 8 | 00
October 24th 1842 received 7½ bushels of Corn at 40 Cent per bushel | | 00
December 24th 1821 Received old Copper 7 pound at sixteen Cents per pound | 1 | 12

aprile 9th 1825 Received in Cash | 5 | 8

Two pages from the business ledger of Daniel Stoehr, showing the cost of stills and the repair work he did on various parts of stills. The page at the right shows the remuneration for his work.

DISTILLERY.

WILLIAM HARRIS,

HAS for Sale at his DISTILLERY, half a mile diſtant from the Borough of York, excellent RYE LIQUOR and GIN, which is eſteemed, by good judges; equal in quality to foreign Geneva, which he will diſpoſe of on reaſonable terms, at his Still Houſe, by the the hogſhead or barrel, or at HARRIS and DONALDSON's ſtore in York, it may be had wholeſale and retail. Thoſe who may pleaſe to favor him with the diſtillation of their own rye, ſhall have ample juſtice done them, with reſpect to both quantity and quality of the liquor.

THE Subſcriber having declined the DRY GOODS buſineſs, requeſts all perfons indebted to him for Shop Goods, &c. to make immediate payment.

N. B. A ſingle man who wiſhes to learn the buſineſs of Diſtillation, or one who underſtands the buſineſs already, and coming well recommended, will meet with ſuitable encouragement by applying to

WM. HARRIS.

Borough of York; Auguſt 20.   t f b

Advertisement in the *Pennsylvania Herald & York General Advertiser*, Aug. 21, 1793. Distilling must have been more lucrative than selling dry goods.

was not regarded as 100 per cent efficient but was recognized as a step in the right direction. Such new advances made great demands on the skill and ingenuity of the coppersmith, and he finally produced a complicated scientific apparatus. One of the final steps was to place a jacket over the bottom half of the still and heat it with steam. With this method, the temperature could be minutely controlled and the need for rectifying was minimized.

The coppersmith, or still maker, always had to be a sort of technician, even an engineer-craftsman. In the eighteenth century, at least, though most coppersmiths advertised the making of stills, there were men who specialized in such work. Daniel Stoehr in Hanover, Pennsylvania, produced 163 stills in his workshop, and the entries in his daybook indicate that stills were his major output. Evidence of the need for craftsmen who were expert at the making of stills is the newspaper advertisement of William Bailey in the *Pennsylvania Herald and York (Pa.) General Advertiser*, September 5, 1792:

WANTED IMMEDIATELY
At this Borough
Journeymen Coppersmiths

Who are compleat Workmen at Stills, to whom 18 dollars per month will be given by the subscriber, and provided with meat, drink, washing and lodging. None need apply but sober industrious persons. Their money shall be paid at the end of each month.

WILLIAM BAILEY
York Borough, August 21

Despite specialization and the constant improvement of distilling apparatus, there were "general" coppersmiths, as late as 1850, who con-

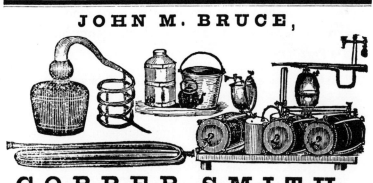

JOHN M. BRUCE,

COPPER SMITH,
No. 110 LOMBARD street, Near Light, BALTIMORE.,

Is prepared to make to order or repair, the following articles: Steam and Water Pipes, for Steam Boats, Stationary Engines, Distilleries and all other purposes, Kettles of all dimensions, Mineral Water Founts, and Pipes, Self Charging Mineral Water Apparatus and Pipes, all complete, on the most improved plan. Steam Drying Cylinders, for Cotton and Woolen Mills, and all other work connected in his line of business. N. B. All work done by me, warranted.

tinued to make stills much like those made a hundred years earlier. The illustration of a still in the advertisement of John Bruce, in *The Baltimore Advertiser and Business Circular* for the year 1850, might well have been used by Francis Sanderson, or some other coppersmith who worked at a much earlier date in Baltimore. The recital of events and developments in still making forces one to conclude that old-fashioned stills were used in 1850 in the backwood hills of Maryland and Virginia, while more modern models were used in cities, such as Philadelphia, New York, and Boston.

D. MISCELLANEOUS OBJECTS

The observer of antique objects made of sheet copper and brass will quickly discover that many of them can be classified as unique pieces. These obviously do not fit into any classification, such as pans or kettles, and are best included in a miscellaneous group. Most of them are rare, but not necessarily expensive. No order of importance is implied in their selection and description.

Butter Churns

Few people today are aroused to nostalgia at the sight of an old butter churn, and only a few have ever seen one made of copper; most of them were made of wood. The following definition appears in the *Encyclopedia Perthensis*:

> A CHURN is a deep wooden vessel, of a conical shape; resting on its base, and having closely fitted into its upper part, a cover of wood, with a hole in its center to admit the handle of the churn staff. This staff consists of a long upright pole, to the bottom of which is fixed a broad kind of foot, perforated at different parts, and calculated to occasion a more universal agitation of the milk in churning. Many attempts have been made to improve this useful implement; but none have been accepted in our dairies, except the barrel churn.

The statement concerning the attempts to improve the function of this simple churning device should be underscored, for a great many

Butter churn made of copper. The funnel on the lid could have been used for adding small quantities of vinegar, which was thought to accelerate the butter-making process.

courtesy *The Spinning Wheel*

ingenious ways were devised to operate it. It was sometimes attached to the limb of a tree, to a dog treadmill, or to a variety of mechanical devices. Making a churn of copper was one way man tried to improve on the wooden model. A copper churn had many good features—it was watertight; an even temperature could be maintained within the churn by placing it in a tub of cold water; it was easier to keep clean than one of wood. But even the combination of all these assets was not enough to make the copper churn popular, and it finally gave way to a barrel-shaped one made of staves of wood.

Sheathing for Ships

Since ships are made of metal in modern shipbuilding, there is no need for the sheathing of ships with sheet metal to protect the hulls from the ravages of marine worms and growths. It was done, however, in ancient times; the Roman Emperor Trajan's galley was sheathed with sheets of lead, and even as late as the seventeenth century English ships were sheathed with lead fastened with copper nails. Eventually, by experimentation and experience, copper was found more satisfactory to the

from *The Anatomy of Nelson's Ships,* by C. Nepean. Longridge.
Published by Percival Marshall & Co., London.

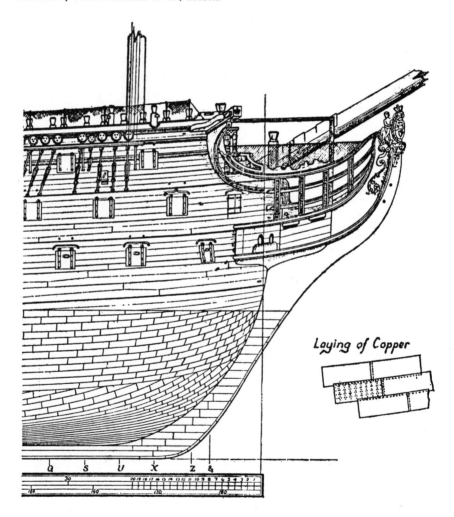

Laying of Copper

purpose than lead. This discovery was one of the reasons Paul Revere became interested in the business of rolling sheet copper. Much of his product was used to sheathe ships of the fledgling navy of the new United States in the beginning of the nineteenth century.

The copper sheets were about fourteen inches wide and four feet long, the sheathing being thicker where it was constantly exposed to the water. Twenty-two ounces to the square foot was regarded as very thick sheathing. The copper sheets were pierced with holes, not only around the edges, but also at intervals of three to four inches over the entire surface. The edge of each piece overlapped each adjoining sheet by about an inch, and all holes were covered with the flat heads of the copper nails. The chemical action of sea water, concussion, and damage while cleaning off barnacles combined to shorten the life of the sheathing. When it was too worn for use, it was removed, remelted, and reapplied.

Though copper has a noncorrosive quality under normal circumstances, an alloy was found that was better for sheathing ships. An Englishman named Muntz took out a patent for an alloy (now called Muntz metal) which was composed of 60 per cent copper and 40 per cent zinc. This substance could be rolled while it was hot, and it withstood sea elements better than did copper. Probably some American vessels were sheathed with Muntz metal in the nineteenth century.

Stencils

The earliest use of a stencil to ornament or otherwise mark an object is not known. The simple utility of the object would suggest that it was used in the eighteenth century, if not before. Stenciling is defined in *An American Dictionary of the English Language,* Springfield, Massachusetts, 1848, as:

> To paint by having the pattern cut out of a thin material, and applied to the surface to be painted; the brush being applied to the stencil permits the interstices alone to be painted.

A sizeable number of tin stencils are found in antique shops and museums. A few copper ones, and a still smaller number of signed copper ones, still exist. They are not masterpieces of workmanship, but are good examples of functional objects which were used in the past.

Stencil of sheet copper, used to produce
individual numbers. Signed
"Wm. D. Zell/Lancaster, Pa."
courtesy Mr. & Mrs. Richard Smith

Stencil of sheet copper used to stencil
data on the end of a flour barrel. Signed
by S. C. Collis of Philadelphia.
Kauffman Collection

Round ones were used on the top or bottom of a barrel, the contents of which was usually flour. The examples illustrated were doubtless used in the last half of the nineteenth century.

Mugs

A few mugs and tankards of copper are found in Europe, but American examples are rare. The scarcity is logical, as not many were made in America. No coppersmith found in this survey advertised mugs, but it is probable that some were made by American coppersmiths. The scant production may be attributed to the unwillingness of the imbiber to drink from a container which was difficult to keep clean, and was likely to impart an unpleasant taste to the liquid served in it. This condition was minimized to some extent by covering the interior surface with a coating of tin, but after long and frequent use the tin coating wore off, once again exposing patches of copper to contaminate the drink.

Copper mug, signed by W. Apple.
A Philip Apple had shops in West Chester
and Philadelphia, Pa., and it is possible
that W. Apple was located in one of
these cities. Signed American copper
mugs are very rare.
Kauffman Collection

Small copper ladle with iron handle.
Length of handle 9 in.; diameter of bowl
2 in. Probably made in Pennsylvania.

Kauffman Collection

Brass dipper with iron handle. Articles
made of brass with cramped joints,
like those used in fabricating objects of
copper, are rare. This one was probably
made in central Pennsylvania, where
objects with similar handles have been
found.

courtesy Mr. & Mrs. Richard Smith

Ladles and Skimmers

Coppersmiths made a reasonably large number of ladles and skimmers, for a number of craftsmen listed them in their advertisements in newspapers. Among these are Gershom Jones, Caleb Allen, and William Billings, all of whom worked in New England.

There is evidence that such products were made there, for Richard Lee, Jr., who marked more of his brass ladles and skimmers than any other craftsman, is known to have lived and worked in Springfield, Vermont. Although his father's name was also Richard Lee, the marked ladles are regarded as the products of the son. In his autobiography, the senior Richard Lee noted that he "peddled pewter and brass" for his son.

The Lee ladles and skimmers were well made, but not very imaginative in form. The bowl was hammered from a thin piece of brass and the handle was shaped from a much heavier piece of the same metal. The mark "R. Lee" was stamped in a cartouche on the underside of the handle; Lee used the same mark on some of his pewter objects. He is much better known for his products of pewter than for those of brass.

In Pennsylvania, no doubt a great many ladles and skimmers were made by craftsmen who worked in copper and brass, although it is possible they did not make the handles, which are usually of iron. It is uncommon to find a ladle or skimmer in Pennsylvania made completely of brass or copper. In recent years this type has been appearing in antique shops, but investigation has disclosed that most are imports from Europe.

There is great variety in the products of Pennsylvania craftsmen. One type of ladle, or dipper, is shaped like a small copper kettle; it is made of a number of pieces joined with the cramped joints used on many of the larger kettles. All of these have iron handles which are attached by two or three rivets.

Another type is shaped like a deep bowl, with a spherical form being used for the ladle and the skimmer. A number of these have been found in central Pennsylvania, and it is believed that this style was produced by a single artisan, or possibly a small number of craftsmen, who worked there. The unusual shape of the iron handle was created

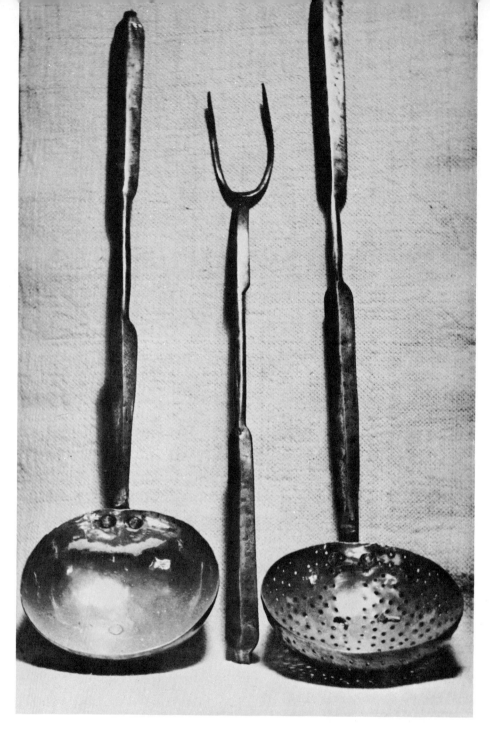

The bowls of the ladle and skimmer are made of brass and are approximately 6 in. in diameter. The handles are 22 in. long. Probably made in central Pennsylvania in the nineteenth century.

Kauffman Collection

Two brass dippers and a brass spatula made in Canton, Ohio, late in the nineteenth century. The iron handles have identical finials.

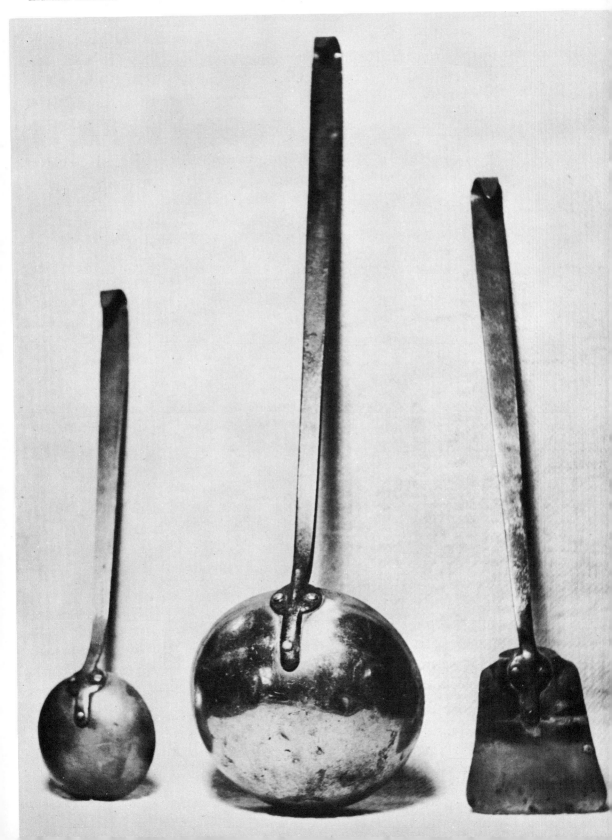

by forging a ridge lengthwise on it, and then tapering the bar to a thin edge along the side of the handle. Sets of such tools have been found, consisting of a ladle, skimmer, fork and, on rare occasions, a spatula.

Some skimmers were so shallow as to be almost flat, and presumably they were used to skim cream from the top of milk. The milk was stored in shallow containers and submerged in the cold water of a spring house; when chilled, the cream became separated and rose to the top, and could easily be lifted with a skimmer. A bowl of this type was usually made of copper or brass and the handles of iron. Some very small shallow ladles were produced by Pennsylvania craftsmen, and for want of a better name they were called "tasters."

Some interesting examples of ladles and skimmers were made in Canton, Ohio, in the late nineteenth century. A number of attractive pieces with brass bowls and iron handles were found stamped on the underside of the handle "F. B. S. Canton, O., Pat. Jan. 26, '86." The uniformity of the bowls and handles indicates that these were made by machine rather than by hand methods; even so, they are survivals of attractive objects seldom used today. At least one spatula has survived with the same marking.

Measures

Perhaps the most important objects in this miscellaneous group are the copper measures, made for both liquid and dry content. Liquid measures are reasonably plentiful; dry measures are extremely scarce.

The common liquid measures found in antique shops range in size from a half pint to two quarts. They usually flare inward toward the top, and have a lip for pouring and a handle for convenience. Some measures show evidence of early production. They have planished surfaces, cramped joints, and a few have details of design which suggest that they were made by craftsmen rather than manufactured.

In the nineteenth century, many sets were made to use in distilleries for the retail trade. This type was obviously made from rolled sheet copper or brass, the joints were seamed with a tool designed for that purpose; there is, however, little variety in their shape or construction details. The interior surfaces of most of them were coated with tin to protect the contents from the distasteful oxide of copper.

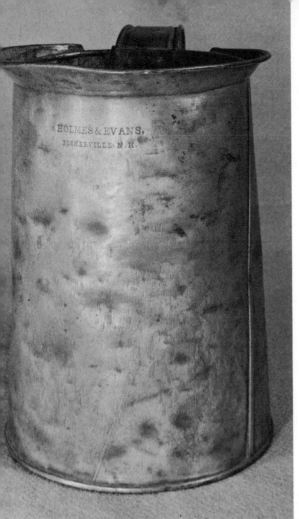

Copper liquid measure; signed "Holmes & Evans/Fisherville, N.H." Signed examples of this type of measure are rare.

courtesy *The Spinning Wheel*

This huge copper measure was found at Chambersburg, Pa., and was reputedly made by William Heyser or his son. It was used in a distillery and the iron bands across the front were to protect the soft copper when the measure was supported on a barrel.

Gabler Collection

There were, however, some important liquid measures made in New England and Pennsylvania which were used as standards by "sealers of weights and measures" in those areas. The form of those made in New England resembled the common tapered form of most liquid measures; some are distinguished by letters "C.M." stamped near the top, signifying the Commonwealth of Massachusetts. The standard liquid measures used in Pennsylvania, New York, and New England were made of a uniform tube of copper, that is, a tube which does *not* taper, and the top and bottom edges were reinforced with bands of brass so that they would not rapidly wear away and become inaccurate.

Only a few examples of dry measures have been found. Some were used in Pennsylvania; another set is known to have been made for use in New York. These sets usually range in size from a half peck to a bushel. They have brass bands around the top and bottom edges to withstand rough usage, and to keep them intact and accurate. The set of measures used in New York has an eagle imprinted on the side, a symbol used by Cluett, an Albany coppersmith.

Standard half-peck measure used by a sealer of weights and measures in Pennsylvania. It was probably made in the early part of the nineteenth century.

Kauffman Collection

Liquid measure used by a sealer of
weights and measures in Pennsylvania.
The tapering tubular is unusual.

courtesy Henry Smith

Lamp filler made of sheet copper in Pennsylvania. The handle is attached with rivets
and the spout with hard solder.

Kauffman Collection

Lamp Fillers

It is probable that coppersmiths working in a particular region produced objects more in demand in their locality than elsewhere. Such were the vessels used to fill lamps with oil in Pennsylvania, particularly around Lancaster and Reading. These diminutive vessels resemble a coffee pot but are much smaller, usually holding a pint, or less, of oil. They have planished surfaces, a cramped joint, and in all details show evidence of having been produced by hand methods. The style suggests they were made in the late eighteenth or early nineteenth centuries. None are known which were signed by the maker.

Drip Pans

Some coppersmiths advertised drip pans. These were usually long, rectangular, shallow pans, possibly two inches in depth. They were used at the fireplace to catch dripping fat and other liquids from roasts rotating on a spit on the hearth. Drippings, if not collected in a pan, might have drained into the fire and caused disastrous damage. Fuller, the author of *The Art of Coppersmithing,* gives directions in his book for making a dripping pan, so they must have been one of the common products of the trade. A few low, oval pans are also known which were probably used for the same purpose.

Funnels

Funnels were made in large sizes, such as quart or gallon; that is, they held such an amount without running over. The earliest types have cramped joints on the side, while later ones have a seamed joint made by a tool for that purpose. The interior surface was usually tinned and the top edge was turned to enclose a wire to make it rigid and safe. A small ring-handle was made for most of them.

Basins

At least one American coppersmith advertised basins. An unmarked specimen has been located, the forming and joinery of which suggest it was made in the eighteenth century. The joint on the side is a cramped type and the bottom is inserted in the same manner. It is twelve and a half inches in diameter and three and a half inches deep.

Copper basin in which "farm hands"
used to wash their hands and faces.

Kauffman Collection

Coal Hods

To make a coal hod required considerable skill, and there is no evidence that the fancy Royal or Nautilus styles were made in America. In
the Boston area, a few hods have been found which were signed by the
famous coppersmith William Hunneman. His product was a straight-
sided bucket with a lip for pouring and a handle halfway down the side
to tilt the hod.

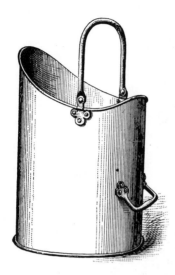

Common Coal Hod

Square-Mouthed or Flat-Bottomed Coal Scoop

Round-Mouthed Coal Scoop

The Tudor Coal Scoop

The only illustration found of coal hods and scoops. The Hunneman product is said to have resembled the one shown at the top left.

from *The Art of Coppersmithing*

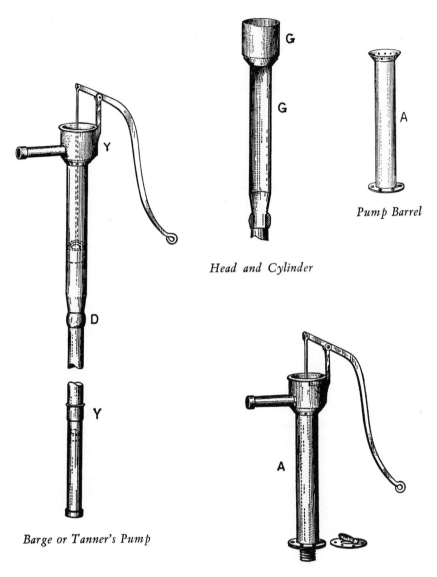

Head and Cylinder

Pump Barrel

Barge or Tanner's Pump

Pump for Pipe or Hose Connection

Various parts of sheet copper for making pumps.

from *The Art of Coppersmithing*

Pumps

Pumps were made of sheet copper and consisted of a head, which was the large portion at the top of the pump, and a long pipe, often eight to ten feet in length. Most often they were a portable type which could be moved from one place to another when certain liquids were to be raised and relocated. They were made principally for brewers, dyers, tanners, bargemen, and oilmen.

Pump made of sheet copper; probably used for dyeing textiles at Old Economy.
courtesy Old Economy at Ambridge, Pa.

The head, at the top, was either a straight-sided cylinder, much bigger in diameter than the pipe, or globular, according to the whim of the coppersmith. A special fitting was attached to the top of the head to hold the handle.

Piping

William Attlee, a coppersmith working in Lancaster, Pennsylvania, in 1795, advertised pipes as follows: "He flatters himself from his knowledge of different methods of making and putting up house pipes, as practiced in Baltimore and Philadelphia, he can give particular satisfaction."

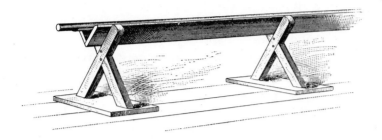

Trough for Forming Copper Pipe

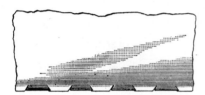

Edge of the Sheet Cramped

Pipe Ready for Brazing

Reed for Placing Spelter on Seam

Portable Supports for Holding Pipe while Brazing

Procedures in making copper pipe. Early pipe has a cramped seam; later pipe has a grooved seam.

from *The Art of Coppersmithing*

The directions for making copper pipe are found in Fuller's *Art of Coppersmithing*. He instructs:

> If the pipe is to be more than 6 feet long we use a trough, made of two planks about 2 inches thick, placed in crossed pieces similar to a saw-buck, and lying at right angles to each other. The sheet is laid in the trough and a straight bar is dropped on the sheet metal, which yields to the falling bar, and the first form is thus given to the sheet. It is then further rounded by placing the other side up over one of the edges of the trough and bringing it together with a mallet. When brought together sufficiently, the joint is laid even on a steel bar fastened at one end of the mandrel block. If the pipe is to be made of thin sheet metal then the joint should be cramped together.

In addition to house piping made of copper, at least one decorative spout header is known to have survived from the eighteenth century, although there is no proof that it was made in America. It has a decorative motif of a sheaf of wheat and is dated 1792. Such a header was used to provide an opening for down-spouting in a funnel-like fashion.

Glue Pots

The form of the teakettle made by American coppersmiths was distinctive to America, and some glue pots were made in the identical shape of the teakettle, lacking the spout. Since the glue pot functioned as a double-boiler, an inner container was necessary. A separate little kettle was made to hold the glue while it was being heated by water in the outer portion of the glue pot. Because the glue could not be brought into direct contact with the heat, the water jacket served to soften the glue slowly and gently without burning it.

Higley Coppers

Copper coins are neither copper nor brassware, but some attention should be given to Higley Coppers in this survey of objects made of copper and brass. The fact that they were made of copper from the Simsbury mine underscores their importance.

In numismatic circles, John Higley is usually regarded as the producer of these coins; however, Richard Moore and Cyril H. Hawley

Old glue pots made of copper are very rare. They were doubtless costly and not many cabinet-makers could afford one.

courtesy Mr. & Mrs. Gil Lyons

contend in their article "The Higley Coppers, 1737-1739," in the bulletin of *The Connecticut Historical Society*, July, 1955, that John Higley's brother, Dr. Samuel Higley, was the producer of the coins.

Samuel Higley was born at Simsbury, Connecticut, attended Yale University, and became a schoolteacher. Later he studied medicine and, in 1719, he and his wife Abigail settled on some land which he had received from his father's estate. He experimented with the process of making steel out of iron and, in 1727, he was given a patent to manufacture the metal for ten years.

In the same year, he bought some land near the Simsbury copper mine and discovered a vein of copper on his property. This he proceeded to "work." He sent his ore to England for smelting, and it yielded from 15 to 40 per cent copper.

Higley's knowledge of steel was, no doubt, of considerable value to him in making the dies for striking the coins. At that time there was little metal money in circulation; thus, with his knowledge of steel and the availability of copper, he made some of the first copper coins in America. His coins were produced from 1737 until he met an untimely death while on a voyage to England with a shipment of his ore. The popularity of the coins caused them to be made by other interested parties.

Higley coins made of copper from the mine near Simsbury, Conn.
courtesy Connecticut Historical Society

Some Higley coins have a deer on the obverse and a broad axe on the reverse side. They have now become rare. Goldsmiths are reputed to have alloyed them with gold because of their purity and excellent qualities for alloying.

Weathercocks

Objects used in America in the seventeenth and eighteenth centuries were widely used in England much earlier. One such object was the weathercock or weathervane, as it is commonly called today. Weathercocks were believed to have been in use in England before the coming

Broadside advertising copper weathervanes. Parker & Gannett were located at this address from 1872 to 1883.
courtesy Abby Aldrich Rockefeller Folk Art Collection, Williamsburg, Va.

BOSTON COPPER
WEATHER VANES,
AND EMBLEMATIC SIGNS.

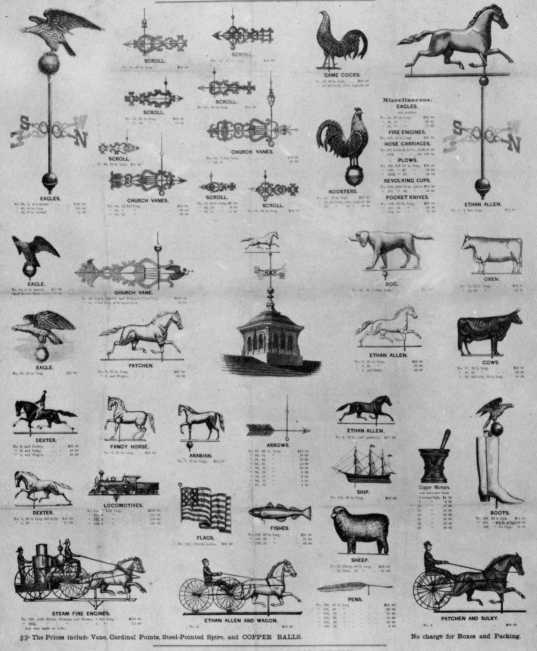

☞ The Prices include Vane, Cardinal Points, Steel-Pointed Spire, and COPPER BALLS.

No charge for Boxes and Packing.

FOR SALE BY
Parker & Gannett, 49 No. Market St., Boston, Mass.

The above Cuts are made from Photographs, and correctly represent our Vanes in every particular.   Our Vanes are made entirely of Copper, and gilded with 23 Carat Gold Leaf.

Vanes and Emblematic Signs of any description, made to order.

Please post in a conspicuous place.

J. E. FARWELL & CO., Printers, 37 Congress Street, Boston.

The running horse was a popular motif for a weathervane. Cast metal dies, into which thin sheets of copper were pounded, were used to create various forms.

courtesy Shelburne Village

of the Normans, though the earliest ones, pierced with the arms of the family who owned the property on which they were located, merely indicated ownership. Later a subsidiary function to show the wind direction was added. For this purpose an arrow was introduced on the front end and the letters N, S, E, W were made a part of the device to easily orient the observer. By the time of Sir Christopher Wren, vanes were made depicting commonplace subjects such as sheep and horses; a vane for a church might use an angel as its motif.

It is a curious coincidence that one of the oldest and one of the most modern copper objects examined for this survey were weathervanes. The oldest one was "bumped out" of sheet copper by Shem Drowne, of Boston, who worked about 1720. The motif is an Indian, in the true culture of early New England. The Indian is wearing a loin cloth, with two leaves missing, and a string of beads, and is drawing an arrow on a bow. This vane was probably one of Drowne's earliest attempts at copperwork. Its charm lies in its design rather than its workmanship.

Hundreds, perhaps thousands, of weathervanes were made between Drowne's Indian and those advertised on the broadside of Parker & Gannett in Boston, late in the nineteenth century. The latter styles also have great charm despite the fact they were partially manufactured—at least, they were hammered into a cast metal form and all of one subject were essentially the same. For reasons of economy, a subject such as a horse was made up of several parts and soldered together.

Engraved Plates

The tools used by the engraver are few and simple. They consist of the graver, the dry-point, the scraper, and the burnisher. The graver is made of a small piece of steel properly shaped and sharpened to remove small threads of metal. Into these minute grooves ink is rubbed so that an impression is created on paper when graver and paper are squeezed together in a press. The dry-point is used to draw designs on the copper preliminary to the engraving process; the scraper is used for removing burrs created by the graver; and the burnisher is used to smooth the surface, particularly if a line is overcut and needs to be removed.

Eighteenth-century presses were made of wood. They had a sturdy frame with a bed on which the plate and paper were laid; pressure was applied by rolling a padded roller over them. Thousands of impressions could be made from one plate, and because engravings were inexpensive to make, they were a poor man's form of art. They were the principal mode of illustrating books in the eighteenth and early nineteenth centuries. Billheads and business cards were other objects produced by this method.

One of the famous American engravers on copper was Paul Revere, who achieved great fame in other areas, particularly in his work in bell and cannon founding. Comments about his ability as an engraver are found in his biography written by Esther Forbes:

> The art of copper-plate engraving Paul Revere taught himself and never mastered. As a silversmith he was unsurpassed in America. The engraving of arms and scrolls which he did directly upon silver is perfection, but his work on copper has little to recommend it except its humor (sometimes unintentional) and historic interest. . . . Paul Revere could not draw, and he knew it. He makes no claims to have done more than engrave his famous plates, but because they were long accepted as original work, he has suffered unfairly. The engravers of his period were as complacent about taking the work of other men as were the dramatists of Shakespeare's day. But few engravers were as completely dependent upon something to copy as Paul Revere.

Miss Forbes notes that Paul Revere was a first-class silversmith but a second-class engraver. Possibly such an evaluation of his work is correct, but in his book, *Paul Revere's Engravings,* Clarence S. Brigham presents another point of view. Mr. Brigham states:

> The plates which Revere made for the *Royal American Magazine* in 1774-1775 constituted one of his most important undertakings in the field of engraving. The magazine had a wide circulation, about a thousand copies, and Revere's name was carried to places he was hitherto unknown. It is true that the designs were copied mostly from English originals, but Revere never professed to be an artist. He was only an engraver and in that respect exceedingly proficient. The copies he made from English originals were faithfully and attractively done, losing none of the beauty of the initial designs.

Although both Miss Forbes and Mr. Brigham have reservations about Revere's ability as an artist, it is difficult to convey to the layman

the high prestige and financial worth placed on his engraved products by todays' collector. Mr. Brigham carefully traces the ownership of Revere's prints as they descended from one family to another, or passed from one collector to another until they were finally deposited in some museum or library to be preserved forever.

In addition to the surviving examples of his work, there is also a day-book in which Revere recorded the charge accounts of his business. The first entry was made in 1761, the final one in 1797. These entries tell for whom various engravings were made as well as their cost and the date of their making. The daybook contains not only data about his work as an engraver, but also about his activity in rolling copper and casting bells. Since the time of his rolling copper barely overlapped his time of work as an engraver, he could not have rolled much of the sheet he used for copper-plate engraving.

Revere produced large numbers of engraved plates at his press, rang-ing over a wide variety of subjects. He produced a simple engraving for a hemp mill, and his largest job was to engrave the plates for *The New England Psalm-Singer,* which consisted of a frontispiece and 116 pages of music. Among his other products are labels for Willard clocks, bookplates, maps, trade cards, the masthead for *The Massachusetts Spy,* and certificates for Masonic lodges. He was an enthusiastic Mason and always helped the Masons in any way he could. His most famous subject, the *Boston Massacre,* was copied from another engraving; he sold more than the man who had engraved the original. Some of his engravings were attractively colored by a Boston artist. Engravings framed in this period have survived in much better condition than those that were rolled or folded for safe keeping.

IV. Products of the Brass Founder

ONE of the most elusive subjects for the antiquarian researcher is andirons. Encyclopedias of the eighteenth century rarely describe them; data about styles and materials from which they were made is uncommon; books that might logically include data about them mention them briefly or neglect them entirely. The famous *Dobson Encyclopedia,* printed in Philadelphia in the 1790s, does not have an entry under andirons nor under "hand-irons," as they were sometimes known. Modern dictionaries contain definitions of andirons, but provide few details which would help the collector identify those he owns or is planning to buy. This obscurity suggests that some attention be given the subject for the benefit of both historian and collector.

A. ANDIRONS

Only a few scattered references have been found that suggest the various uses and names of andirons. Among them, the *Encyclopedia Perthensis,* a late eighteenth-century Scottish publication, gives the following definition:

> ANDIRON. (Supposed by Skinner to be corrupted from Hand-iron; an iron that may be moved by the hand, or may supply the place of the hand). Irons at the end of a fire grate, in which the spit turns; or irons on which wood is laid to burn.—If you strike an entire body, as an andiron of brass, at the top, it maketh a more trebel sound, and at the bottom a baser.

Another definition that throws some light on the function of and-irons is found in *The American Dictionary of the English Language*, Springfield, Massachusetts, 1848.

> An iron utensil used in Great Britain where coal is the common fuel, to support the ends of a spit; but in America used to support wood in fireplaces.

A reference, including a definition, is found in a supplement to Ure's *Dictionary of Arts, Manufactures, and Mines.*

> Andirons, or handirons, also called firedogs. Before the introduction of the raised and closed fireplace stoves these articles were in general use. Strytt, in 1775, says, 'These awnd-irons aroused this day and are called cob-irons; they stand on the hearth, where they burn wood, to lay it upon, their fronts are usually carved, with a round knob at the top; some of them are kept polished and bright; anciently many of them were embellished with a variety of ornaments.'

Records and surviving examples of andirons indicate that they were used in Europe as early as the fifteenth century. The earliest ones were made of cast iron; perhaps their production was coeval with the first

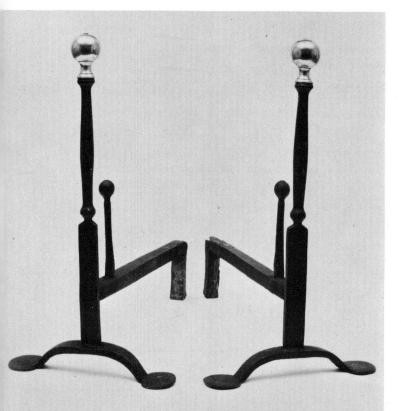

Andirons of the seventeenth or early eighteenth century, made of brass and iron. These are products of a whitesmith, who turned the baluster and attached the brass finials.

courtesy Henry Francis du Pont
Winterthur Museum

casting of iron into other useful objects for the home. The vertical shaft of the andirons was often embellished with figures. By constant cleaning and dusting, even those made of cast iron tended to become slightly polished. Later ones, made of wrought iron, though not ornamented with figures, also became bright after years of dusting and polishing. Actually some andirons were finished "bright" by the whitesmiths, and it was easy to keep them in their original bright and smooth condition. If the vertical shaft of an andiron was turned round on a lathe, this is prima facie evidence that the object was the product of a whitesmith. He also turned the brass finial, which was mounted on the top of the shaft and polished brightly.

Unfortunately, nothing is known about the production of andirons in America in the seventeenth century. The earliest homes, of wattle and daub, built in Jamestown, Virginia, and Plymouth and Salem, Massachusetts, contained fireplaces. However, the use of andirons is uncertain and the suggestion that there was an American production of andirons in those early times is not even entertained. The primitive houses of Jamestown were replaced by brick structures, possibly as early as 1640; presumably andirons of cast iron were used in the fireplaces of these houses. Such an hypothesis has considerable support, for by the middle of the seventeenth century the iron furnace at Saugus, Massachusetts, was producing pig iron, and it is probable that such objects as andirons were made there.

At least one andiron, almost intact, was found among the artifacts recovered by archeologists working at Jamestown. This one is a massive piece of cast iron, the front of which is embellished with a depressed panel and a cherub's head in bas-relief.

Although the cast-iron andirons of the seventeenth century were functional, from an esthetic point of view they were bulky, and when houses and furniture became more refined, a demand for more delicately designed andirons arose. Inasmuch as blacksmiths were among the first craftsmen to come to America, and importations included bar and strip iron, it is likely that some of these men turned to making andirons of wrought iron. Most of their products were probably modest and functional, but if a wealthy landowner or an influential official of his Majesty's government wanted andirons that were elegant and decorative, blacksmiths tried to meet his demand.

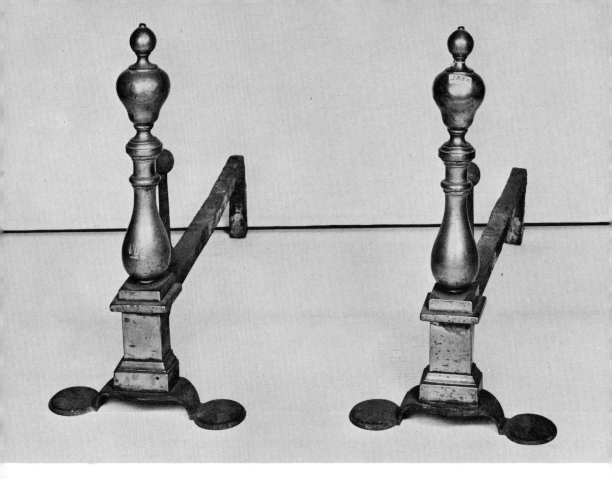

Very early set of American brass andirons. The low bow in the legs and the penny feet suggest they were influenced by early andirons made of iron. The horizontal supports for the logs are made of iron.

courtesy Joe Kindig, Jr.

One of the ways in which the decorative quality of the early wrought iron andirons was improved was by ornamenting the shaft and base with scrolls, and topping the shaft with a round knob, sometimes of brass. Alternatively, the entire shaft could be made of brass, mounted on a base of forged iron. An iron base was better able to withstand the deteriorating effects of the heat than brass and also required less polishing. The horizontal bar which supported the wood was always made of iron.

Andirons made of wrought iron with some decorative details made of brass were widely used in eighteenth-century America; unfortunately, none have been identified as products of American craftsmen. Some, in the knife-blade style with the initials "I C" stamped on them, are thought to have been the products of a Pennsylvania craftsman. No documented proof has yet come to light, though a sizeable number of this type have been found in Pennsylvania.

These knife-blade andirons· are forged of iron and have a tapering shaft, thick at the top where the shaft is narrow, and thin at the bottom where the shaft is wide. The shaft is mounted on a forged-iron base, which terminates in round feet, called "penny-feet." On the top of the shaft is usually mounted a brass finial in the shape of a ball, urn, or diamond and flame pattern. At the bottom of the shaft, a brass plate is mounted usually with no ornamentation except a reeded edge across its top.

A contemporary form of iron andiron resembles the contour of the shaft of the knife-blade style, but was turned round on a lathe. These andirons are also topped with turned brass finials, more ornamented and larger in proportion to the length of the shaft than the finial on the knife-blade style. The base or legs were often very low, but usually

Brass andirons of the mid-eighteenth century. Although of a more sophisticated pattern than earlier ones, the low legs and penny feet are retained in these.

courtesy Joe Kindig, Jr.

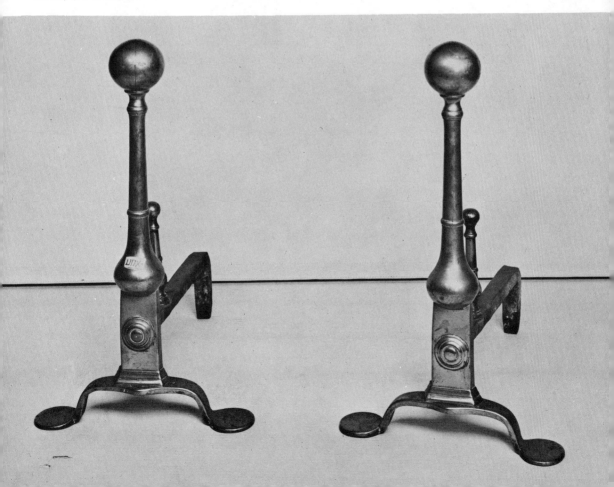

An elegant pair of brass andirons of the late eighteenth century. On the back of one leg is stamped "Revere & Son," on the back of the other is stamped "Boston."

courtesy The Metropolitan Museum of Art, The Sylmaris Collection, Gift of George Coe Graves, 1930

terminated in penny-feet. Both these types were compatible with the furniture styles of the seventeenth century.

The building of country mansions on the eastern seaboard, such as Mt. Vernon, Kenmore, Brandon, Berkley, and Gunston Hall, and the concentration of new wealth in cities, such as Boston, New York, Philadelphia, and Williamsburg, created a need for more elegant andirons than those made of iron, or of iron and brass. These homes were furnished with the more graceful styles of Queen Anne and Chippendale furniture, and more delicately proportioned andirons were desired.

Brass andirons with unusual finials; possibly made in the South.

courtesy Old Salem, Inc.

Because many of Britain's wealthy families were then burning coal in their grates, and no longer used andirons, English production of them was slowed down. It is thought that many of the elegant andirons used in the eighteenth-century mansions of America were produced by American craftsmen. An advertisement of Daniel King in the *Pennsyl-*

Copy of a bill rendered by Daniel King to John "Calwalater" (Cadwalader in the receipt) for several of his products. The most important item is "fier Dogs With Corinthen Coloms." The final item, "3 pound of Roting Stone," was rottenstone for polishing brass.
courtesy Historical Society of Pennsylvania

vania Gazette, March 9, 1767, supports this belief. This advertisement, which enumerates a seemingly endless variety of products for the time, states:

> He has likewise a new and curious Set of Patterns for Brass Fire
> Dogs, neater and more to order than any yet made on the Continent.

King's use of the word "Continent" must be regarded with reservations, for an unusually small quantity of such items was imported from the Continent at that time. He probably meant Britain.

The transition from the early style of andirons to the elegant ones of the mid-eighteenth century must have been attended with many trials and errors, but two outstanding designs evolved which mark the zenith in the style of American andirons. One design, possibly the earlier of the two, is described as a baluster turning with a variety of finials and foot patterns. This one was obviously influenced by the design used in the baluster of a tilt-top table of the period. On the top of this bulbous baluster turning was a diamond and flame finial, and on the bottom was a square plinth with molded edges on its top and bottom. The entire shaft was mounted on brass cabriole legs which terminated in feet snaped like a ball-and-claw, a penny, or a snake's head. The ball-and-claw style is regarded as especially desirable. A few of this type are known as "hairy-claw" because the hair of an animal is reproduced in the brass casting. The most elegant of the baluster type have a pattern which suggests a twisted baluster and sometimes the plinth is decorated with an engraved design.

About 1760, a new architectural style—called "Adam" or "Classical" —was brought to the attention of England and America by the Adam brothers. In this new concept there was an attenuation of classic forms which was well suited to the design and function of andirons. The documented proof of the early arrival of the new style in America is found in the bill which Daniel King of Philadelphia rendered to the famous John Cadwalader of that same city on September 4, 1770. The invoice lists, among other objects made for Cadwalader, "one Pare of the Best Rote fier Dogs With Corinthen Coloms, £25." The sum of £25 for one pair of andirons seems incredible today. Evidently Cadwalader wanted the best. (He paid the cabinetmaker, Thomas Affleck, only £10 each for his great sofa and mahogany desk!)

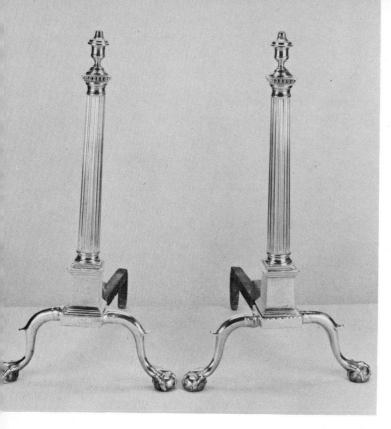

Brass andirons made and signed by Daniel King of Philadelphia, Pa.; in the Corinthian column style that he made for Cadwalader.

courtesy Henry Francis du Pont Winterthur Museum

Fortunately, one pair of andirons signed by King has survived but nothing is known about the Cadwalader andirons beyond the description in the invoice. It is likely that this costly pair (five additional pairs are listed in the invoice) had tall columns, possibly thirty inches high, probably fluted, round or square, and surmounted by a finial shaped like an urn, with columns mounted on cabriole legs of cast brass, terminating in ball-and-claw feet.

Not everyone could afford such expensive andirons and, of course, many rooms were modestly furnished. Thus a short type of andiron was widely used in the last half of the eighteenth century and the early part of the nineteenth century. Some of these short andirons had a round or faceted plinth, longer than that of earlier andirons, and a turned shaft, shorter than those used on earlier models. The turned portion above the plinth sometimes consisted of a large, turned ball with a few smaller balls for a finial. The turned portions of other models were in the shape of an urn, lemon, or acorn. Some had a flaring finial, resembling a church steeple, and are called "steeple-type" andirons. A sizeable number of this short type are signed. Among the makers are Molineux of Boston and Wittingham of New York.

William Rollinson Wittingham was a brass founder in Birmingham, England, and emigrated to America in 1791. He landed in Philadelphia and was advised to establish his new business in Paterson, New Jersey, where it was proposed to create a "Society for the Encouragement of Useful Arts." After three years there, he moved to New York City. He is listed as a brass founder in Duncan's *New York City Directory* for 1795; his last listing was in 1808; and he died in 1821. His son, Richard Wittingham, is first listed as a brass founder in 1806 and his name is in the directories until 1819.

The most frequently found andirons, signed by an American craftsman, were made by Hunneman of Boston. Instead of a shaft mounted on cabriole legs, most of his had no legs and consisted of two turned shafts connected to the iron bar which held the wood. The front shaft was about fifteen inches high; to the rear, offset about six or eight

Brass andirons made by James Davis, who worked in Boston, Mass., from 1803 to 1828. Note the "lemon" finials and the "snake" feet.

courtesy Old Sturbridge Village

inches, was a shorter shaft, shaped like the front one, but on a reduced scale. The two shafts were joined by a heavy brass bar. Thus, the two columns, combined with the back foot of the andiron, provided the three supports necessary to keep the andiron in an upright position. Although these are marked products of an American craftsman, they lack the charm and elegance of earlier andirons. A pair of tongs is known, the handle being identical in design to the andirons made by Hunneman, and stamped, "Boston." This is one of the few tongs known that is signed by an American craftsman.

One of the latest types of andirons, usually called "Empire," consists of a turned shaft with many curves, so that the design lacks definition

Brass andirons signed by Wittingham, New York.

courtesy Joe Kindig, Jr.

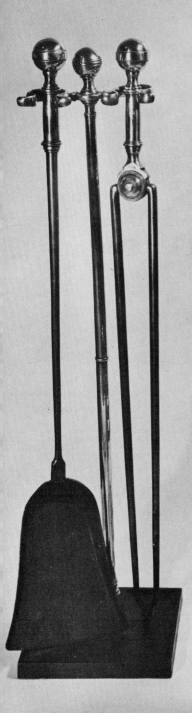

Pair of typical Hunneman andirons and a set of
fire tools, probably made by Hunneman; tongs are
stamped "Boston."

courtesy Teina Baunstone

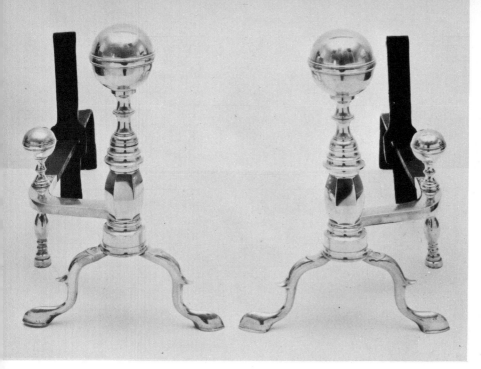

Pair of brass andirons made and signed by Hunneman, with brass shaft, brass log stop, brass cabriole legs, and iron billet bar. Few examples of this style bearing the Hunneman imprint are known. William C. Hunneman and family were located in Boston, Mass., from 1798 to 1845.

courtesy Henry Francis du Pont Winterthur Museum

and charm. They are frequently mounted on thin cabriole-type legs having balls for feet. They vary in size, but the top portion usually appears too heavy for the legs; in simple language, they are top-heavy. After 1840, brass founders rarely mention andirons and those in existence gradually disappeared; no doubt some were sold for junk metal while others were stored out of the way in the attic.

Such were the major styles of andirons. Excerpts from *The Cabinet Encyclopedia* by Rev. Dionysius Lardner give additional perspective on their use, focusing attention on the comparative status of andirons in England and America. Because of the abundance of wood in America, and its scarcity in England, Americans burned wood in their fireplaces, and the British turned to coal. Hence andirons were used more widely in America in the eighteenth and nineteenth century than in England. The advertisements of brass founders in American papers show andirons high on their list of products, indicating that a great many were made here. Lardner, writing in 1833, amplifies the situation thus:

As the taste for luxuries in England was cultivated the enterprise of the whitesmith increased, and, the consumption of pit-coal becoming general, the transition from andirons to fireplaces composed of connected bars was obvious and easy; the new contrivance, for a time exhibiting more or less traces of its origin. . . . In the houses of the nobility the grates were, of course, of a more expensive and ornamental description, still retaining however, as their most conspicuous feature, two ornamented pillars, or standards, in front, similar to those which exhibited the taste or ingenuity of the manufacturer of the ancient andirons. . . . Moveable fireplaces of this description may be met with about 200 years old. America, whose immense forests have hitherto been regarded as inexhaustible, and where in consequence, andirons, or dogs, have been most largely in demand, has latterly manufactured metallic stoves and ornamental fire-places to a large extent. Even in New

This advertisement of William Zane in the *Pennsylvania Gazette* of Oct. 10, 1792, notes that, although he imported many objects of cast brass from Europe, his andirons were made in America. Such evidence helps to confirm that brass andirons, previously thought to be European, were made in America.

WILLIAM ZANE,

At the sign of the Canister and Hand-saw, between Market and Chesnut-streets,

Has just imported, in the late arrivals from Europe, a large and general assortment of IRONMONGERY, CUTLERY, SADDLERY, &c. Among which are

SHEET iron, pots, kettles, pye-pans and skillets; cart and waggon boxes; blistered and Crowley's steel; flat-irons; coffee-mills; frying-pans; patent iron tea and fish-kettles and sauce-pans; a great variety of locks and hinges; ivory, horn and iron combs; fish-hooks; pins, Whitechapel needles; sailmakers do. common and gilt coat and vest buttons of various patterns; a large assortment of common and best plated knee and knee-buckles; a great variety of knives and forks; razors, cases and strops; shaving-boxes; scissars; taylors shears; common and taylors thimbles; fowling-pieces, gun-locks; coal-sifters; curry-combs and brushes; elegant japanned tea-waiters, caddies and bread-baskets; a variety of bellows; brass and iron weights in setts; gold scales and scale-beams; iron and japanned snuffers & trays; Turkey oil and rag stones; Scotch ditto; shoe rubbers; brass head and iron shovels and tongs; a great variety of shoe and knee chapes; London and Bristol pewter, consisting of dishes, plates, basons, spoons, &c. brass and iron wire; huntsmens horns and squirrel chains; brass and bell-metal kettles; brass table chafing-dishes; iron ditto; brass locks, cocks, hinges, nails, scutcheons, drawer handles, &c. brass and iron candlesticks; a general supply of carpenters and shoemakers tools; tacks, nails, sprigs and screws of different sorts and sizes; smiths anvils, vizes, beck-irons, sledge and hand hammers, and riveting ditto; chain traces; spinning-wheel irons; sleigh bells; redwood, copperas, allum, venetian red, yellow ochre and glue; saddlers straining-irons, girth, diaper and straining-web, sadded and plated buckles and tips; saddlers hammers, stirrup irons and bridle bitts; brass warming-pans; spelter; brass and paper ink-stands; steelyards; curriers knives and steels; screws of many sorts and sizes, &c.

AMERICAN MANUFACTORY,

3, 4, 6, 8, 9, 10 and 20d. nails; screw augers; spades, shovels and wood axes; shingling hatchets; black balls; crooked combs; Dutch ovens; wool and cotton cards; copper and iron teakettles; plow lines, traces, bed-cords and laces, sash-cord, fishing and chalk lines; wrapping and seine twine; spinning-wheels; a great variety of brass andirons, brass head and common iron ditto; red clover, timothy and hemp-seed, with many other articles not enumerated.   Tf.

York this species of fuel [anthracite stone coal] is getting into general use; it burns with intense heat, but without flame or smoke . . . In Philadelphia the use of this fuel is still more general; and the saving, in some cases, is said to be more than thirty per cent upon the former expenditure in the maintenance of wood fires.

Fire tools (shovels and tongs) were an important appendage to the fireplace, and intimately related to the design of andirons. Signed tongs have been identified as the products of the same craftsman who made andirons, as the bill of Daniel King to John Cadwalader confirms. Two items on his bill were, "3 pares of the best Brass Tongs and Shovel at 2-10 per pare," and "3 pares of tongs and shovel with stell legs at 2-10 per pare."

This description of the fire tools made by King is particularly interesting because it specifies that 3 pairs were made completely of brass. All-brass "period" tools of this type have become extremely rare; those combining brass and steel are more common. It is known that the all-brass andirons were appropriate for use with the elegant furnishings of

Copy of a bill rendered by Daniel King to John Cadwalader for several objects of brass. The "Chimeley hucks" were probably jamb hooks for holding fire tools upright.

courtesy Historical Society of Pennsylvania

Brass andiron made by Molineux of
Boston. Note the forged iron
vertical rod with coarse threading.
Kauffman Collection

the Cadwalader residence. Fire tools made of brass and steel might have
been intended for use with andirons made of the same metals. Curiously, the price of both types was the same.

In addition to the matching finials on andirons and fire tools, the
finials on chimney hooks, or jamb hooks, often matched the other two
items. Jamb hooks were fastened on each side of the fireplace so that
fire tools could be leaned against them while the bottom ends rested on
marble blocks, shaped and recessed to accommodate them.

The transition from a wood-burning fireplace with its tools to a coal
grate was slow in America and little of the original equipment was
discarded. The coal grate was set on the andirons and the tools, particularly the shovel, were used to handle coal. The coal grate probably was
used widely in the big cities, such as New York and Philadelphia, where
all fuels had to be imported, and the balance was tipped in favor of coal

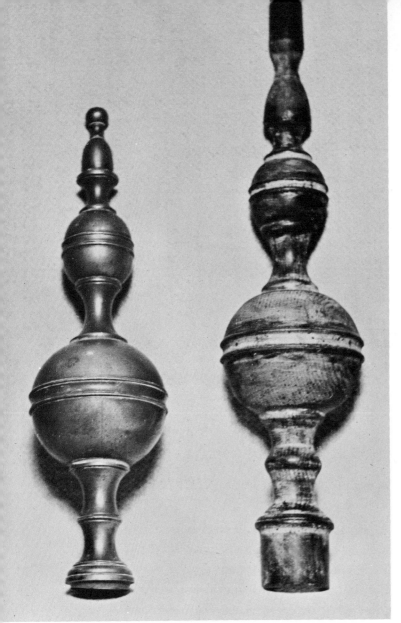

because it had certain advantages over the burning of wood. In other areas, the severity of the impact of the coal grate is suspect, particularly in smaller cities, such as Norwich and Albany, New York, and Rutland, Vermont, which were near extensive supplies of wood and distant from coal supplies. The number of fireplaces which were closed off with the andirons still in them in the late nineteenth and early twentieth centuries suggests they were used for burning wood right up until the time they were abandoned.

Although efficient devices for heating houses have been invented in recent years, the warmth of an open fire with a pair of polished brass andirons holding the logs is as refreshing an experience today as it was one, two, or three centuries ago. The style and beauty of the andirons have no influence on the heat, but a person with esthetic sensitivity will always appreciate the designs and workmanship of old "fire dogs."

In examining andirons and fire tools, there are various clues that will help in determining if an example is old or new. While it is not impos-

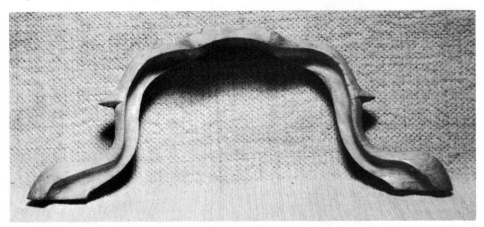

Pattern for base of an andiron. The recessed portion greatly reduces the quantity of metal needed for casting.

Kauffman Collection

Rough casting of the base of an andiron similar to the Molineux example, showing the gates and the sprues. A great deal of work was necessary to make such a casting smooth and attractive.

Kauffman Collection

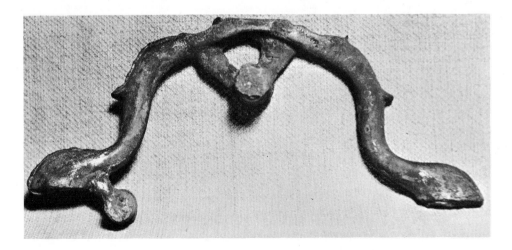

Brass andiron, complete except for rear portion of the iron support for logs. The design and workmanship are of fine quality.

Kauffman Collection

Top view of the Molineux andiron showing the brass plate which covers part of the iron log support. "Molineux" and "Boston" are stamped on the plate, the word "Boston" being obscured by the secondary brass turning. Note the design filed in the end of the brass plate.

Kauffman Collection

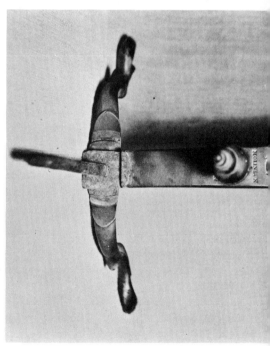

sible that even an experienced connoisseur may be deceived, there is specific basic evidence to look for before making a final decision in regard to age.

The first, and most conclusive step is to ascertain if a shaft has two vertical joints opposite each other from top to bottom. On the square shaft, the joint is probably on the corner and will be somewhat difficult to detect. The presence of this point is not absolute proof of great age, but is proof that the object was made by the traditional method. It is possible, but improbable, that modern reproductions are made in this manner.

Another part to examine is the forged iron rod within the hollow shaft. Old ones are usually square, or square with chamfered corners. They should have the forge marks of the hammer and a very coarse thread on the top where the finial is attached. This examination can be made by twisting and removing the finial.

A more elusive criterion is the weight of the andiron. Brass was relatively scarce and expensive in the eighteenth century and an old specimen is likely to be lighter in weight than a new one. The procedure of casting the shafts in halves facilitated the production of parts which were light in weight.

Finally, there should be some surface deterioration which normally occurs with age. Pits, dents, and scratches are usually found on any old metal objects which had been in use for about a hundred years.

None of these criteria is conclusive, but several combined should lead to a sound decision on the age of an andiron.

B. BELLS

Bells and bellmaking have received scant attention in the history of craftsmanship in metals in early America. This neglect is difficult to understand, for bells have been made here since the middle of the eighteenth century. The earliest advertisement found in this survey was placed in the *Pennsylvania Gazette*, August 17, 1749, by John Stow, who later became one of the partners to cast the famous Liberty Bell. Other bellmakers of the eighteenth century were Daniel King of Philadelphia, Philip Syng of Annapolis, and Paul Revere of Boston.

Not only were bells an important product of the industrial scene in early America, but they also served a significant function in the social customs of the country. The Declaration of Independence was proclaimed by the ringing of bells, and other events of great joy were

Invention.	Inventor.	Residence.	Date.	No.
Bell, Æolian chiming	H. Herrmann	New York, N. Y	Feb. 7, 1871	111,537
Bell, Alarm	S. C. Bond	Hainesville, Ill	May 9, 1871	114,521
Bell, Alarm	L. F. Bruce	Bridgeport, Conn	Aug. 3, 1869	93,168
Bell, Alarm	L. Holmes	Paterson, N. J	May 18, 1869	90,173
Bell, Alarm	T. and G. A. Pemberton	Birmingham, England	Apr. 19, 1870	102,035
Bell, Alarm	C. Penfield	New Britain, Conn	Jan. 12, 1869	85,760
Bell, Alarm	W. M Preston	Roxbury, N. Y	Apr. 2, 1872	125,328
Bell, Alarm	C. A. Slack	Frenchtown, N. J	Feb. 9, 1869	86,876
Bell, Alarm	C. Wiley	Hannibal Centre, N. Y	Mar. 23, 1869	88,106
Bell alarm, Door	C. C. Gerhardt and G. S. Lander.	Wyandotte, Kans	Apr. 16, 1872	125,731
Bell and bell wheel, Rotating	J. Rogester	Baltimore, Md	July 13, 1869	92,470
Bell and burglar-alarm, Door	D. L. Collins	Antwerp, N. Y	Nov. 20, 1866	59,820
Bell and burglar-alarm, Door	E. H. Crane	Burr Oak, Mich	June 26, 1866	55,823
Bell and burglar-alarm, Door	M. A. Genung	Granville, Ohio	June 17, 1862	35,603
Bell and caster-stand, Call	F. A. Blatterlien	West Meriden, Conn	Nov. 8, 1870	109,101
Bell and gong striking apparatus	C. and G. M. Stevens	Boston, Mass	May 21, 1872	126,992
Bell and slop-bowl, Call	N. Lawrence	Taunton, Mass	June 28, 1870	104,859
Bell and table-caster, Combined	H. A. Dierkes	New York, N. Y	Dec. 7, 1869	97,617
Bell and vessel, Call	N. Lawrence	Taunton, Mass	Aug. 30, 1870	106,840
Bell attachment	A. E. Taylor	Ogdensburgh, N. Y	Oct. 23, 1860	30,509
Bell attachment, Alarm	A. Sherwood	Auburn, N. Y	Aug. 26, 1873	142,287
Bell, Call	H. H. Abbe	East Hampton, Conn	Jan. 2, 1866	51,764
Bell, Call	E. C. Barton	East Hampton, Conn	Aug. 20, 1872	130,690
Bell, Call	N. L. Bradley	West Meriden, Conn	Aug. 25, 1863	39,697
Bell, Call	E. G. Cone	East Hampton, Conn	Oct. 27, 1868	83,468
Bell, Call	H. A. Dierkes	New York, N. Y	Aug. 8, 1871	117,871
Bell, Call	H. A. Dierkes	New York, N. Y	Mar. 26, 1872	125,029
Bell, Call	H. A. Dierkes and J. Fretts	New York, N. Y	Mar. 21, 1871	112,907
Bell, Call	W. H. Nichols	East Hampton, Conn	July 16, 1867	66,874
Bell, Call	W. H. Nichols	East Hampton, Conn	Aug. 27, 1872	130,818
Bell, Call	E. Parker	West Meriden, Conn	Mar. 29, 1864	42,107
Bell, Call	D. W. Sexton	East Hampton, Conn	May 3, 1864	42,604
Bell, Call	H. Stratton	West Meriden, Conn	Feb. 11, 1873	135,860
Bell, Call	H. A. Thompson	Hartford, Conn	June 5, 1866	55,392
Bell, Call	C. Volger	Wilmington, Del	June 20, 1871	116,241
Bell, Car	A. Borrowman	New York, N. Y	Apr. 16, 1867	63,843
Bell, Car	J. Sweeney	New York, N. Y	Nov. 27, 1866	60,083
Bell, Cast-iron	E. G. Cone	East Hampton, Conn	Aug. 6, 1867	67,500
Bell, Ceremonial	J. H. Smith	Keokuk, Iowa	Jan. 10, 1871	110,875
Bell, Chime and alarm	G. R. Meneely	West Troy, N. Y	Jan. 2, 1872	122,397
Bell, Cow or sheep	S. Newton		Dec. 22, 1804	....
Bell-crank	M. C. Ames	Hartford, Conn	May 7, 1872	126,369
Bell, Door	W. Allport	New Britain, Conn	Dec. 29, 1868	85,352
Bell, Door	W. Allport	New Britain, Conn	Apr. 12, 1870	101,609
Bell, Door	H. D. Blake	New Britain, Conn	Apr. 9, 1872	125,530
Bell, Door	F. Blakemore	Philadelphia, Pa	July 2, 1872	128,458
Bell, Door	A. T. Brooks	New Britain, Conn	Dec. 31, 1867	72,791
Bell, Door	A. T. Brooks	New Britain, Conn	June 30, 1868	79,308
Bell, Door	N. F. Cone	La Crosse, Wis	Sept. 8, 1863	39,796
Bell, Door	N. F. Cone	La Crosse, Wis	Feb. 23, 1864	41,683
Bell, Door	J. P. Connell	Kensington, Conn	Mar. 21, 1871	112,903
Bell, Door	J. P. Connell	Kensington, Conn	June 18, 1872	127,959
Bell, Door	J. P. Connell	Kensington, Conn	Oct. 15, 1872	132,199
Bell, Door	M. L. Delavan and J. Dyson	New Britain, Conn	July 23, 1867	67,030
Bell, Door	M. A. Genung	Granville, Ohio	Mar. 10, 1863	37,863
Bell, Door	E. H. Goldman and D. W. Hisey.	Kansas, Ill	May 24, 1870	103,446
Bell, Door	T. Lyons	Hartford, Conn	Aug. 11, 1868	80,983
Bell, Door	W. T. Munger	New Britain, Conn	June 20, 1871	116,082
Bell, Door	W. H. Nichols	Chatham, Conn	Jan. 30, 1866	52,365
Bell, Door	W. H. Nichols	East Hampton, Conn	Sept. 22, 1868	82,434
Bell, Door	C. S. Nickelson	Canton, N. Y	Oct. 24, 1865	50,616
Bell, Door	O. A. North	New Britain, Conn	Apr. 27, 1869	89,331
Bell, Door	O. B. Oakley and H. Rosekrans	San Francisco, Cal	Sept. 1, 1868	81,672
Bell, Door	M. B. Ogden	Fond du Lac, Wis	Aug. 23, 1864	43,924
Bell, Door	C. Penfield	New Britain, Conn	July 30, 1867	67,212
Bell, Door	C. Penfield	New Britain, Conn	Jan. 12, 1869	85,759
Bell, Door	C. W. Saladee	Circleville, Ohio	Mar. 16, 1869	87,794
Bell, Door	E. B. Sims	Antwerp, N. Y	Sept. 16, 1873	142,953
Bell, Door	A. A. Stuart	Cedar Rapids, Iowa	May 20, 1873	139,206
Bell, Door	A. L. Swan	Cherry Valley, N. Y	Nov. 19, 1872	133,269
Bell, Door	A. Turnball	New Britain, Conn	June 13, 1865	48,242
Bell, Door	W. H. Watrous	Hartford, Conn	Mar. 20, 1866	53,366
Bell, Door and alarm	G. O. Lackey	Akron, Ohio	Oct. 25, 1870	108,708
Bell, Diving	J. A. Weisse	New York, N. Y	Apr. 27, 1869	89,453
Bell, Electro-magnetic alarm	M. G. Farmer	Salem, Mass	May 4, 1852	8,920
Bell, Electro-magnetic alarm	C. Williams, jr., and J. Redding	Somerville and Charlestown, Mass.	Feb. 7, 1871	111,707
Bell, Electro-magnetic fog	A. Barbarin and B. F. Simms	New Orleans, La	July 15, 1856	15,323
Bell, Enameled	F. Raymond	Woodhaven, N. Y	June 29, 1869	92,095
Bell, Fog	A. C. Rand and R. R. Johnson	Buffalo, N. Y	Apr. 13, 1858	19,949
Bell for doors, Alarm	E. Barton	East Hampton, Conn	Sept. 9, 1862	36,436
Bell for fire-engines, Alarm	J. P. Parke	Philadelphia, Pa	Dec. 19, 1808	....
Bell for horses	J. Barton	Cairo, N. Y	Mar. 18, 1834	....
Bell for horses, Alarm chime	C. Kirchkof	Newark, N. J	Sept. 29, 1863	40,108
Bell, Gong	I. A. Bevin	Chatham, Conn	Oct. 9, 1866	58,580
Bell, Gong	L. S. Carpenter	East Hampton, Conn	Apr. 20, 1869	89,024
Bell, Gong	H. A. Foss	New Britain, Conn	May 28, 1872	127,333
Bell-head, Rotary	S. M. and W. M. Fulton	Pittsburgh, Pa	Nov. 30, 1869	97,383
Bell-holder, Stationary	S. Croll	Philadelphia, Pa	Feb. 14, 1871	111,729
Bell, Horse	J. Barton	Middle Haddam, Conn	Feb. 14, 1854	10,532
Bell, House	H. Barton	East Hampton, Conn	Oct. 9, 1866	58,576
Bell, House	J. Barton	East Hampton, Conn	June 15, 1858	20,538
Bell, House	A. L. Swan	Cherry Valley, N. Y	Dec. 26, 1871	122,200
Bell, House	A. Turnball	New Britain, Conn	June 12, 1866	55,528
Bell joint	B. P. Walker	Wolverhampton, England	May 4, 1869	89,820
Bell-lever box	B. W. Hopper	Astoria, N. Y	Jan. 8, 1869	91,019

Invention.	Inventor.	Residence.	Date.	No.
Bell-levers, Attaching caps to bases of	E. W. Brettel	Elizabeth, N. J	Aug. 2, 1870	105,900
Bell, Locomotive alarm	B. Briscoe	Detroit, Mich	Mar. 2, 1869	87,462
Bell-machinery for hotels, &c	T. D. Jackson and A. Judson	Rochester, N. Y	Oct. 17, 1846	4,816
Bell, Magnetic alarm	A. Eckert	Trenton, Ohio	Oct. 10, 1854	11,780
Bell or gong, Door	H. H. Abbe	Chatham, Conn	July 11, 1865	48,637
Bell or gong, Door	A. G. Dexter	San Francisco, Cal	June 13, 1865	48,234
Bell, Portable house	A. W. Hale	New Britain, Conn	Aug. 31, 1858	21,335
Bell, Pressure	J. Barton	Middle Haddam, Conn	Apr. 8, 1856	14,593
Bell-pull	S. Bonsall and L. Hillebrand	Philadelphia. Pa	Mar. 3, 1868	75,118
Bell-pull	S Bonsall and L. Hillebraud	Philadelphia, Pa	Dec. 15, 1868	84,998
Bell-pull	C. J. Bradbury	Boston, Mass	Feb. 28, 1860	27,330
Bell-pull	J. Garvey and M. H. Kimball	San Francisco, Cal	Nov. 3, 1868	83,622
Bell-pull	J. Garvey and M. H. Kimball	San Francisco, Cal	Nov. 3, 1868	83,623
Bell-pull	H. Homer	New York, N. Y	Sept. 5, 1865	49,757
Bell-pull	W. T. Munger	New Britain, Conn	June 10, 1873	139,687
Bell-pull	W. M. Preston	Roxbury, N. Y	Aug. 20, 1872	130,742
Bell-pull	J. J. C. Smith	Somerville, Mass	Jan. 18, 1870	99,020
Bell-pull	A. L. Swan	Cherry Valley, N. Y	Nov. 7, 1871	120,682
Bell-pull	A. L. Swan	Cherry Valley, N. Y	Aug. 19, 1873	142,057
Bell-pull, Noiseless	J. F. Cory	New York, N. Y	Nov. 3, 1868	83,606
Bell pulls and trips, Construction of	S. L. Covell, jr	Troy, N. Y	July 16, 1867	66,801
Bell-ringer, Automatic	E. N. Scherr	Philadelphia, Pa	Mar. 1, 1859	23,118
Bell-ringer, Steam	W. H. Beach	Chicago, Ill	Apr. 19, 1864	42,428
Bell-ringer, Steam	G. B. Snow	Buffalo, N. Y	June 11, 1872	127,933
Bell-ringer, Steam	J. West and O. M. Parker	Quincy, Ill	June 25, 1872	128,441
Bell-ringer, Steam,	J. West and O. M. Parker	Quincy, Ill	Jan. 7, 1873	134,719
Bell-ringing apparatus	J. R. Baird	Vincennes, Ind	Nov. 17, 1857	18,623
Bell-ringing apparatus	J. Harrison	Troy, N. Y	Aug. 28, 1860	29,784
Bell-ringing apparatus	R. Kinsley	Springfield, Mass	June 11, 1861	32,520
Bell-ringing apparatus for locomotive, Automatic	J. S. Lamar	Augusta, Ga	July 9, 1872	128,601
Bell-rope supporter	W. C. Marshall	Hartford, Conn	Aug. 10, 1869	93,461
Bell ropes, Eye for railway-car	W. M. Walton	Newark, N. J	Dec. 21, 1869	98,130
Bell, Self-adjusting fog	H. L. De Zeng	Geneva, N. Y	Aug. 26, 1856	15,605
Bell, Sheet-steel	J. E. Tencate	Pittsburgh, Pa	Jan. 9, 1872	122,679
Bell, Signal	G. F. and D. H. Benckert	Philadelphia, Pa	Oct. 11, 1859	25,714
Bell, Signal	J. A. Woodward	Philadelphia, Pa	Nov. 15, 1859	26,137
Bell, Signal or alarm	G. H. Hoagland	Port Jervis, N. Y	July 21, 1857	17,836
Bell strap, Cow	J. H. and A. Hughs	Wautoma, Wis	Dec. 19, 1871	122,020
Bell, Table or call	A. W. Turner	New York, N. Y	Jan. 30, 1866	52,344
Bell to straps, Attaching	D. W. Welch	Middle Haddam, Conn	Aug. 10, 1869	93,652
Bell-yoke attachment	C. H. Mencely	Troy, N. Y	May 9, 1871	114,585
Bells and adjustable clappers for ringing fog	D. Jones, jr	Saint John, New Brunswick	Nov. 27, 1849	6,915
Bells, &c., Apparatus for sounding house	J. Corduan	Brooklyn, N. Y	Mar. 29, 1859	23,353
Bells by steam, Ringing	G. B. Snow	Buffalo, N. Y	July 11, 1854	11,307
Bells, Casting	A. Jusberg	Galva, Ill	Aug. 27, 1867	68,206
Bells, Constructing and hanging	E. Dewey	New York, N. Y	Apr. 10, 1839	1,114
Bells, Construction and tono of	R. Leslie		Feb. 2, 1793	
Bells, Device for ringing street-car	C. Carr	Boston, Mass	Apr. 5, 1870	101,580
Bells, Die for making	A. Patterson	Birmingham, Pa	Mar. 5, 1867	62,678
Bells, Electro-magnetic machine for ringing	C. Robinson	New York, N. Y	Dec. 6, 1864	45,347
Bells for cows, &c., Brazing and bronzing	S. Booth	Berlin, Conn	June 1, 1832	
Bells, Hanging	G. E. Baker	Waukegan, Ill	July 10, 1866	56,160
Bells, Hanging	H. Belfied	Philadelphia, Pa	Apr. 12, 1859	23,639
Bells, Hanging	T. H. Bell	Washington, D. C	Apr. 17, 1860	27,880
Bells, Hanging	J. Currier	Boston, Mass	Jan. 23, 1834	
Bells, Hanging	N. G. Du Bois	Brooklyn, N. Y	Jan. 12, 1858	19,082
Bells, Hanging	G. Equillon	Paris, France	Oct. 26, 1869	96,092
Bells, Hanging	S. Fuller	Boston, Mass	Dec. 26, 1833	
Bells, Hanging	G. W. Hildreth	Lockport, N. Y	June 19, 1855	13,089
Bells, Hanging	M. R. Jones	Troy, N. Y	Mar. 19, 1872	124,685
Bells, Hanging	A. Laroye	Sas Slykens, near Ostend, Belgium.	Mar. 21, 1871	112,932
Bells, Hanging	A. Lynar	New York, N. Y	Dec. 24, 1819	
Bells, Hanging	G. R. Meneely	West Troy, N. Y	Sept. 7, 1858	21,422
Bells, Hanging	G. R. Meneely	West Troy, N. Y	Oct. 9, 1860	30,338
Bells, Hanging	J. Russell	New York, N. Y	Oct. 10, 1829	
Bells, Hanging	E. W. Vanduzen	Cincinnati, Ohio	Oct. 23, 1866	59,098
Bells, Hanging	E. W. Vanduzen	Cincinnati, Ohio	Oct. 23, 1866	59,099
Bells, Hanging	J. B. Young	Harper's Ferry, Va	July 4, 1854	11,236
Bells, Hanging door	J. O. Harris	Ottawa, Ill	June 21, 1864	43,243
Bells, Hanging house	E. Stetson	New Bedford, Mass	Aug. 17, 1843	3,226
Bells, Machine for making wire	R. W. Norton	New Haven, Conn	Aug. 30, 1870	106,951
Bells, Machinery for operating fog	J. Haynes	Pembroke, Me	Apr. 2, 1861	31,886
Bells, Machinery for ringing fog	A. Morse	Portland, Me	Aug. 27, 1861	33,156
Bells, Manufacture of corrugated	G. S. Saxton	Saint Louis, Mo	Dec. 17, 1867	72,422
Bells, Manufacture of cow	G. C. Albaugh	Louisville, Ky	Feb. 26, 1861	31,521
Bells, Manufacture of cow	W. T. and L. B. Tibbals	Cobalt, Conn	Aug. 31, 1869	94,453
Bells, Method of making smoke	J. S. and T. B. Atterbury	Pittsburgh, Pa	Aug. 14, 1866	57,063
Bells, Mold for casting	E. Jones	Troy, N. Y	Dec. 18, 1855	13,948
Bells, Molding	W. H. Davis	Brooklyn, N. Y	Sept. 15, 1868	82,094
Bells, Molding and casting	B. Hanks	Albany, N. Y	Nov. 4, 1816	
Bells on steamers, Mode of operating pilot	J. R. Hopkins	Lincoln, Me	Nov. 17, 1857	18,641
Bells or other hollow castings, Machine for turning or plaining the inside of.	O. Jones	Troy, N. Y	Oct. 4, 1870	107,918
Bells, Ringing	J. Harrison	New York, N. Y	Mar. 8, 1864	41,843
Bells, Ringing	J. Harrison	New York, N. Y	Aug. 6, 1867	67,537
Bells, Ringing	J. Harrison	East Hampton, Conn	May 20, 1873	139,147
Bells, Ringing	B. Kitt	Cincinnati, Ohio	June 5, 1860	28,586
Bells, Ringing	T. V. Stran	New Albany, Ind	June 29, 1852	9,081

Two pages from the *Index of Patents Issued from the United States Patent Office from 1790 to 1873, inclusive*. Other pages have data about other types of bells. There are approximately 200 patents listed on the two pages.

celebrated in a similar manner. The bell also has proclaimed the un-happy news of death. As recently as the early part of this century, it was customary in rural districts to ring a church bell to announce the death of a member of the community, the number of tolls indicating the age of the deceased.

Before discussing the making of bells in America, let us look briefly at some of the famous bells of Europe. Bells have an ancient origin but two observations, other than age, stand out in their history. One is the tremendous size in which bells have been cast.

Communities and even countries seemed to vie with each other in the production of large bells.

In England, large bells have been affectionately known by the name "Tom." One such bell was the great "Tom of Lincoln," which weighed

Memorial bell dedicated to Robert Fulton with an embossed inscription: "T. W. LEVERING, fecit Philadelphia A.D. 1816. NOW FULTON IS GONE. HE IS NO MORE BUT HE LEFT HIS GENIUS TO CARRY US FROM SHORE TO SHORE. UNION STEAM-BOAT." The bell is 16 in. high and 14½ in. in diameter.

formerly in the late Arthur J. Sussel Collection

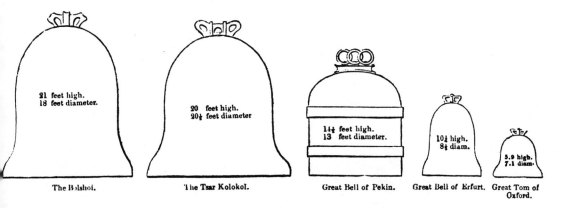

21 feet high.
18 feet diameter.

The Bolshoi.

20 feet high.
20¼ feet diameter

The Tsar Kolokol.

11¼ feet high.
13 feet diameter.

Great Bell of Pekin.

10¼ high.
8¼ diam.

Great Bell of Erfurt.

5.9 high.
7.1 diam.

Great Tom of Oxford.

Comparative dimensions of celebrated bells of the world. Reputedly, the shape has nothing to do with the quality of the sound.

from *The Pictorial Gallery of the Arts*

10,000 pounds and continued in service for two hundred years. In 1835, it was replaced by another bell weighing 12,000 pounds. The "Great Tom of Oxford" weighs 17,000 pounds and in 1856 an even larger bell was cast for the Houses of Parliament.

These English bells are small, however, compared with other bells made in Europe. In Erfurt, Germany, is located a bell which is ten feet tall. The European champion in bell making is Russia. The "Tsar Kolokol" bell weighs 400,000 pounds and contains enough metal to cast thirty bells the size of the one in St. Paul's Cathedral in London. The clapper, which is not considered part of the bell, weighs about 4,000 pounds. The clappers on these large bells were moved by ropes attached to the bottom end, which groups of men pulled back and forth.

The second noteworthy feature about bells in Europe was the custom followed by conquering armies of seizing the bells of an area which they had subdued and recasting them into cannon. It is believed that metal in many of the bells has been alternately used in bells and cannons. This practice was followed as recently as World War I in 1914-1918.

The subject of casting bells into cannons, and vice versa, focuses attention on the metal of which bells and cannons are made. This substance was called bell metal when it was cast in a bell, and gun metal when cast in a cannon.

Home Moravian Church Bell: This bell was made by the Moravian brother, Matthias Tommerup, a noted bell founder, who came to Bethlehem, Pa., from Denmark in 1761. The bell, cast in 1771, was delivered to the Salem Moravian Congregation during Passion Week in 1772. It was rung for the first time on April 21, 1772. The bell is noted for its clarity of tone, due to its alloy, part silver, which was donated by the brothers and sisters of the congregation. It weighs 275 pounds.

The bell was first set up on the northeast corner of Salem Square near the Gemein Haus, second place of worship for the early Moravians. After Home Moravian Church was finished and dedicated in 1800, the bell was moved to its steeple and has remained there ever since.

courtesy Old Salem, Inc.

Although bell metal and gun metal are neither copper nor brass, they are examples of the many alloys which can be made by combining copper with other metals. An alloy is a substance consisting of two or more metals, combined to create a metal with qualities none of them had alone. Both gun metal and bell metal were made of copper and tin, but with slightly different ratios. Bell metal used 75 parts of copper and 25 parts of tin, while gun metal was made of 90 parts of copper and 10 parts of tin. Although there is a difference in the ratio of tin to copper in the two metals, the contents are so similar that either alloy could serve for both bells and cannons. It is likely that some bells were cast of brass, an alloy of copper and zinc; and some cannons were definitely cast of bronze.

The definition of bell metal found in *A Supplement to Chambers' Cyclopedia or Universal Dictionary of Arts and Sciences,* London, 1753, does not mention the ratio of the two metals used:

> Bell-metal is a composition of tin and copper in due proportion; which has the property, that it is more sonorous than any of its ingredients taken apart.

Perhaps the reason for not stating the ratio of tin to copper was that there was no unanimous agreement among practical bellmakers on this matter at that time.

This definition points to the sonorous quality of the tin-copper alloy as one of its major assets. Although bell founders probably varied the contents of bell metal to create unusual effects, they cast most of their bells (except those made of cast iron) out of the tin-copper alloy. Tales have been told of royalty and peasants alike contributing small objects of silver and gold toward some special bell, but additions of these metals in small amounts had little, if any, influence on the appearance of the bell or its sonorous quality.

In addition to possessing the quality to produce a pleasant sound, bell metal must also vibrate under impact—it must have elasticity. The sound of a bell arises from the vibration of its various parts. The thud of the clapper changes the contour of the brim from round to elliptical. The point which the clapper strikes is momentarily extended, and then, in reaction, bends slightly inward as the clapper strikes the opposite side of the bell. Thus, by striking and changing the shape of the bell exciting sounds are set into motion on the air waves.

Finally, the bell must be made of a substance which is very resistant to corrosion. Most bells are under roofs but, to disseminate their sounds, they cannot be completely enclosed. They must therefore remain subject to various climatic conditions, ranging from the salt in sea-air to the dust and smoke of a city. That so many bells have survived attests to their resistance to corrosion.

The combination of art and science in bellmaking requires a knowledge of many minute details. For example, bell founders have a diapason or bell scale, otherwise called a musical interval, which they use to measure the size, thickness, weight, and tone of their products.

Thomas Martin named the various parts of a bell in *The Circle of the Mechanical Arts:*

> The bell itself consists of its sounding bow, which is terminated by an inferior circle, which diminishes thinner and thinner as it approaches to the brim or that part on which the clapper strikes, and which is required to be left rather thicker than the rest both above and below; also the outward sinking or properly the waist of the bell, or the point under which it grows wider to the brim and the upper vase, or top or dome of the bell, or the point under which it grows wider to the brim and the upper waist of the bell, or that part which is above the waist. The pallet is inside the vase or dome to which the clapper is suspended. The vent and hollowed branches of metal which unite the cannon to receive the iron keys by which the bell is hung to its beam or support, where it must be exactly counterpoised. The height of a bell is in proportion to its diameter as twelve is to fifteen, or in the proportion of the fundamental sound of its third major, from which it follows that the sound of a bell is principally composed of the sound of its extremity or brim as a fundamental of the sound of the crown, and which is an octave to it, and that of the height, which is third.

A number of systematic steps were followed in making a large bell in the eighteenth and early nineteenth centuries. The first was the proportioning of the bell, which was of critical importance, particularly when a chime or peal of bells was made. The geometrical and mathematical procedures involved in this step will not be detailed here.

"Revere" church bell. The ridges were made by a sweep but "Revere Boston" had to be applied in the wax by hand.

owned by The Henry Ford Museum, Dearborn, Michigan

The second step was making a mold for a big bell. A hole was dug in the ground, deeper than the height of the bell to be cast, and big enough so that workmen could walk around the mold in which the bell was to be cast. A pole was placed in the center of the hole to which templates or sweeps were later attached to form the precise interior and exterior shape of the bell. A hollow form of bricks was built around the pole, smaller in diameter and shorter in length than the intended size of the bell. The bricks were covered with a composition of sifted earth, brick or stone dust, horse dung, hair, and hemp. A pattern identical to half the cross-section of the interior shape of the bell was then attached to the center pole and swung around the mound of bricks and dirt to create the inside contour of the bell.

Next a layer of wax, mixed with tallow, was applied to the formed portion, called the "core," to create a perfect model of the bell. The surface was made uniform, and various lines and moldings were scraped into the wax with another template, similar to the one used for the core, but larger and differently shaped. Such additions as letters or decorative motifs were cut to complete the wax model of the bell.

Finally, a shell of material similar to the mixture used for the outer portion of the core was applied to the wax. The first thin layer was brushed on so that all the small corners were properly filled; later layers were applied with a board or trowel. Many layers were applied, but not before the earlier applications were partially dry. This portion of the mold was called the "shell."

After all parts of the mold were finished and in place, a fire was started within the core to melt away the wax and to further dry the core and the shell. After the wax was gone, the shell was removed and thoroughly dried by burning straw under it. When replacing the shell it had to be *perfectly* centered over the core, and the entire mold was reinforced by filling the hole with sand or loose soil so the shell could not burst from the pressure and heat of the molten metal.

On the ground level, above the top level of the bell, a furnace was erected into which the metal was placed for melting. In the eighteenth century, about twenty-four hours were required for this operation. After the metal was fluid, a hole was opened near the bottom of the furnace and the molten metal flowed through a trough into the top of the bell cavity. When the metal was cast and cooled, the bell was removed from the pit and all irregularities trimmed from the casting.

The casting of bells in such an air-tight enclosure sometimes caused trouble. Since air could be trapped in the casting, creating holes or pocks, there was a great need for improving the casting technique. By the eighteenth century a great many inventions and new procedures had eased this venting problem, and others. One improvement was used by Andrew Meneely's Sons, who were awarded a silver premium on their bells entered in the World's Fair in New York in 1853-1854. (No gold medals were awarded that year.)

Meneely's success in casting bells was attributed to the use of two iron molds on the ground level instead of a core and shell for casting. These iron

The Liberty Bell, Independence Hall, Philadelphia, Pa. Made by Pass and Stow in Philadelphia in 1753.

courtesy National Park Service

molds were preforated for ventilation, and to allow the loam with which they were lined to adhere better than to a smooth, unbroken surface. After these iron molds were lined with loam and swept to shape with a template, casting was done as in the earlier technique of bell making. The holes provided ample opportunity for trapped gases to escape, and many small flames burned over the outer surface of the iron mold. This improved procedure in casting bells is only one evidence that the Industrial Revolution of the nineteenth century was developing rapidly.

The Meneely firm was particularly successful in casting chimes and peals of bells. The term "chime" usually implies that any number of bells are attuned with each other although, strictly speaking, a chime is a set of bells, the tones of which, beginning with the largest (commonly called the "tenor"), follow each other in diatonic succession. A "peal," as generally understood in America, consists of three or more bells attuned in harmonic succession, which may be rung successively or simultaneously, but will not permit a tune being played upon them. Thus, a set of bells upon the eight notes of the common scale would be a "chime"; a set upon the first, third, fifth, and eighth of the scale would be a "peal."

The Meneelys also patented a rotating yoke, on September 7, 1858. This device reduced the chance of breaking a bell by automatically rotating it so that the clapper struck a new point each time the bell was rung. In addition to church bells, the Meneelys cast academy, factory, steamboat, locomotive, plantation, and fire-engine bells.

From the standpoint of this survey of bells and bell making, the most important feature is the name of the maker on the bell. Doubtless, the most important bell in America is the Liberty Bell in Independence Hall in Philadelphia, Pennsylvania. Many people think this bell was cast in Europe, but the names of Pass and Stow, cast on its outer surface, confirm the fact that this bell was cast in America in 1753. The following item from the *Pennsylvania Packet*, May 8, 1754, also attests to the American production of the bell:

> Last week was raised and fixed in the State House steeple, the new bell cast here by Pass and Stow, weighing 2,080 pounds with the motto, 'Proclaim Liberty through all the land to all the inhabitants thereof.'

Although Pass and Stow cast the most famous bell in America, the most famous bell founder was Paul Revere. Revere is affectionately known to American children for his ride to warn his countrymen that the British were coming. Later many of them learn that Revere was one of America's outstanding silversmiths; only a few, though, discover that he was also the country's most illustrious bell founder.

Before 1792, Revere had been engaged in the casting of cannon, but in that year he cast his first bell. His initial product did not have good tone quality, still it was used for many years and is now the precious possession of St. James Episcopal Church in Cambridge, Massachusetts. In the years from 1792 until 1828, Revere's stock book lists 400 bells, ranging in weight from 50 to 2,885 pounds. Most of his products cannot be located today, although about 100 have been discovered by Edward and Evelyn Stickney, who researched these bell locations with other data in their monograph called *Revere Bells*.

Starting in 1800, the following Revere industries are recorded in the various *Business Directories* of Boston.

Revere, Paul	Bell and Cannon founder	1800
Revere, Paul		1805
Revere, Paul & Son		1806
Revere, Paul & Sons, Charter Street		1809
Revere, Paul & Son, Kirby Street		1813
Revere, Paul	house	1816
Revere, Paul & Son (Joseph)	Bell and Cannon casting	1818
Revere, Joseph W.	Bell Mfg. & Copper Dealer	
	Water Street corner Adam	1821
Revere, Joseph	Bell Mfg. & Copper Dealer	1826
Revere Copper Co.		1846

From the listings in the *Business Directories*, it is clear that Paul Revere started the business of casting bells and was later joined by his son Paul, and still later, by his son Joseph. The first bells were marked either "Revere," "Revere Boston," or "Revere and Son Boston," followed by a date in each instance. After Paul Revere, Sr., died in 1818, the bells were marked "Revere Boston" with a date following; after 1824, no date appeared. The last product listed in the stock book was in the year 1828. A few bells were sold by the Revere Copper Company after

C. J. STEWART,

BELL HANGER

AND

LOCKSMITH,

Lombard street,

Two doors W. of Howard,

BALTIMORE,

ASTRAL LAMPS

Re-bronzed, and all kinds of Brass Work repaired.

Also, Manufacturer of

PATENT LEVER

LOCKS,

OF HIS OWN INVENTION,

FOR

BANKS, PRISONS, &c.

ALSO

PAD LOCKS,

For stores, of the same description, and of superior quality.

Advertisement of C. J. Stewart in a Baltimore *Business Directory* of 1850. Bells such as he advertised were used in houses over a long period of time. Stewart also listed some of his side lines.

that date and records prove that some Revere bells were bought by various churches in the 1830s.

The Stickney treatise provides the following data concerning the surviving Revere bells:

Bells actually cast while Paul was alive	37
Bells cast by Joseph and his associates	53
Bells cast by Paul Jr.	1
Bells cast by grandson Paul	2
Total	93

The large bells, made principally for churches, are given precedence over other types in this survey because they were of such importance to the bell founders that many makers cast their names on their products. Yet advertisements of such founders as Daniel King show that bell founders made several types of bells. King's advertisement in the *Pennsylvania Gazette*, April 20, 1767, lists church bells, criers' bells, house bells, and horse bells among his products.

House bells, one of the chief products of the bell founders, played an important part in the architecture and social customs of people of substance in the eighteenth and nineteenth centuries. No data are available on how these bells were produced, but their size (four to six inches in diameter) indicates that their production was not a major technological problem. They could easily have been cast on the floor of the foundry, and finished without the use of much space or equipment.

Despite the absence of particulars about their production, we do know how they were used. These house bells were mounted on springs, which were activated by wires pulled from the various rooms in a house. A servant was attracted by the sound of the bell, but unless a distinctive tone indicated a special room in the house, he had to see the bell ring to determine where in the house he was needed. Sometimes the wires to the bells were exposed as they were strung along the walls and ceilings of the various rooms, but in the nineteenth century, metal tubes were placed within the walls and the wires encased within the tubes. This practice improved the appearance of the rooms, and is also reported to have improved the function of the pulling device.

Just as there was competition among the men who made the bells, there was competition among the men who installed them. Some bell hangers claimed their method of installing pulling devices was the best. Alexander Smith, a whitesmith in Philadelphia, states in his advertisement in the *Royal Gazette*, September 19, 1778:

> He also hangs bells after a new, best, and least expensive plan, never before made use of. As he has worked in some of the first shops in London, he flatters himself to give satisfaction to those who may be pleased to employ him in any of the aforesaid branches, as they may depend upon having their work done with fidelity and dispatch. N.B. As the making of Jacks, and hanging Bells has yet been imperfectly performed in this place, he hopes

that a little experience of his performance will entitle him to the friendship of his employers, which shall always be acknowledged with gratitude.

On August 16, 1756, a professional bell hanger inserted the following advertisement in the *New York Gazette or the Weekly Post-Boy*. This was the first illustrated advertisement of a craftsman to appear in a New York City newspaper.

> Bell Hanger.—Lately come to this city from Philadelphia, John Eliot, who hangs House and Cabin Bells, in the neatest and most convenient manner, as done at London, with cranks and wires which are not liable to be put out of order, as those done with pullies. He also gives ready money for broken Looking-Glasses; and may be heard of at John Haydock's in the Fly, opposite Beekman's Slip. N. B. His stay in town will be but short.

Brace of Conestoga wagon bells. The bars below the bells were fastened in the hames or on a part of the horse-collar designed for that purpose. Such bells are very resonant.
courtesy Pennsylvania Farm Museum of Landis Valley

The competition between bell hangers continued as long as house bells of this type were used. During the nineteenth century, the American Patent Office in Washington was besieged with various patents concerned with the methods of ringing bells. Among the inventions were noiseless bell pulls, bell machinery for hotels, machines for making bell wire, and table or call bells. Throughout the nineteenth century, there were approximately 200 inventions relating to bells of all types, eighteen of which were directly concerned with bell hanging.

Little is known about criers' bells, such as King advertised in 1767. More is known of the horse bells so widely used in Pennsylvania. Though there was probably more romance than utility involved in their use, braces of Conestoga wagon bells are much sought by collectors of Americana today.

Braces of horse bells were of many sizes and contained a varying number of bells. Some had as few as three bells while others had as many as six on each brace. These bells were really miniature church bells with a stud on the top for attaching them to an iron brace or bracket. Slots were cut through the bracket, and the stud of the bell extended through far enough to be engaged by slipping a piece of wire through the stud. The bells were mounted horizontally on the bracket which had vertical parts attached to the collar or hames of the horse's harness.

A premium was placed on the ownership of a complete set of bells. One traditional story is that when a wagon driver became mired in the mud and accepted help from a fellow teamster to get him out, the mired driver was obligated to give a brace of bells to his benefactor.

Imperfect sleigh bell. The metal was too cool when the casting was poured and chilled below the flowing temperature before the cavity was filled.

courtesy Edwin Battison

Top and side views of three sleigh bells. The designs and openings of the bells were cut into the patterns and transferred to the metal when the castings were made. The initials "W. B." presumably stand for William Barton.

Kauffman Collection

Thus, the owning of many braces of bells was the sign of a clever wagon driver, while the lack of them was evidence that the driver frequently needed help.

The function of the bells was reportedly to warn drivers as they approached each other in woodland so that one would drive to the side of the road permitting the other to pass. It is also said that when a team with tinkling bells arrived in a village, children followed the wagon to observe its contents and pick up gossip from the driver.

A third definition for a bell was given by Samuel Johnson in *The Dictionary of the English Language,* London, 1755:

> A small hollow globe of metal perforated, and containing in it a solid ball; which, when it is shaken by bounding against the sides, gives a sound.

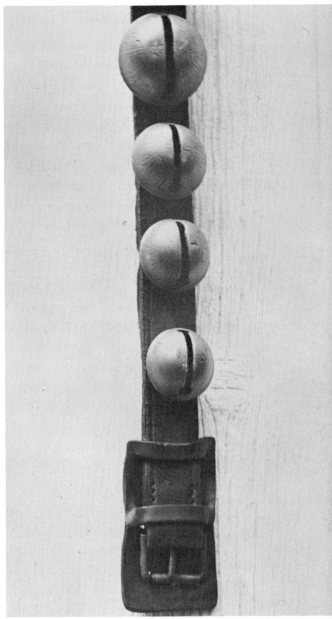

Complete set of sleigh bells mounted on a leather strap with a buckle for joining the ends under the horse's belly. The close-up of the buckle shows a piece of leather under the buckle to keep it from rubbing against the horse.

courtesy Pennsylvania Farm Museum of Landis Valley

This describes another type of horse bell made by American founders. Many of these bells bear the initials of the maker. They range in diameter from approximately two inches to four inches. Some were beautifully engraved with designs; some were engraved with the number of the bell, for they were used in graded sets; and some, the cheapest variety, were just plain castings. These bells were usually attached to a leather band which hung around the horse's neck or to a larger band which went over the horse's back and buckled under the stomach. They were used on horses principally when drawing a sleigh, their function being to warn other travelers of the sleigh's location. The finest specimens are highly regarded by today's collectors.

These round bells were called either "crotal bells" or "sleigh bells." According to information in the *Oxford English Dictionary*, the English word "crotal" was derived from the Latin *crotalum* or the French *crotale*. "In Irish Antiquity, Crotal was applied to a small globular or pear-shaped bell or rattle, the nature and use of which is obscure." It must have been a strange word for a farmer to call his bells, and it is likely that more were called "sleigh bells" than "crotal bells."

The making of sleigh bells was a tedious task which often ended in failure. First a pattern had to be made of the same shape and size desired for the finished bell. A similarly shaped core of baked sand had also to be made, but smaller than the pattern, so that when the metal flowed into the cavity formed by the pattern and around the core, adequate space was provided to cast a complete and perfect bell. A small ball of metal was sealed within the core of sand so that after the casting was made, and the core-sand shaken out, the ball remained to cause a jingling sound when the bell was shaken. An imperfect casting could be caused by not having the core properly placed, or by the molten metal chilling in the damp sand before the entire cavity was filled.

William Barton is reported to have been the first American to cast sleigh bells in East Hampton (Belltown), Connecticut, in 1808. In 1828, Barton moved to Cairo, New York, and continued to make bells there. One of his apprentices, named Bevin, returned to East Hampton in 1832, and went into bell founding for himself. Since that time bells have been made in East Hampton; the Bevin Brothers Manufacturing Company was operating there as of 1967.

C. GUN PARTS AND CANNON

Although the subject of firearms has received considerable attention in recent publications about Americana, it is evident that little is known about how they were made in the various historical eras of our country. Because the first guns made here were fabricated by men who were trained in Europe, many cannot be positively identified as the product of a European or American craftsman. There is considerable support of the theory, however, that early gunsmiths on the frontier made their guns with little assistance from other craftsmen, even though many gun parts were made of cast brass. Gunsmiths were trained by the apprenticeship system; presumably they were taught to carve wood, forge iron, cast brass, file locks, and engrave metal. Such a variety of skills suggests that they were not masters of their trade, but surviving examples of their work clearly show that they produced a fine product, distinguished in design and superior in craftsmanship.

The thesis for the complete production of the gun is based primarily on the inventories of early gunsmiths' tools. In these records, one finds lists of equipment for doing all the work connected with gunmaking. The gunsmiths owned anvils to forge iron, gravers to engrave designs, tools to cut and carve wood, and facilities for casting brass. Although no really ancient inventories of any gunsmiths have been located in America, the contents of the inventory of John Philip Beck, a gunsmith in Lebanon Township, Dauphin County, Pennsylvania, in the late eighteenth century, includes all the tools needed for the complete following of his trade. Among his tools were listed nine crucibles, scrap brass and copper, smith bellows, and flasks for casting metal. The premise for his casting brass is firm, for it is not likely that he cast iron from the heat of a forge (which he also owned). Indeed, there would have been little reason for him to have cast iron, for the iron parts of his products were not formed by the casting process. It is not likely that he cast objects of pewter for, at that time, pewter was cast in bronze molds, and not in flasks such as he is known to have had. The parts he was likely to have cast of brass were trigger guards, butt plates, lock-bolt plates, patch-box

Obverse and reverse of a brass patch box for a Kentucky rifle; signed by the maker, "Henry / Boulton" (Pa.). Signed parts of this type are extremely rare.
Kauffman Collection

covers, and possibly toe plates. The outer surfaces of all such parts in the guns he made smooth and polished, but the underside is invariably rough, the typical texture of a piece of brass cast in sand.

The intestate inventory of Thomas Earle, a famous New England gunsmith of the eighteenth century includes items similar to those found in the Beck inventory. Among the Earle tools and materials were flasks for casting metal and a considerable quantity of scrap brass. These two examples could be repeated many times by continued research of the subject in an area from North Carolina to New England, and westward into Ohio. The Ohio gunsmiths were particularly dependent on their own resources, being far removed from the importing and manufacturing centers on the eastern seaboard. If any of the gunsmiths working on the frontier used imported parts, those parts were probably locks, but they were rarely made of brass.

By the end of the eighteenth century the picture of gun production was changing in America; craftsmen were becoming specialists, and brass founders were casting brass parts of gunsmiths. This trend in the early part of the nineteenth century shows up in an advertisement which Fellows and Myers inserted in the *Berks and Schuylkill Journal,* December 13, 1718, offering a number of products including brass castings for gunsmiths.

NEW BRASS FOUNDRY

Fellows and Myers

Inform the Public that they have just commenced the business of

Brass Founding

In all its various branches, in West Penn Street at the corner opposite the sign of the Golden Swan, and next door to J. Ritter & Co's German Printing office.

They will furnish the brass work for any kind of machinery, castings for gunsmiths and clock makers, cocks for stills, andirons, bells, etc., etc. And all kinds of brass work mended and repaired at the shortest notice.

As they mean to execute work with dispatch and elegance, they hope to merit the patronage of the public.

Reading, December 13
N. B. One or two apprentices wanted to the above business.

The availability of gun parts of cast brass from brass founders indicates that the earlier practice of the gunsmith making the entire gun had by then disappeared. He was now becoming a fabricator of parts made by other craftsmen, such as lock-makers and barrel-welders. His product continued to have a distinctive style and its function was not impaired by the new manufacturing procedures, but the charm of earlier guns, made by such men as Eyster, Beck, Resor, Berry, Beyer, Schroyer, and other makers of Kentucky rifles, was lost. By the middle of the nineteenth century, gun factories such as those of Henry Leman in Lancaster, Pennsylvania, and J. Henry of Boulton, Pennsylvania, produced guns entirely out of their own manufactured parts.

Every gun collector knows that parts such as butt plates, patch-box covers, and trigger guards bearing the names of the manufacturer are extremely scarce. A few lock plates of cast brass are known bearing such names as James Golcher, The Pennsylvania Rifle Works, A. Ernst, and Fredrick Sell. Most of these brass lock plates are of the flint-lock era and are usually found on very fine guns, such as those by Ernst and Sell. The two brass lock plates illustrated are of the percussion type, equally as rare as the flintlock type.

Brass lock plates, made for use on Kentucky rifles. *Left:* by the Pennsylvania Rifle Works; *right:* by James Golcher.

Kauffman Collection; courtesy The Stackpole Company

A patch-box cover is illustrated bearing the imprint of the Henry Company gun factory at Boulton near Bethlehem, Pennsylvania. The only other marked parts found in any quantity were produced by Tryon in Philadelphia. At best, the total quantity of signed cast brass parts of guns can be counted in the dozens rather than the hundreds. In most objects, other than locks, the name is imprinted on the underside of the part, which must be removed for examination and identification.

There was quite some difficulty in casting brass parts for guns. Some of them are very thin, and great skill was required to cast perfect specimens. The thin cross section of patch-box covers must have been particularly trying to cast, and many times the metal must have chilled in the damp sand before a perfect product was obtained. Butt plates and trigger guards were thicker, and the chances for casting a perfect product at the first attempt were greater. All of these gunsmith-casters must be commended for their work, for rarely does one find indifferent workmanship in gun parts made of cast brass.

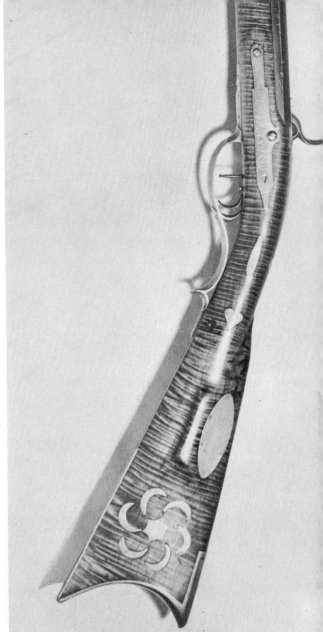

A profusion of brass inlays in the stock of a Kentucky rifle made in Bedford County, Pa.

Farber Collection; courtesy The Stackpole Company

Extravagantly engraved patch box of brass on a Kentucky rifle.

formerly in the S. E. Dyke Collection

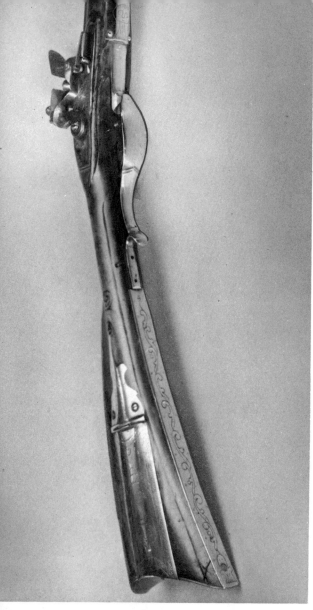

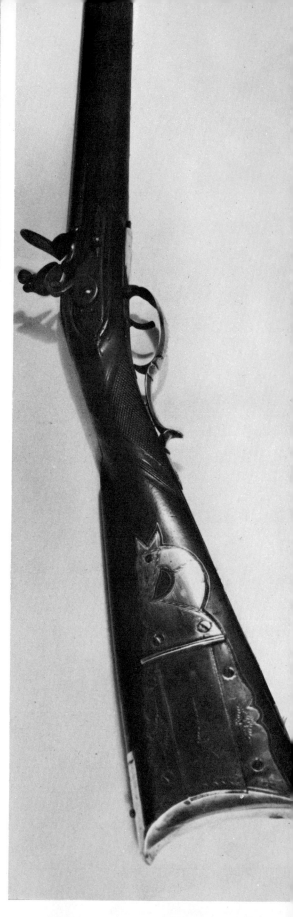

Butt end of a Kentucky rifle showing
an extravagantly engraved toe plate
on the under edge. Above the
trigger guard another brass plate is inlaid
with the head of an Indian engraved on it.

Kauffman Collection

Brass patch box on the product of a New
England gunsmith. Patch boxes were not
widely used there, and this one is an
attractive example of the work done
there.

formerly in the Kauffman Collection

Brass wire inlay in the stock of a
Kentucky rifle.

Clegg Collection; courtesy The Stackpole
Company

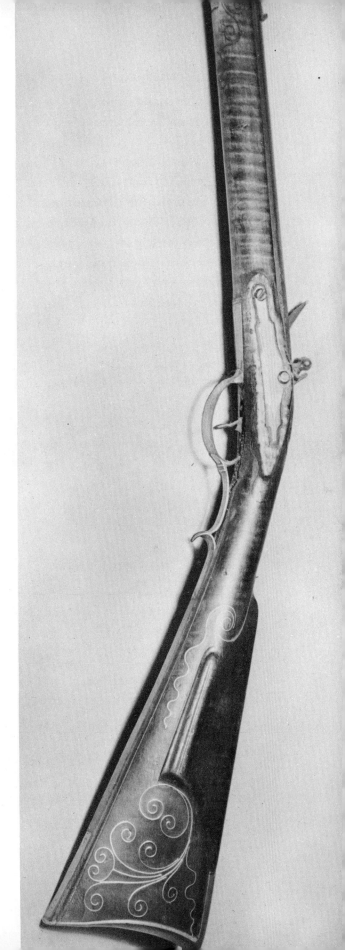

Occasional pistols and even fewer long guns have barrels made of cast brass. In the eighteenth century, it was difficult to drill a small hole through a long, solid piece of metal. Holes were formed in iron barrels by welding a strip of metal into a tube. The undersize hole formed by this method was later enlarged and rifled according to the whims of the gunsmith or the customer for whom the gun was made. Brass barrels could not be manufactured in this manner, so that extremely few of them were made.

The craftsmen most famous for pistol barrels of brass are P. and D. Moll, of Hellertown, Pennsylvania. These men worked in the early part of the nineteenth century and produced a sizeable number of pistols with brass barrels. Most of their products are boldly marked on the

Kentucky pistol with brass barrel and other metal parts made of brass. The weapon is fully identified by the engraving on the top facet of the barrel, "P & D Moll / Hellertown" (Pa.).

Smith Collection; courtesy The Stackpole Company

top facet of the barrel, their identification including both their initials and their names, and the town where they worked. Other gunsmiths made pistols with brass barrels, too, but a brass-barreled pistol is a rarity in arms collections today. The other parts made of brass on such pistols are of the standard style. The most desirable stocks are made of curly maple wood; they are usually referred to as "Kentucky pistols."

If one describes the quantity of information about making guns as "meager," the data about making cannon in America might be described as "nil." There is a strong possibility, of course, that contemporary European practices were followed in America in the eighteenth century; thus, some information on the subject might be logically included from European sources.

In the discussion about metal used to make bells, it is pointed out that a long tradition existed in Europe which permitted invading armies to confiscate the bells of areas they conquered and recast them into cannon. Such action indicates that one metal could be used for making both bells and cannons. However, when considering the best metal for cannons, there is evidence that a metal called "gun metal" was the ideal one. This metal is described in Chambers' *Cyclopedia or, an Universal Dictionary of Arts and Sciences,* as follows:

Manner of Casting Great Guns, or Pieces of Artillery.

The casting of cannons, mortars, and other pieces of artillery, is performed like statues and bells; especially as to what regards the mould, wax, shell, furnaces, etc.

As to the metal, it is somewhat different from both; as having a mixture of tin, which is not in that of statues; and only having half the quantity of tin in bells, i.e. at the rate of ten pounds of tin to an hundred of copper. A cannon is always shaped a little conical, being thickest of metal at the breech, where the greatest effort of gunpowder is made, and diminishes thence to the muzzle: so that if the mouth be two inches thick of metal, the breech is six.

The length is measured in calibers, i.e. in diameters of the muzzle. Six inches at the muzzle requires twenty calibers, or ten feet in length; there is always about a sixth of an inch allowed play for the ball.

Though little mention is made of casting cannons of brass in the literature of the subject, brass was apparently widely used for that purpose throughout the eighteenth and nineteenth centuries. The trade card of Paul Revere and Son states that, "They cast Bells and Brass Cannon of all Sizes," and Benjamin Loxley is reported to have cast brass eight-inch mortars, howitzers, cannons, and shells in Philadelphia in 1776. Daniel King cast a brass three-inch howitzer to be paraded in the Federal Procession in Philadelphia on July 4, 1788, later finishing it and firing it on the Union Green.

If the materials for making cannon in America are uncertain, the actual production is equally difficult to establish, particularly in the eighteenth century. Some comment on the subject is found in *A History of American Manufactures from 1608 to 1860* by J. Leander Bishop who states:

> In April, 1776 Benjamin Loxley made proposals for casting eight-inch mortars, howitzers, cannon, and shells for Congress or the Committees of Safety. Some of the brass guns of Major Loxley were tested by Daniel Joy of the Reading Furnace, who was also engaged in casting and boring iron nine-pounders at the rate of one daily, to be followed by others of larger size. The iron pieces appear to have stood the proof better than brass. . . .
>
> During the same month James Byers, who had cast brass guns for the Government was requested to hold himself in readiness to remove his apparatus and utensils at a moment's warning on the approach of the British. Morgan Busteed, Samuel Potts, and Thomas Rutter each made proposals to cast cannon in the course of that year. There was a cannon-foundry at Southwark, but we do not know who owned it. In August 1777, the Board of War informed President Warton that the furnace for casting cannon stood idle for want of copper, and requested permission to use a load which had been sent from French Creek, but was claimed by the State.

There is little reason to doubt the veracity of Bishop's comments about the casting of cannons for the American Revolution. However, such information must be given a secondary status, and the researcher is better satisfied with a recently found primary source which substantiates such activity in Philadelphia. A letter written by Daniel King to the Pennsylvania Council of Safety on July 26, 1776, has been found in the Force Manuscripts, in the manuscript division of the Library of Congress. The contents of the letter are as follows:

> Sir: As you are not unacquainted with the Resolution of the late Committee of Safety to have a number of Brass Field Pieces cast and the necessity which gave rise to it, it will be needless to enlarge thereon, but as the board have not had the success they wish in their attempt to cast Iron Cannon, it becomes more necessary for the board to promote and forward the said intention to the utmost of their power. The absence of Capt. Sexley with his artillery company, who has the chief Management and Superintendence of the

foundry [presumably King's brass foundry] has occasioned the entire stoppage of that important business.

The Council of Safety have, therefore, a request to return Capt. Sexley to the Cannon Foundry as he will be likely to serve his country more effectually in that station than any other. A day's delay in this business may be attended with the most serious consequences, we do therefore hope it will be done as soon as possible.

By modern standards, it might be surmised that Capt. Sexley was peeling potatoes or cleaning the barracks in the service of his country. Hopefully he was released to get back to his brass foundry, but posterity will probably not know the answer to King's letter. Nevertheless, the letter can be regarded as documented evidence that King was casting brass cannon at that time.

The brief for King's activity is further substantiated by another letter in the manuscript collection of the Library of Congress which states that: "By order of the Board, Mr. R. Towers Company was desired to deliver to Daniel King one old cannon in the State House Yard to be bore."

The frequent mention of the name Daniel King in connection with brass founding places him as one of Philadelphia's most important

Brass howitzer bearing the inscription "D. King / Philada. 1793."

courtesy Smithsonian Institution

craftsmen in the second half of the eighteenth century. Documents and artifacts survive, indicating his activity there at that time. A newspaper advertisement tells that he invented a new type of door knocker, and an invoice shows that he made a pair of andirons with Corinthian columns for the Cadwalader family of Philadelphia. In addition, he was selected to represent the trade of brass founding in the Federal Procession on July 4, 1788. The names of people who represented the various trades in that procession show most of them to be outstanding tradesmen; it is significant that King represented the brass founders. Benjamin Harbeson, an outstanding coppersmith and merchant in Philadelphia, represented the coppersmiths in that notable event.

The trail of industrial drama continues, with the name of Daniel King appearing on some brass howitzers; but because they were made in 1793, there is some uncertainty as to which Daniel King made them.

Advertisement of Daniel King in the *Pennsylvania Chronicle* of Apr. 20, 1767, enumerating his various products. He must have been a busy man, but in his spare time he "also rivets broken *China*, in the *neatest* Manner."

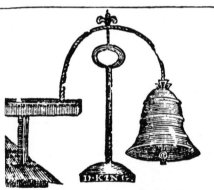

DANIEL KING,
BRASS-FOUNDER,
AND
BRAND-MAKER,

At the Corner of *Norris's Alley*, in *Front Street*, between *Chesnut* and *Walnut Streets*;

TAKES this Method to inform his Customers and the PUBLIC in general, that he has, after considerable Expence and Trouble, discovered a new Method of making Brands either of Copper or Iron, which far excel any yet made for Neatness and Service; he will warrant them, and make them for less than the customary Prices.

He has likewise a new and curious Set of Patterns for Brass Fire Dogs, neater and more to Order than any yet made on the Continent.

He makes Brass Fenders of all Sorts, in the neatest Manner, Fire Shovels and Tongs, Candlesticks, Sconces, all Kinds and Sizes of Chandelers or Branches, for Places of Worship or Shop Use, Bells of all Sizes, *viz.* Church Bells, Criers Bells, House Bells, Horse Bells, &c. Cylinders for Pumps, for Land and Sea Uses, of all Sizes; all Sorts of Brass Work for *West-India* Sugar-Mills, Brasses for Grist-Mills, Wind-Mills, Saw-Mills, and Cart Boxes; all Sorts and Sizes of Brass Cocks, all Sorts of Founders Work for Coppersmiths, Gunsmiths, &c. Brass and Pinchbeck Buckles for the Army, Town or Country Use, with all Sorts of Brass Furniture.

Said KING, continues to make his new-constructed Brass Knockers for Front Doors, which he will warrant agreeable to his former *Advertisement*; they are both neat and strong, and have given entire Satisfaction to those Gentlemen who have had them.—Please to take Notice they are not that Sort which have an Iron Staple over them.

N. B. Gentlemen and Ladies who will please to favour him with their Custom, may depend on being faithfully served; and as he has many Hands at Work, he is thereby enabled to carry on his Business extensively; but is determined, however, to undertake no Work, but what he can get done according to his Engagements, unless some unavoidable Accident should happen. He continues to give the best Prices for old Copper and Brass.

*** He also rivets broken *China*, in the *neatest* Manner. *Philad. April* 20, 1767.

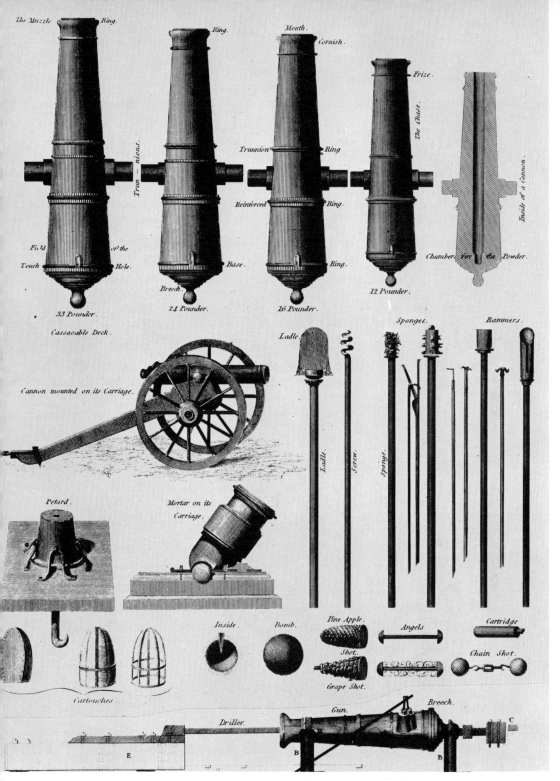

Illustrations and terminology concerning cannons of the early nineteenth century.

from *A Dictionary of Mechanical Science, Arts, Manufactures and Miscellaneous Knowledge*. Fisher, Son & Co. London, 1827.

At that time, Daniel King Jr. was listed as a brass founder, and it is entirely possible that the elder Daniel King had by that date relinquished the operation of the brass founding business to his son.

Don Berkbile, in the *Military Collector and Historian* (Spring 1961), wrote of nine early howitzers. Five of them were of a light type, approximately sixteen inches long and weighing thirty-eight pounds, some of which are marked "D. King, Germantown," with "U.S." stamped on the trunnions and the tops of the barrels. The other four, of heavier type, seventeen inches long and weighing sixty pounds, bore the impression "D. King, Philada. 1793."

It is particularly helpful to study the advertisement of Daniel King, illustrated here. King had a business of considerable stature in Philadelphia as early as 1767, and it is not surprising that he had facilities for casting and boring cannons at the time of the Revolution. Unfortunately, it is not known today just how extensive the buildings were in which brass founding was done. Cannons were cast in a vertical position in a hole which was slightly deeper than the cannons were long. In this procedure, the scoriae, or impurities, frequently rose to the top of the casting where they could be sawed away without impairing the shape and function of the casting. Casting in a hole was also a safe procedure; if the mold burst, the hot metal was confined to the hole and could not endanger the lives of workmen.

The earliest cannons were cast with a core which created the bore. This procedure was unsatisfactory because the surface of the bore was rough, and the scale on the surface of cast brass was difficult to remove with the machinery available at that time. About the middle of the eighteenth century, a machine was invented in Europe to bore cannons which were cast in a solid cylinder. At first, the cannons were mounted in a vertical position, and the power for boring was supplied by a windmill or by horses. At the turn of the nineteenth century, a boring machine was invented which bored cannons held in a horizontal position, and simultaneously cleaned the outside. This device was at first operated by water power, but was later powered by a steam engine.

Many improvements in the casting and finishing of cannons were made in the nineteenth century. Although production methods became more efficient, the products lacked the ornamentation and charm of most cannons cast in the eighteenth century.

D. MOLDS FOR CASTING OBJECTS OF PEWTER

In recent years collectors of Americana have become interested in
the various tools and techniques used by the men who produced the
objects which they are collecting. This technological information is not

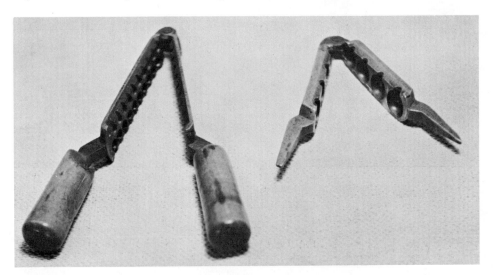

Open and closed molds for rifle bullets and for buckshot, made of cast brass. A fairly
large number of brass molds have been found in America bearing the initials "I. M."
but nothing is known about the person designated.

Kauffman Collection

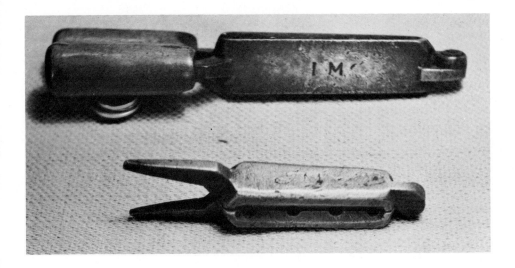

Three spoon molds made of bronze and brass. The smallest is approximately 4 in. long. The middle one has a side gate designed to produce more perfectly formed spoons in the casting process.

Kauffman Collection

only an important fund of knowledge in itself, but also leads to a better understanding of the objects in question. This interest has been nurtured by the establishment of shops in restored villages such as Williamsburg, Virginia, and Old Sturbridge, Massachusetts. In these villages, blacksmiths are working at their forges, weavers are weaving cloth, and potters are making pots. A few pewterers make spoons, but none shows the wide scope of the trade.

The most likely reason for this omission is that almost no tools of the trade have survived. The molds used by pewterers to cast such objects as teapots, mugs, tankards, basins, and plates are sadly missing. Although a few of these molds were made of cast iron in the nineteenth century, most of the earlier ones were of brass or bronze. These metals are good conductors of heat; they deteriorate slowly; and they can be reheated many times without impairing their quality. Of the few brass molds surviving today, none can be identified as the products of an American founder. However, some of them were undoubtedly produced in America, since a number of brass founders list them among their products. One founder mentioned molds for pewterers, while two or three others specified that they made molds for casting spoons of pewter. The scarcity of spoon molds in England and the reasonably good supply of them in America confirm the hypothesis that many were made here in the eighteenth and early nineteenth centuries.

The earliest advertisement found for objects made of copper and brass for the pewterer was placed in the *Pennsylvania Gazette* on May 3, 1753, by James Smith, who included pewter-spoon molds in his usual line of cast brass objects. On November 26, 1774, Jacob and Solomon Proby advertised the making of spoon molds in the *South Carolina Gazette;* and Hedderly and Riland placed the following advertisement in *Paxton's Philadelphia Directory* in 1819.

> Cast and hung Church, Ship, and House Bells, of any weight, Stair rods, Andirons, and all kinds of brass work in general, made and repaired. Fan Sashes and Brackets made.
> Pewterers's moulds made at the shortest notice.

Up until about 1825, all objects made of pewter were cast in molds. Molds consisted of a number of plates or pieces, carefully fitted together so that the molten metal would not leak out when the part was poured and also so that the mold could easily be disassembled to remove the cast part. Such objects as teapots and tankards consisted of a number of parts, each of which required a complete mold to produce.

The production of these molds was a meticulous business, for the castings could not have any flaws. The round ones had also to be carefully turned to shape on a lathe after they were cast. Ingenious holding devices were used for turning the molds, and making them smooth was a slow, laborious task. After the various parts were turned and smoothed, they were held together by clamps or hinges. Sometimes the hinges were made of iron since iron resisted wear longer than bronze or brass, and the mold would retain a tighter fit for a longer time.

Today a careful search by collectors, museums, technologists, craftsmen, and others is being made to find molds for making pewter objects, but only a relatively few are being located. The most frequently found mold is one for casting spoons. They are popular today as a survival from the era in which things were produced by hand methods, and also because many people like to try to cast spoons in the old molds.

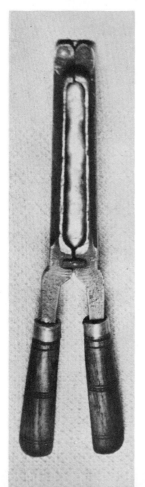

Two molds for casting pewter buttons. *Left:* closed mold, showing trough into which the metal is poured to form buttons underneath it. *Right:* Open mold, showing the shape and size of the buttons cast in it; the wooden handles are missing.

Kauffman Collection

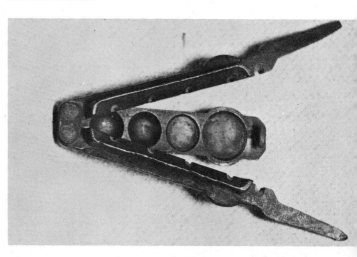

Though most of the spoon molds have a stud or a handle on each of the two parts, few people know the function of these studs, which is to attach the mold to tongs.

One old mold was recently found which was attached to a pair of blacksmith's tongs. The tongs functioned as a clamp, in keeping the two parts together, and also as a hinge, when the two parts were to be separated to remove the spoon. Possibly the only documented method for using the mold appears in *The Cabinet Cyclopedia*, by Rev. Dionysius Lardner. Although this sketch and data about the making of a spoon was printed in London in 1834, it is very likely that similar procedures were followed here.

The molds are described as of brass, "formed with great nicety and used with great facility." Lardner explains:

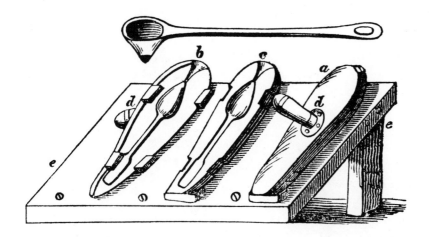

The annexed sketch represents two pairs of spoon moulds, which is generally the number managed by a single caster, the metal being left to cool a little in the one last filled while the spoon is removed, by means of a pair of pliers, from the other. A shows the mould as closed up and ready for the reception of the metal by way of an orifice at the upper end; B C are the two parts of another mould separated: D D are handles, by which the upper part of the mould is removed: E E is an inclined board fixed upon the workbench, near to which the caster sits, and within reach of the metal-pot: F is the ladle, partly covered with a lid of sheet iron, which prevents the scum or dross from passing into the mould. The metal used for this purpose is made much harder than that which is

Brass mold for casting pewter buttons. "USA" is engraved on the bottom surface of each cavity and was reproduced on each button. The wooden handles are missing.

courtesy Don Berkbile

Pennsylvania-type pewter porringer on the inner half of the brass mold used to cast the vessel. The body and handle were cast in one piece, unlike most porringers.

Kauffman Collection

rolled into sheets: the spoons are accordingly stiff, and admit of a
high polish; but they are at the same time proportionably liable to
break, if bent considerably, though by no means so brittle as to fail
with ordinary usage.

None of the molds for casting objects of pewter can be regarded as
plentiful today. Molds for pewter spoons turn up occasionally; some
molds for making bullets have survived, and a few for making buttons
are found in antique shops and museums. The buttons produced in
these molds had either flat or curved tops, and all of them were in one
piece, including the eye. Little filing or smoothing was necessary on the
buttons after the casting was taken from the mold.

Two halves of a Pennsylvania-type porringer mold are owned by two
different museums; the Brooklyn Museum owns a mold for casting
pewter basins; the Henry Ford Museum owns a mold for casting plates;
Colonial Williamsburg has a mold for 13-inch deep plates; and Old
Salem at Winston Salem, North Carolina, has several molds for basins
or plates. A few other molds are now in private collections throughout
the country.

A variety of devices were used to clamp the plate and basin molds
together while the molten metal was poured into the inner cavity. Several have two straps of iron across their outer surface, hinged at one

A plate mold in a closed position. Although the exterior surface is rough, the interior
surface is probably as smooth as when it was finally polished a long time ago.
Kauffman Collection

Bronze mold for casting pewter plates. Although others are known, none has the grooves in the bottom half of the mold to produce ridges on the bottom of the plate. The purpose of the ridges is not known.

Kauffman Collection

end, and fitted with handles on the other end. The handles were squeezed tightly together while the plate was cast and pulled apart to release the plate.

Anyone who has tried to cast spoons of pewter in bronze or brass molds is aware of the problems in this operation. The metal often "chills" before the mold is completely filled, or, if the mold is very hot, and not fitted together perfectly, the molten pewter flows through the cracks between the two halves as fast as it is poured into the mold.

The problems of casting are greatly compounded by the use of a mold such as the one illustrated for casting inkstands of pewter. Turning the parts of this mold on a lathe was an advantage over fitting them by hand, filing, and scraping, as was necessary in fitting the two parts of a spoon mold together. But, after much use, the various parts of the inkstand mold became worn and refitting was necessary, an operation which was probably more difficult than the original work.

The mold for casting the body of the tankard was similar to the one used for the inkstand and both procedures involved about the same problems. Casting the handle, hinge knuckle, and thumbpiece, however, was one of the most complicated operations performed by the craftsmen. A perfect fit between the various mold parts was imperative; the correct temperature of the metal was a critical matter; and the

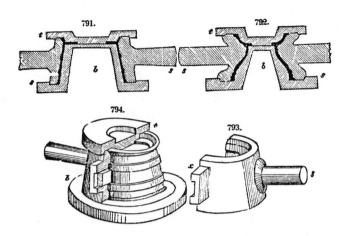

"Figs. 791 to 794 represent the moulds for casting pewter inkstands. These moulds are
. . . each made in four parts; the black portions represent the sections of the inkstands
to be cast. The moulds each consist of a top-piece or *cap t*, a bottom or *core b*, and two
sides or *cottles s s*. In Fig. 794 the one side is removed in order to expose the castings,
and the top-piece *t* is supposed to be sawn through to make the whole [procedure] more
distinct. It will be seen [that] the top and bottom parts have each a rebate like the lid
of a snuffbox, which embrace the external edges of the two side-pieces *s s*, and the latter
divide, as in the bullet mould, exactly upon the diametrical line of the inkstand, which
is a circular object is, of course, the largest part; the positions of the parts are therefore
strictly maintained.

"When the mould has been put together, laid upon its side, and filled through *x* the
ingate, or as it is technically called, the *tedge*, it is allowed to stand about a minute or
two, and then the top *t* is knocked off by one or two light blows of a pewter mallet; the
mould is then held in the hand, and the bottom part or core is knocked out of the casting
by the edge; lastly, the two sides are pulled asunder by their handles, and the casting is
removed from the one in which it happens to stick fast; but it requires cautious handling
not to break it. The face of the mould is slightly *coated* with red ochre and white of
egg to prevent the casting adhering to the same, and to give the works a better face. The
first few castings are generally spoiled, until in fact the mould becomes properly warmed."
from Appleton's *Dictionary of Machines, Mechanics, Engine-Work, and Engineering.* New York, 1866

disassembly of the mold parts had to be easy and uncomplicated so
that the surface of the castings was not impaired.

The casting of molds for making pewter vessels was a demanding
and, hopefully, a remunerative occupation. Although some of the surviving molds could have been made by American brass founders, none
of them is marked, and one can only presume that the pewterers in

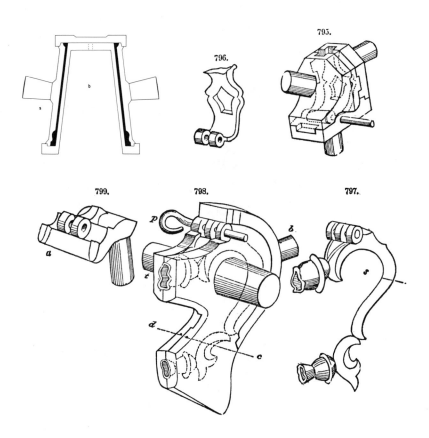

"Most of the works made in the very useful material, pewter, are cast in gun-metal moulds, which require much skill in their construction; thus, a pewter tankard, with a hinged cover and spout, consists of six pieces, every one of which requires a different mould. Thus:—

"1. The body has a mould in four parts, like that for the inkstand, but it is filled in the erect position through two ingates, which are made through the top-piece *t* of the mould.

"2. The bottom requires a mould in two parts, and is poured at the edge.

"3. The cover is cast in the same manner; and thus far the moulds are all made in the lathe, in which useful machine these castings are also finished before being soldered together.

"4. The spout requires a mould in two parts.

"5. The piece, Fig. 796, by which the cover is hinged to the handle, requires a much more complex mould, which divides in four parts, as shown in Fig. 795, and much resembles, except in external form, the remaining mould: namely,

"6. For the handle, which mould, like the last, consists of four pieces, fitted together with various ears and projections. They are represented in their relative positions in Fig. 798, with the exception of the piece *a*, Fig. 799, which is detached and shown bottom upwards. Fig. 797 shows the pewter handle separately, with the three knuckles for joining on the cover; and on reference to Fig. 798, of the five parts through which the pin *p* is thrust, the two external pieces belong respectively to the sides *c* and *d* of the mould; the others are parts of the casting, and the two hollows are formed by the two solid knuckles fixed to the detached piece of the mould *a*, Fig. 799."

from Appleton's *Dictionary of Machines, Mechanics, Engine-Work, and Engineering.* New York, 1866.

various communities along the Atlantic seaboard patronized their fellow craftsmen in brass. The absence of such marks on molds points out that much research still remains to be done on this remarkable facet of brass founding.

E. MISCELLANEOUS OBJECTS OF CAST BRASS

In considering the sizeable number of objects made of cast brass in America in the eighteenth and nineteenth centuries, it must be regretfully reported that little is known about their manufacture or about the craftsmen who fashioned them. The signed bells, andirons, and other pieces discussed in this survey are exceptions; vast quantities of objects in museums and private collections await identification by methods not yet known.

Why so few objects were signed is explained in part by the difficulties encountered in marking objects of cast brass. Unlike copper, pewter, and silver, which could be imprinted easily with a die struck by a hammer, brass castings were harder and much larger; some other way had to be devised to place the maker's name on his product. The traditional method was to carve the name of the maker into the pattern of the object, which would then be perfectly reproduced in the casting. This procedure required considerable skill on the part of the pattern-maker, with the result that such a procedure was rarely followed, a fact confirmed by the quantity of surviving unmarked objects. John Taylor of Richmond, Virginia, and Martin Gay and Hunneman of Boston used this method and had their names carved into the pattern for the top surface of the handles of the skillets they cast. It is not claimed that

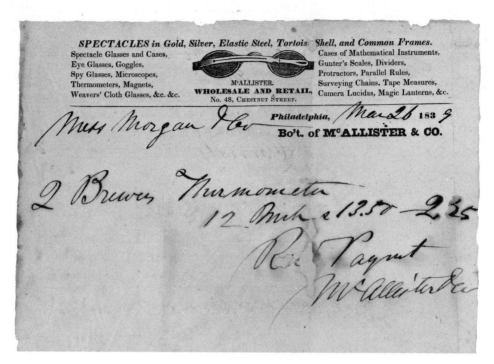

Bill rendered by McAllister of Philadelphia, Pa., a dealer in many objects made of brass. Some items stamped by the company name and, presumably, were made there.

Kauffman Collection

names could not be imprinted with a die, but the traditional and most appropriate method was to carve the name of the maker into the pattern.

This lack of signatures on objects of cast brass is unfortunate, particularly in regard to candlesticks and furniture brasses. Advertisements in newspapers show that both these items were made in America, but none have been found in this survey which can be positively identified as products of American craftsmen. A few marked examples of other objects have been found in museums and private collections, but much work remains to be done on the identification of objects of cast brass.

The products of John Taylor, Brass and Pewter Founder of Richmond, Virginia, are listed in his advertisement in the *Virginia Gazette*, June 5, 1793. A few of his products have been identified. His enumeration includes

> "bell metal skillets, pans and mortars, copper tea-kettles, pans, and coal boxes of all sizes; a great variety of coach mountings, and any fancy patterns, executed with neatness and dispatch, pewter candle molds, dishes, plates, and basins, brass candlesticks of the latest fancy patterns; mill inks, copper rivets, and brass cocks; bells

of all sizes from 2 oz. to 500 pounds, spelter and plumber's solder; branding irons, mathematical instruments made and repaired; skeletons for umbrellas made and repaired, and all kinds of Repairs executed in the neatest manner, on the shortest notice, and on the most reasonable terms."

This enumeration is included here, not because it was the longest of the advertisements examined, or because it contained many unusual items, but because it lists many of the usual items made by brass founders in the eighteenth century, and because Taylor worked outside the densely populated areas of Boston, New York, Philadelphia, Baltimore, and Charleston. Frankly, no one list did include all the items to be discussed, a selection that includes furniture brasses, tomahawks, faucets, pie crimpers, skillets, lancets, sundials, surveyors' compasses, door knockers, jamb hooks, buttons, balances, candlesticks, clocks, and scientific instruments.

Furniture Brasses

Furniture brasses are included in this miscellaneous group of objects to indicate the paucity of information about these numerous and important objects. While a great deal is known about the various styles, information about where, how, and by whom they were made is fragmentary. Such information is not found in old encyclopedias or dictionaries, and even modern definitive books about cased furniture have no index entries for "brasses," "furniture hardware," or "plates and pulls." One of the few informative sources about furniture hardware is found in the *Winterthur Portfolio One, 1964,* in which Charles Hummel discusses the "English Hardware Catalogue of Samuel Rowland Fisher," a merchant in Philadelphia in the last half of the eighteenth century. This discussion is directed principally toward the pattern of brasses in the Fisher catalogue and those with similar patterns found on furniture made in America. The very presence of this catalogue, and a sizeable number of others, indicates clearly that a great many of the brasses used on American furniture were made in England. Possibly a study of old English dock records would throw some light on the quantity of brasses shipped to America, but it would be an unusual find that would explain other details we would need to know for exact attribution.

To separate imported brasses from those produced in America invites confusion. A number of early brass founders advertised furniture hardware, but, to date, no distinction has been made between pieces made in England and those cast in America. It would seem likely that some of the famous cabinetmakers in Philadelphia, Newport, and Charleston patronized American craftsmen in brass, but there is no evidence to support such an assumption.

The present inability to make definitive attributions resulted from the fact that virtually no brasses were marked by their makers, either in England or America. A few examples have been found with a letter on them; and some bearing the name "S. Parker" are on a piece of furniture owned by Colonial Williamsburg. A brass founder by the name of Parker worked in Philadelphia in the eighteenth century, and it is highly possible that he made those brasses. A decision, however, about this matter depends on discriminating judgment rather than positive identification. Much research remains to be done before confidence in identification can be achieved.

Furniture brasses.

courtesy Metropolitan Museum of Art

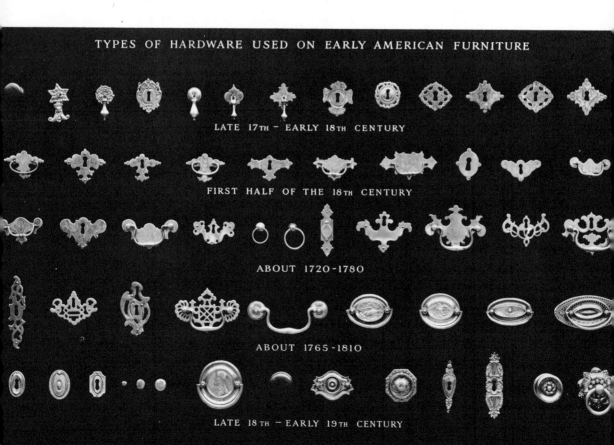

TYPES OF HARDWARE USED ON EARLY AMERICAN FURNITURE

LATE 17TH - EARLY 18TH CENTURY

FIRST HALF OF THE 18TH CENTURY

ABOUT 1720-1780

ABOUT 1765-1810

LATE 18TH - EARLY 19TH CENTURY

Current knowledge, obtained principally from newspaper advertisements, suggests that few furniture brasses were produced in America before the middle of the eighteenth century. They were difficult to cast and, since they were easily available from England, American craftsmen probably directed their efforts toward the making of larger and less difficult objects. Philip Syng mentions furniture brasses in his advertisement in Annapolis in 1759, as did Daniel Jackson of Boston in 1763, and Daniel King in Philadelphia in 1767. No brasses were available from England during the Revolution, of course; and after the war, the disposition of Americans to patronize American craftsmen must have placed the local brass founder in a better competitive position with England than ever before.

Many forms of brass hardware for furniture were made in the eighteenth century, but the plate-pull is the *pièce de résistance* to the collector and the dealer in antiques. It consisted of a flat brass plate, two

Front and back views of brass pulls marked "S. Parker," with a close-up of the name on the back of one of the pulls. Very few pulls were marked and the origin of these has not been positively established. A brass founder named S. Parker did work in the Philadelphia area in the eighteenth century.

courtesy Colonial Williamsburg

posts, and a bail. All of these parts were cast and because of their small size, each presented a problem in production. The greatest difficulty lay in casting the plates, which were reasonably long and wide, and very thin. Probably there were patterns of wood or metal. These may have been enclosed in sand to reproduce a replica of the model, or cast between two metal plates of iron, preheated so that the brass would flow through the thin cavity without cooling before the cavity was filled. Molten metal was apt to solidify before such a thin cavity could be filled, and the incidence of imperfect castings must have been high. The front surface of the casting was made smooth, the edges filed on a bevel, and all parts were polished before they were fitted on the furni-

Advertisement of Philip Syng enumerating the various brass products that he made and sold.

PHILIP SYNG,

BRASS-FOUNDER, *from* PHILADELPHIA,
Living near the Town-Gate in ANNAPOLIS,

MAKES (or Repairs) all Sorts of Brafs-Work, such as Candlefticks, Heads or Knobs of all Sizes for Shovels, Dogs, &c. Furniture for Defks and Chefts of Drawers, Knockers for Doors, Boxes for Carriages, Mill-Braffes for Saw or Grift Mills, Plate-Warmers, Fenders, Stirrups, &c. &c. He alfo cafts Bells of different Sizes; and gives the beft Prices for old Brafs and Copper:

He has to fell cheap, a very good 30 Hour Clock.

The faid *Syng* lens fome Time ago, but to whom he has forgot, the Third and Seventh Volume of the Spectator. Whoever has them, is defired to return them.

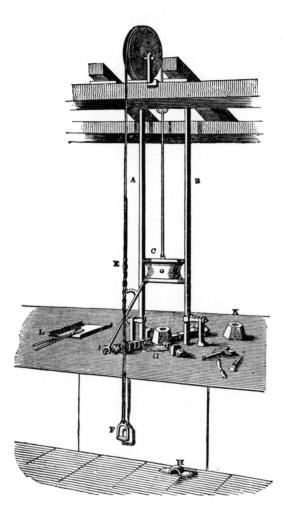

Sketch of stamp for cutting out small objects from thin sheet brass. *A* and *B* are wrought-iron pillars, about 8 ft. high, placed so that their angular edges serve to guide the hammer, *C*, the ends of the hammer being grooved for that purpose. The hammer is about 18 in. across and weighs about 100 lbs. It is suspended by a rope over the pulley at the top of the mechanism; a handhold is arranged at *E* and at the lower end the rope is attached to a stirrup, *F*. When the stamp is not in use, the hammer is fixed into position with the bar, *I*.

Such objects as plate–pulls, escutcheons, door plates, and curtain pins were made on this device. Some parts were reinforced with iron rings or discs, giving them an appearance of being very sturdy when they were actually very light.

from *The Cabinet Cyclopedia*

ture. Escutcheons were made in the same manner, but instead of holes for posts, an opening for a key was provided.

The clue to early eighteenth-century production, and authentic reproduction, is a rough surface on the back side of the plate. Some modern reproductions are stamped from sheet brass, which is smooth on both sides.

Late in the eighteenth century, a desire for more ornamented plates, combined with advanced technological skill, led to the stamping of plates for furniture of Hepplewhite and Sheraton styles. A male and female die were needed to produce these plates. The dies were placed in a device which held one die firmly in position and directed the second die to fall downward on the first, with a thin sheet of brass between them.

The dies of the brass stamper, which vary in size and weight depending on the size of the article to be produced, were made of steel or cast iron. The top die, or "hammer," as it was called, often weighed about 100 pounds. Dies made of steel were more costly to produce, but they lasted longer than those of cast iron, and gave better definition to the design created in the product.

Sometimes several "passes" had to be made to produce a good plate, and sometimes the metal had to be softened to prevent cracking at high points in the design. There were dies to make designs in the center of plates, such as hands, eagles, lions heads, and leaves. Dies also formed a shaped edge, which not only gave the plate rigidity, but also raised the pattern in the center so it would clear the surface of the wood on which it was mounted. Some of the stamped designs needed handwork to sharpen the imprinted pattern, which still could be made more rapidly and more cheaply than the brass cast plate-pulls used throughout most of the eighteenth century. The latter type also had posts and a bail.

Door Knockers

The door knocker of cast brass presents the same problem as the plate-pull, as far as identification of makers is concerned. They were illustrated in catalogues of English brass founders and were advertised by American craftsmen. Jackson, Syng, and King advertised door knockers, but the King advertisement introduced an historical sidelight

Typical S-shaped door knocker of the eighteenth century. The bottom striking plate is missing. None of these has been identified as the product of an American brass founder.

which may eventually lead to the identification of his product. It seems that in Philadelphia, in the 1760s, a number of door knockers were wrenched off the doors by vandals. These were apparently fastened to the door with an iron staple. King comments as follows in his advertisement in the *Pennsylvania Chronicle*, March 7, 1767.

> Said KING continues to make his new-constructed Brass Knockers for Front Doors, which he will warrant agreeable to his former *Advertisement*; they are both neat and strong, and have given entire Satisfaction to those Gentlemen who have had them.—Please notice they are not that sort which have an Iron Staple over them.

Because none have been found with King's signature on them, King's special form continues to be a mystery. There was, however, a type of door knocker used in the eighteenth century which he might possibly have made. This pattern, in the shape of a modified S, was particularly attractive and functional, and the quantity of surviving examples suggests that it was the most popular form of its time. It was attached to the door with a bolt which went entirely through the door and was fastened on the inside with a nut. The bottom plate on which it was "banged" was attached in the same way.

Later, a shield shape was used as a plate to which a knocker was attached, and some clever pattern-maker, striving for popular appeal, created an eagle knocker design early in the nineteenth century.

Skillets

One of the survivals of ancient English culture in America was the brass or bronze skillet. This vessel was the saucepan of medieval times and probably served a variety of purposes on the hearth. The diameter of the top was greater than the bottom. The bottom was almost flat and to it were attached three short legs. It had a long tapered handle, on top

Cast posnet or skillet by John Taylor, Richmond, Va., *circa* 1793. A number of similar ones by Taylor are known; however, marked American examples of this form are rare.
courtesy Old Salem, Inc.

of which usually appeared a motto, or the name and residence of the maker, such as "Jno. Taylor, Richmond." Although the various parts seem to be separate entities, close observation will disclose that the skillet was cast in one solid piece. Great skill was required to cast one of these vessels. It is curious that Taylor was making them as late as 1793, for they were essentially a utensil of the sixteenth and seventeenth centuries. Imported examples are not particularly rare, but examples bearing the name of an identified American craftsman are uncommon.

Tomahawks

Few objects known today exhibit the dual symbolism found in a tomahawk. One end was a cutting edge, useful in scalping, while the other end held an opening for tobacco to be smoked when peaceful conditions were to be established. Although it is regarded as the weapon of the American Indian, most early metal tomahawks were made in Europe; it is doubtful if the Indian's technology ever advanced to the point where he made his own tool or weapon of brass or bronze. The earliest ones were made of iron in a variety of ways, but in the nineteenth century a sizeable number were cast of brass or bronze. A definitive book, *American Indian Tomahawks*, by Harold Peterson, was published by the Museum of the American Indian, Heye Foundation, 1965. A paragraph from his book discusses the implement since 1700.

> About 1700, specialized forms in iron began to appear which were called axes, hatchets, or tomahawks at the time, but which are normally called tomahawks today. First came those with auxiliary spikes, then almost immediately those combined with pipes. All were strong implements, useful as a tool, a weapon, or a ceremonial implement. It was about this time that other specialized forms were developed. . . . Later years saw the decline of the weapon: softer metals replaced iron and steel, hafts were reduced in diameter, blades were made slimmer, and all semblance of an edge disappeared.

The tomahawks described in the last sentence of this paragraph are those which fall within the scope of this study. These may have been used by white men as well as Indians, for a weapon or for more peace-

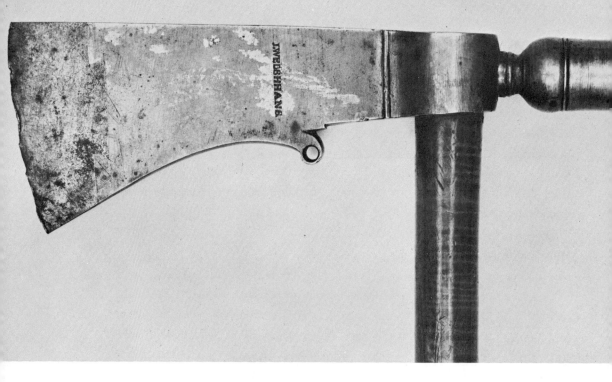

Tomahawk of cast brass with a steel blade inserted in the left-hand end to improve its cutting quality. Signed tomahawks, such as this one, are very scarce items of Americana today.

courtesy Joe Kindig, Jr.

ful purposes. On some examples, the soft brass and bronze heads were made more functional for cutting by inserting a piece of steel in the edge; a male and female dovetail joint was cut into the two parts, and they were held together by silver solder. Finally this feature was dropped, and the entire implement was made of the softer metals. It is concluded that the ones without steel inserts were for Indian ceremonial use only. A small hole in the bottom of the bowl continued through the handle so that it could be used as a pipe. The object had considerable charm as a pipe; as a weapon it was effective, often deadly. It is thought that the Indians learned to throw them and their penetration could have been considerable when the blade struck the body at the best angle.

The hafts were made of wood; one in the Kindig collection has a haft of curly maple and is marked "J. Welshhans." The use of curly maple for this one is significant, for gunsmiths by the name of Welchhans worked in York, Pennsylvania, and they used curly maple for their gun stocks.

Lancets

Although lancets were not made completely of cast brass, the cases were usually fine examples of the founder's art and thus are a legitimate part of this survey. Considerable interest has been shown lately in collecting these dangerous little instruments. Many were made and signed by American craftsmen, men who were cutlers or specialists in the making of lancets.

Their function is interestingly described in the *Encyclopedia Perthensis:*

> The LANCET is sharp-pointed and two-edged, chiefly used for opening veins in the operation of bleeding; also for laying open abscesses, tumors, etc. The late Dr. Brown often said in his lectures when declaiming against phlebotomy that "this little mischievous instrument has murdered more of the human race, than all the swords, spears, javelins, battering rams, cannons, and other instru-

Lancet and brass case marked "John Vogeler/Salem, N.C." Vogeler was a versatile craftsman and, in addition to making the lancet, he probably engraved his name on it. The form is quite different from the common form made by craftsmen in Philadelphia and New York.

courtesy Old Salem, Inc.

ments of war, that ever were invented." Without giving full credit
to this hyperbolical assertion it must be allowed that copious bleed-
ing has been by far too frequently prescribed in many diseases.

The small size of these objects indicates they were difficult to cast so
that the parts fitted properly. They usually consisted of a case with a
sliding cover which could easily be removed. Their traditional form
was dictated by the shape of the spring. It had a bow in the rounded

Lancet made in the style produced by craftsmen working in New York and Pennsylvania.
This one was made by Tieman, of New York City, in the middle of the nineteenth
century.
Kauffman Collection

end to make it effective on the short stroke which the blade had. Some
signed ones were made by Geo. Tieman & Co., No. 67 Chatham Street,
New York. Tieman is listed as a cutler in the *Business Directory of
New York City* for 1841-1842. How long before and after that date he
worked is not known.

Jagging Irons

The jagging irons of the eighteenth century are one of the most
mysterious gadgets made of cast brass. Little is known about how they
were used, who made them, or where they were made. Their mystery
and their curious manner of fabrication cause them to be desirable
collectors' items, and many a collector has a small drawer full of them,
waiting for someone to inform him about them. The most logical suggestion as to their purpose is that they were used to cut decorative strips

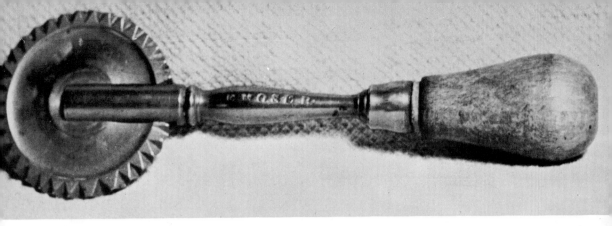

Jagging iron of bronze, marked "Moser," presumably the maker. Nothing is known about Moser but, since that is a common name in Pennsylvania, it was probably made there. The workmanship is of high quality. The diameter of almost 3 in. is unusual.
courtesy Mr. & Mrs. Richard Smith

of dough with serrated edges for partially covering open-faced pies. Although today they are used for thin cakes and cookies, their original purpose could have been very different. They certainly were not crimpers, as they are commonly called now, for they could not function as the crimpers of the nineteenth century.

About the middle of the nineteenth century a device called a "Pie Rimmer and Pastry Cutter" was patented. This device continued to have the serrated wheel of the earlier jagger and, in addition, had a wheel which was passed around the outer edge of the pie plate to cut and press the dough together. It also created an attractive ruffled edge. Today's housewife does the same with her nimble thumb.

Jagging irons and pie crimper. The older type utensils on the right and left are usually called "jagging irons" while the mid-nineteenth-century type in the center is called a "pie crimper."
courtesy Mr. & Mrs. Richard Smith

The late jagging irons are made of iron and brass, while earlier ones were made of bone, wood, brass, iron, or bronze or a combination of these various substances. Some of the wheels were made from large pennies.

Buttons

The manufacture of buttons was an important industry in the eighteenth and nineteenth centuries. It is known that brass buttons were made in America early in the eighteenth century. The method of making them is described in *A Dictionary of Arts, Manfactures, and Mines,* by Andre Ure:

> Metal buttons are formed of an inferior kind of brass, pewter, and other metallic compositions; the shanks are made of iron wire, the formation of which is a distinct trade. The buttons are made by casting them round the shank. For this purpose the workman has a pattern of metal, consisting of a great number of circular buttons, connected together in one plane by very small bars from one to the next; and the pattern contains from four to twelve dozen buttons of the same size. An impression from this pattern is taken in sand in the usual manner; and shanks are pressed into the sand in the center of each impression, the part which is to enter the metal being left projecting above the surface of the sand. The buttons are now cast from a mixture of brass and tin; sometimes a small portion of zinc is added, which is found useful in causing the metal to flow freely in the mold, and makes a sharp casting. When the buttons are cast, they are cleaned from the sand by brushing; they are broken asunder, and carried to a second workman at the lathe, who inserts the shank of the button into a chuck of a proper figure, in which it is retained by the back center of the lathe being pressed against the button with a spring. The circumference is now, by filing as it turns around, reduced to a true circle: and the button is instantly released by the workman's holding back the center, and it is replaced by another.

The buttons were later engraved, or contoured by other means, and finally burnished. The description of the procedures used in producing the buttons indicates that it was a sizeable industry, though few of the eighteenth-century buttons have survived until today. Only a handful that can be identified as products of American craftsmen exist in the fine private or museum collections of buttons. Later buttons were

Some important buttons connected with the early history of the U.S. The top left button is known as the "Inaugural Button"; the initials of President Washington are in the center; around the edge is a chain of links, each of which contains the initial or initials of one of the thirteen colonies. The other buttons are of the eighteenth century and are connected with either President Washington or the nation.

courtesy Mr. & Mrs. Benjamin Landis

stamped in a manner similar to the stamping of late furniture brasses. More of these exist than the earlier type, but they cannot be regarded as a common commodity.

The best-known early producer of brass buttons in America was Caspar Wistar, a German emigrant living in Philadelphia during the first quarter of the eighteenth century. Though he was primarily known as a manufacturer of glass, his work in the making of brass buttons earned him the appelation of "maker of brass buttons in Philadelphia." His fame spread far and wide; deeds for property which he owned in Lancaster, Pennsylvania, now filed in the court house there, refer to him as the "brass button maker of Philadelphia."

Counterfeits of Philadelphia brass buttons were sold in New York City that were found to be of inferior quality and easily broken. Henry Whiteman called his products "New York Buttons," and probably warranted them to be as good as those from Philadelphia. In 1769, Richard Wistar, Caspar's son, advertised that he "continues to make Philadelphia Brass Buttons" and warranted them for seven years.

Scientific Instruments

Objects made of cast brass ranged from pie crimpers of the kitchen to scientific instruments devised by the keenest minds of America in the eighteenth and nineteenth centuries. Observation, though, reveals that

Surveying theodolite, made by Augustus Platt, Columbus, Ohio, probably in the second quarter of the nineteenth century. The telescope is 13¾ in. long; the needle is 3½ in. long; the limb is 5¼ in. in diameter. Augustus Platt and his father, Benjamin, also a well-known instrument maker, moved to Columbus about 1817.

courtesy Ohio State Museum

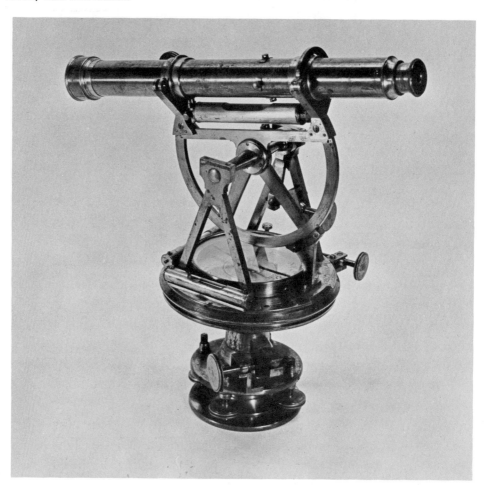

Surveyor's compass, marked "John Vogeler, Salem, N.C." John Vogeler (1783-1881) served his apprenticeship under Christoph Vogeler, his uncle, and is known to have made guns. He called himself a silversmith and a watchmaker and opened his shop in Salem about 1806.

courtesy Old Salem, Inc.

all parts were not made of cast brass; some were made of glass, wood, and iron, if the movement of the part entailed much motion and wear. An instrument is defined by *The Oxford English Dictionary*, revised edition 1955, as,

> "A thing with or through which something is done or effected, a means. A tool, implement, weapon. (Now usu. dict. from a tool as being used for more delicate work or for artistic or scientific purposes."

There is some unanimity among scholars to call the group of instruments in this discussion "scientific" instruments; however, in earlier times they were called "nautical," "optical," and/or "mathematical" instruments, and, on occasion, "philosophical apparatus."

Until recent times there has been little interest in these curiosities of the past; now the age of technology focuses attention on them. Harvard College, in the eighteenth century, had a collection of such instruments and exhibited them in a sort of museum located near to its library. In the broadside published after the fire which destroyed them on January

Surveyor's compass, brass with silvered dial; pine case with iron loops and hooks; made by C. Hurtin in Goshen, N.Y. Inscribed in script on face of dial between the compass point designations "C. Hurtin / Goshen / AD 1794 / N° 18." Overall length 13⅜ in.; diameter 6⅛ in.

courtesy Department of Collection, Colonial Williamsburg

25, 1764, they were described as, "Curiosities natural and artificial, both of American and foreign produce." After the fire, the college started collecting again, but over the years such apparatus fell into disfavor and was scattered throughout the college's various attics and basements.

In recent years they were re-collected and, in 1949, an exhibition of scientific instruments at Harvard was followed by a book about them, *Some Early Tools of American Science*, written by I. Bernard Cohen. Instruments described and illustrated in it are relevant to the fields of astronomy, physics, natural history, chemistry, and mineralogy. The

Page from the *Index of Patents issued from the United States Patent Office from 1790 to 1873, inclusive,* showing the number of patents issued for compasses. W. J. Young was a prolific producer of such instruments and two patents were issued to him during this time, one in 1832, the other in 1834.

Index of patents issued from the United States Patent Office from 1790 to 1873, inclusive—Continued.

Invention.	Inventor.	Residence.	Date.	No.
Commutator, Electric	L. B. Firman	Chicago, Ill	Mar. 24, 1868	75,743
Compass	P. Roessler	New Haven, Conn	Sept. 19, 1865	50,037
Compass	H. Stewart	Clinton, Mass	Apr. 21, 1868	77,123
Compass	O. Stoddard	Detroit, Mich	Aug. 27, 1872	130,879
Compass and magnetic needle	J. Hauks	Troy, N. Y	July 22, 1833	....
Compass, Azimuth	E. S. Ritchie	Brookline, Mass	Aug. 1, 1865	49,157
Compass, Beam	J. Lyman	Lenox, Mass	Feb. 21, 1871	111,954
Compass, Beam	M. Toulmin	New Orleans, La	Sept. 16, 1873	142,823
Compass, Correcting the deviation of the mariner's	L. F. A. Arson	Paris, France	May 31, 1870	103,701
Compass for determining variations from local causes.	J. R. St. John	New York, N. Y	Mar. 2, 1852	8,785
Compass for mining	J. Blomgren	New York, N. Y	Oct. 25, 1870	108,555
Compass, Instrument for determining 'the variation of the.	E. S. Ritchie	Brookline, Mass	Jan. 3, 1865	45,753
Compass-joint	T. Alteneder	Philadelphia, Pa	Feb. 14, 1871	111,715
Compass joint, Measuring	T. Alteneder	Philadelphia, Pa	July 16, 1850	7,501
Compass, Liquid	J. and G. H. Bliss	Brooklyn, N. Y	Jan. 24, 1871	111,169
Compass, Liquid	E. Blunt	Brooklyn, N. Y	Dec. 5, 1865	51,290
Compass, Magnetic	H. W. Hunter	New York, N. Y	May 6, 1862	35,156
Compass, Marine	S. Custer	Salem, Va	June 26, 1866	55,827
Compass, Marine	E. S. Ritchie	Brookline, Mass	July 19, 1870	105,492
Compass, Mariner's	J. Ball	Buffalo, N. Y	Mar. 6, 1835	....
Compass, Mariner's	J. and G. H. Bliss	Brooklyn, N. Y	May 24, 1870	103,286
Compass, Mariner's	J. and G. H. Bliss	Brooklyn, N. Y	May 24, 1870	103,287
Compass, Mariner's	H. Colby	Rochester, N. Y	May 1, 1847	5,096
Compass, Mariner's	S. Custer	Salem, Va	July 16, 1867	66,805
Compass, Mariner's	J. S. Pender	New York, N. Y	Sept. 27, 1864	44,451
Compass, Mariner's	E. S. Ritchie	Brookline, Mass	Sept. 9, 1862	36,422
Compass, Mariner's	E. S. Ritchie	Brookline, Mass	Apr. 7, 1863	38,125
Compass, Mariner's	E. S. Ritchie	Brookline, Mass	Apr. 7, 1863	38,126
Compass, Mariner's	E. S. Ritchie	Brookline, Mass	Apr. 10, 1866	53,875
Compass, Mariner's and surveyor's	W. C. Poole	Lancaster, Pa	July 31, 1840	1,707
Compass, Mariner's or surveyor's	W. Russell	New Bedford, Mass	Dec. 1, 1809	....
Compass, Mariner's time	R. Reeder	Cincinnati, Ohio	Feb. 9, 1847	4,964
Compass-needle, Magnetizing	S. Custer	Salem, Va	July 16, 1867	66,806
Compass needle, Marine and surveying	M. Smith	New York, N. Y	June 15, 1830	....
Compass or theodolite, Surveying	J. Eames	Newry, Me	Feb. 11, 1835	....
Compass-protractor	F. H. West	San Francisco, Cal	Sept. 25, 1860	30,137
Compass, quadrant, and protractor	F. Whiteley	Stanardsville, Va	Dec. 6, 1836	99
Compass, Self-registering ship's	R. H. Peverly	Chelsea, Mass	June 3, 1856	15,017
Compass, Ship's	James, Earl of Caithness	Middlesex County, England	Nov. 5, 1867	70,520
Compass, Ship's	J. Prime	Washington, N. C	Feb. 12, 1856	14,251
Compass, Ship's	G. W. Wood	Brooklyn, N. Y	Mar. 21, 1871	112,999
Compass, Solar	H. O. Cook	New York, N. Y	Aug. 12, 1873	141,766
Compass, Solar	B. S. Lyman	Philadelphia, Pa	July 18, 1871	117,184
Compass, Surveying	G. W. Dickinson, jr	Breckenridge, Va	Feb. 21, 1860	27,210
Compass, Surveying	W. J. Young	Philadelphia, Pa	Jan. 17, 1832	....
Compass, Surveying	W. J. Young	Philadelphia, Pa	Jan. 11, 1834	....
Compass, Surveyor's	N. Bassett	Wilmington, Del	June 28, 1836	....
Compass, Surveyor's	S. Kern	Strasburgh, Va	July 28, 1846	4,675
Compass, Surveyor's	J. Locke	Cincinnati, Ohio	July 16, 1850	7,510
Compass, Surveyor's	H. B. Martin	Santa Rosa, Cal	June 7, 1864	43,036
Compass, Surveyor's	S. R. Miller	Front Royal, Va	Oct. 22, 1835	....
Compass, Universal	S. Dew	Romney, Va	Apr. 13, 1822	....
Compasses and calipers	J. E. Earle	Leicester, Mass	Aug. 1, 1854	11,420
Compasses and calipers	F. P. Pfleghar and W. Schollhorn.	New Haven, Conn	Jan. 9, 1866	51,967
Compasses and calipers, Combined beam	W. Burrows	New York, N. Y	Dec. 29, 1868	85,430
Compasses, Card for liquid	E. S. Ritchie	Brookline, Mass	June 2, 1863	38,762
Compasses, Binnacle for mariner's	G. W. Richey and H. E. Bixby	Saint Louis, Mo	July 4, 1871	116,631
Compasses, Card for mariner's liquid	E. S. Ritchie	Brookline, Mass	Jan. 24, 1871	111,254
Compasses, Construction of	T. Hagerty	Richmond, Va	July 30, 1872	130,036
Compasses, Construction of	T. Hagerty	Richmond, Va	July 30, 1872	130,037
Compasses, Construction of spring	T. Hagerty	Richmond, Va	July 30, 1872	130,038
Compasses, Electro-magnetic attachment to ships'	A. Foucaut	Orleans, France	July 19, 1870	105,562
Compasses insensible to local attraction, Rendering.	J. S. Gisbone and W. Simpson	Birkenhead and Liverpool, England.	Mar. 8, 1864	41,839
Compasses, Local-attraction indicator for ships'	H. Glover	Brooklyn, N. Y	Sept. 17, 1872	131,435
Compasses, Mode of fixing mariners'	L. Langley	Gosport, Va	June 23, 1828	....
Compasses, Pencil-attachment for	C. Schott	Nashville, Tenn	July 12, 1870	105,376
Compasses, Pencil-attachment to	C. L. Tyler	Ithaca, N. Y	Nov. 2, 1869	96,366
Compasses, Preventing the deviation of ships'	J. W. Girdlestone	Strand, England	Oct. 25, 1870	108,585
Compasses used in calking seams	G. Dowling	Fair Haven, Conn	June 11, 1867	65,654
Compensating or equilibrium spring	C. Shea	Newark, N. J	Oct. 12, 1869	95,736
Composing-stick	L. Buschmann	Newark, N. J	Oct. 21, 1873	143,875
Composing-stick	A. F. Cloudman and G. W. Coffin.	Brooklyn, N. Y., and Charlestown, Mass.	Oct. 18, 1870	108,451
Composing-stick	J. M. Eaton	Charlestown, Mass	Aug. 10, 1869	93,426
Composing-stick	F. W. Murray	Cincinnati, Ohio	Mar. 16, 1869	88,800
Composing-stick	R. W. Thing	Boston, Mass	Jan. 26, 1869	86,257
Composing-stick	W. T. Tillinghast	Dayton, Ohio	May 22, 1866	54,979
Composing-stick	J. L. Wait	East Cambridge, Mass	May 19, 1868	78,033
Composing-stick	J. Wilson	Beston, Mass	Aug. 6, 1872	130,170
Composing-stick	R. C. Young	Middletown, Conn	Oct. 18, 1870	108,549
Composing-stick, Printer's	S. W. Brown	Syracuse, N. Y	May 22, 1860	28,436
Composing-stick, Printer's	A. Calhoun	Hartford, Conn	Aug. 31, 1858	21,321
Composing-stick, Printer's	O. F. Grover	Middletown, Conn	July 15, 1856	15,358
Composing-stick, Printer's	P. S. Hoe	New York, N. Y	Nov. 5, 1872	132,722
Composing-stick, Printer's	J. and W. Tidgewell	Middletown, Conn	June 2, 1857	17,457
Composing-stick, Printer's	W. T. Tillinghast	Dayton, Ohio	Jan. 27, 1857	16,500
Composing-stick, Printer's	D. Winder	Cincinnati, Ohio	Apr. 7, 1857	17,007
Composite pipe	A. P. Stephens	Brooklyn, N. Y	May 26, 1868	78,336
Composition-box	T. B. Gunning	New York, N. Y	Oct. 3, 1871	119,603
Composition handle or pull	W. B. Gleason	Boston, Mass	Mar. 22, 1870	101,119
Compositor's stand	F. Vallee	Philadelphia, Pa	Apr. 8, 1873	137,639
Compost	E. Blanchard	Greenfield Mills, Md	Aug. 9, 1859	24,988
Compost for soil	A. B. Martin	Baltimore, Md	June 2, 1819	....
Compound engine	A. Hartupee	Pittsburgh, Pa	Apr. 16, 1872	125,812

contents of the book disclosed unsuspected interest in scientific matters in the eighteenth century and doubtless sparked further contemporary interest in the subject.

In 1964, the *Bulletin of the U.S. National Museum, # 231*, was authored by Silvio Bedini, entitled "Early American Scientific Instruments and Their Makers." This valuable publication provides detailed information about surveyor's compasses, circumferentors, theodilites, and their variants, with a brief listing of instruments owned by the Smithsonian Institution. The author also listed the names of about 200 craftsmen who made scientific instruments. While the listing is in no wise complete, it does provide an excellent base for further study of the subject.

A biography of the famous instrument maker, David Rittenhouse, written by Brooke Hindle, and published by the Princeton University Press in 1964, is another illuminating publication which adds luster to the work done in instrument making in America and indicates that the apogee of interest in this exciting field has not yet been reached.

The fact that Rittenhouse was a maker of instruments, not a brass founder, raises the question, "Where is the connection between the two?" This question has not yet been completely resolved though it is likely that a number of procedures were followed in the two trades. Some of the brass founders advertised that they made mathematical instruments; John Taylor of Richmond, Virginia, was one of them. Some instrument makers probably bought parts of cast brass from brass founders, and completed the work on the instrument at hand. It is likely that other instrument makers cast their own parts, fabricated additional parts from sheet brass and other metals, and made the entire product themselves.

There was a distinct trade of instrument makers in America as early as 1730 when Anthony Lamb advertised in the *Pennsylvania Gazette*, December 3, as follows:

ANTHONY LAMB

Mathematical Instrument maker from London, now makes in New York, compasses, quadrants, forestaffs, notinners, sectors, protractors, all sorts of scales, gauging rods, and rules in wood, iron, brass, and silver. Also any other small work at wholesale or retail.

Combined clock and planetarium by
David Rittenhouse; presumably made
for his own use.

courtesy Joe Kindig, Jr.

Needless to say, the man who was the maker of complete scientific instruments had to be extremely knowledgeable and skilled. In addition to his proficiency in sawing, filing, fitting, soldering, engraving, and polishing, he had to have a mind ("systematic," they would have called it in the old days) which was able to make mathematical computations, to understand and possibly initiate scientific concepts, and to possess an esthetic sensitivity so that his products were attractive. A number of instruments are appearing on the market today, many of them signed. Most of them will become of increasing importance in the future to American historians and connoisseurs.

Steelyards

The large number of steelyards found in private collections and museums today suggests that those partially made of brass should be included in this survey. Steelyards are ancient instruments for measuring

This steelyard has a beam and a weight of brass, the rest of it being made of iron. Many are marked by the makers, but few makers have been identified. This one is marked "Starratts / Pat⁽ᵈ⁾ / July 9ᵗʰ '67."

courtesy Old Sturbridge Village

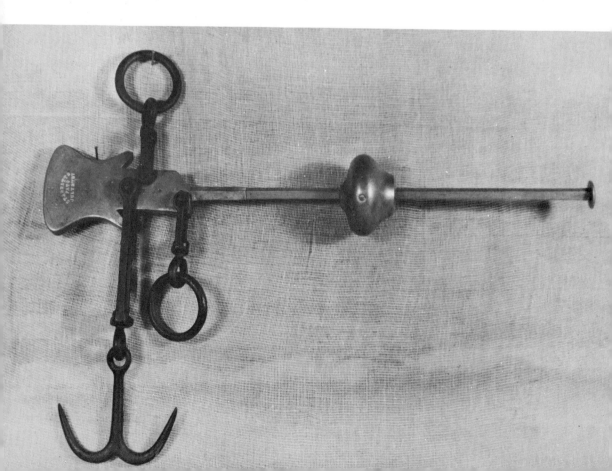

weight; there are three different forms—steelyards with movable weights, steelyards with proportional weights, and steelyards with fixed weights.

The type most commonly found today is the one with a movable weight. These have two arms of unequal length. On the short arm, to the left of the fulcrum of the one illustrated, hooks or a pan was suspended. (In this case, two hooks.) On the longer arm graduations are indented, with a movable weight which can be brought into equilibrium with the object to be weighed. The versatility of the one illustrated is increased by having two fulcra, so that by inverting the device and changing the location of the fulcrum, a large range of objects could be weighed.

Balances

Although most of the balances available today were made in Europe, many were made in America in the middle of the nineteenth century. These can usually be identified by the name and location of the maker imprinted on the horizontal beam at the top of the balance. The *Business Directory of New York City for 1841-1842* lists the following men as makers of scales and balances at that time.

Brown, John L., 234 Water Street
Chatillion, George, 16 Frankfort Street
Jones, William, 86 Fulton Street
McDonald, R. A. & Co, 83 Fulton Street
Nichols, S. Jr. 252 Water Street
Wade, Ezekiel, 17 Peck Slip

A marked beam is illustrated on which is stamped "J. Marden," who was listed as a "Manufacturer and wholesale dealer of Patent Platform Scales, Patent Balances and Scale Beams," in *Matchett's Baltimore Directory 1842*, page 29.

The common balance consists of a beam with arms of equal length with pans or dishes suspended on each end by heavy wires or chains. The beam is supported by a column of brass, usually turned in an attractive shape. On the top of the column is a fulcrum on which the beam rests, permitting the ends to move up and down freely. The requirements of the balance are: 1. That it shall take a horizontal position when the weights in the two pans are equal; and 2. That it must

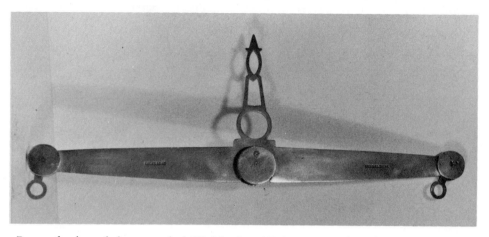

Beam of a brass balance marked "J. Marden / Baltimore." When the point on the top of the beam was in a perfect vertical position, the weights on the two pans were equally balanced.

Kauffman Collection

American balance made by J. Maxwell of Albany, N.Y. The central column is made of wood.

courtesy Old Sturbridge Village

American brass balance of the mid-nineteenth century. The name of the maker is blurred, but Philadelphia can be deciphered as the place of manufacture.

have sensitivity and stability. "Sensitivity" means that the beam may move as freely as possible, and particularly that its action may not be impeded by friction from the fulcrum on which it rests. The fulcrum was frequently made of steel or a hard stone, such as agate. "Stability" means that the balance must return to a position of equilibrium when no weight or object is on either plate or dish. Balances of all sizes and degrees of accuracy were made. Some were used for common transactions in weighing while others, which were very sensitive, were used in pharmacies, for assaying, and in physical research. Today their function is strictly decorative.

Sundials

A sundial was an instrument for telling time by measuring the shadow of the sun. Its lay-out was determined by mathematical computation, and each one had to be suited to the latitude of the area where it was to be used. Lines were engraved on its upper surface in such a manner that the shadow of the upper edge of a plane, mounted perpendicularly on the top surface, indicated the true "sun" time of the day. The vertical plane which cast the shadow was called a "gnomon." The line on which the gnomon was erected was called the "sub-style."

Brass sundial stamped "B. Harbeson"; made in 1763. Very few brass products of the Harbeson family of craftsmen are known; however, the variety of their products suggests that other items will be found. The intaglio stamp on this dial resembles the one used by the Harbesons on handles of copper teakettles.

courtesy Philadelphia Museum of Art

An infinitesimal number of American sundials have survived. A few cast in brass by the clockmakers of the Chandlee family are in museums and private collections. A signed dial by B. Harbeson is extant—one of very few brass products of this maker known to exist. There are a few signed examples made of pewter.

Lighting Devices

While American brass founders of the eighteenth and nineteenth centuries are known to have made lighting devices, no signed pieces have been located in the museums and private collections of the country. The focus here is principally on candlesticks and candelabra. A number of brass founders advertised these, as John Robertson did in the *South Carolina Gazette,* December 16, 1760:

JOHN ROBERTSON

> John Robertson brass-founder, in King Street begs leave to return thanks to those gentlemen and others who have been pleased to favour him with their custom, and at the same time informs them that he continues to make in the neatest manner, all sorts of brass candlesticks, and church lustres and branches; also cabinet, desk drawer, couch chair and chaise mountings; brass tongs shovels and fenders, bells, brass weights, etc. etc. Likewise all sorts of brasses used by gunsmiths, blacksmiths, etc.
> N.B. He also makes all sorts of mill and other machinery work, soldiers regimental belt, shoe, and knee buckles, and clamps. Ready money will be given for old brass, copper, pewter, bell metal, or lead by said Robertson.

This advertisement, and others similar to it, establish the fact that candlesticks and candelabra (lusters and branches) were made here, and attention turns to the popular use of cast brass for these articles. In the first place, brass was used for both functional and decorative articles in the Americas because of its attractive color. Objects of brass helped to create a rich decor wherever it was used, particularly in the living room or parlor, where the gleam of polished brass made a pleasing contrast to interior walls painted blue, green, white, or other light shades. In the second place, the metal was tough and could withstand many years of hard use. It also was relatively easy to cast and finish on the lathes available in the workshops of brass founders or whitesmiths.

Thousands of old brass candlesticks are in use in America today. Where they were made is unresolved, even though the method of producing them is known. Most of the columns were cast in halves (in a manner similar to casting andirons) and were soldered together with hard solder. The similarity of this solder to the color of brass often conceals the joint, but close examination will usually show that they were made of two pieces. The procedure of casting halves was a good one for only one half pattern had to be made and brass could be saved by removing the inner portion of the pattern. The weight of the whole stick was thus much lighter than a casual observer would suspect. The base was cast as one piece, and after filing and burnishing, threads were cut on the column and in the base so they could be easily joined or disjoined. These threads were usually quite coarse and are not likely to

Left: Pair of English candlesticks made of brass in the second quarter of the eighteenth century, of the "George I" type; engraved at one side on upper surface of base near center with the initials "A.C." These have been electrified. *Right:* Early American brass candlestick of the "George I" style.

left: courtesy Henry Francis du Pont Winterthur Museum; *right:* Kauffman Collection

A mid-eighteenth-century English brass
candlestick; circular, swirled base with
spaced clusters of ridges forming a wavy
outline; slim shaft with two swirled,
half-spherical knops; cylindrical candle
cup with molded rim and base; electrified;
height 8¾ in.

courtesy Henry Francis du Pont Winterthur
Museum

A mid-eighteenth-century English brass candlestick;
close-up of impressed name "Joseph Wood" which
appears on the under side of the base on two
corner lobes; electrified; height 7½ in.

courtesy Henry Francis du Pont Winterthur Museum

A mid-eighteenth-century brass candlestick; in the "Chippendale" style; perhaps American; scalloped base; round baluster shaft, scalloped candle nozzle; height 10 in.

courtesy Henry Francis du Pont Winterthur Museum

Pair of bell metal candlesticks in the "Classical" style; probably English; *circa* 1775; round, stepped base with gadrooned edge; knopped stem similarly gadrooned and urn-shaped cup with flaring gadrooned edge; height 11⅛ in.

courtesy Henry Francis du Pont Winterthur Museum

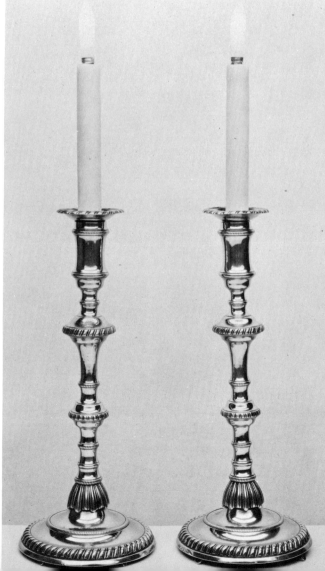

fit threads cut with a modern tap and die set. The interior surfaces at
the base of most "period sticks" was scraped smooth, and by now has
acquired a patina which aids in separating old from new.

Candlesticks of the first quarter of the eighteenth century (sometimes described as "George I") often had square, low-domed bases with
canted corners. The shaft of the column was composed of a large, pan-
eled, inverted-vase form and a small faceted knop. The candle cups
were also square with canted corners and a molded rim. Great variation
is found, but most of them have some characteristics in common. A few
were signed by the makers.

The designs in the middle of the eighteenth century became more
frivolous, but possibly not more attractive. Preferences depended on

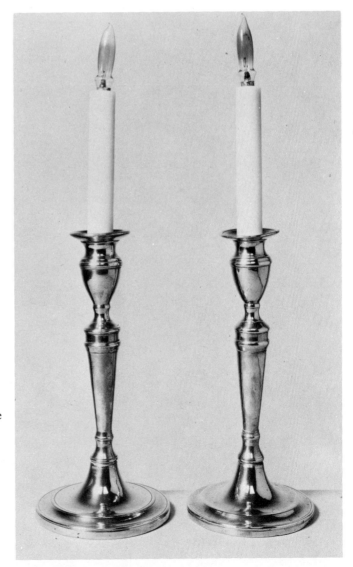

Pair of brass candlesticks in the
"Classical" style; probably English; made
in the last quarter of the eighteenth
century; round base; simple shaft
flaring upward; urn-shaped candle cup
with wide rim; height 9 in.

courtesy Henry Francis du Pont Winterthur
Museum

the tastes of the various owners. One of the candlesticks illustrated was signed by Joseph Wood. It has a square, ridged, low-domed base with rounded, lobed corners, and an additional lobe in the middle of each side. It has a baluster stem with knop and cone with lobed knob. The candle cup is long and cylindrical with a molded base and circular scalloped rim.

Near the end of the century a classical style became popular, keeping pace with andirons and other accessories. Many had round bases with a simple vase-shaped shaft flaring upwards. The candle cup was urn-shaped with a wide rim for catching molten wax.

The first half of the nineteenth century brought a profusion of styles. Many had round bases and shafts with a dishtype base and only a vestigial wax catcher under the candle cup.

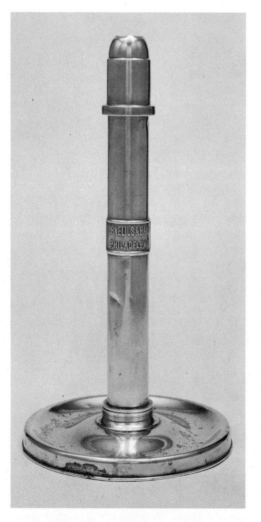

A mid-nineteenth-century brass candlestick; circular base with molding on edge; deep, concave pan; cylindrical shaft, removable cap; spring platform for candle; shaft stamped in front "Cornelius & Baker/Philadelphia" inside a rectangular metal frame; height 9 ⅛ in. "Cornelius and Co. Lamps" and "Isaac F. Baker, lamp mfg." are both listed at 176 Chestnut Street. As early as 1810, a Christian Cornelius had been listed as silverplate worker and later appeared as a patent lamp manufacturer.

courtesy Henry Francis du Pont Winterthur Museum

By the middle of the nineteenth century, some patented devices appeared. About 1845, an Englishman named Palmer invented the spring candlestick. The candle was held in place by a locking cap at the top and, as the candle burned, the spring forced it up through the opening in the locking cap. Candlesticks and similar devices became products of the Industrial Revolution around the middle of the nineteenth century and deterioration in style eliminates them from further attention here.

The style and quality of candelabra parallel that of candlesticks. They were elegant and charming in the eighteenth century, unattractive in the nineteenth. None can be identified as the product of an American craftsman, but they are one of the important products of the period. In the future possibly some manner of identification will be evolved to give American craftsmen their true identity in the medium of cast brass lighting devices.

Clocks

The making of clockworks, particularly for grandfather clocks, falls within the scope of this survey, for most of them were made of brass. Just how many were made in America, and how many were imported from England will never be known. The trade of clockmaking covered a wide range of aptitudes, from the man who bought all the parts, engraved his name on the face, and advertised in the local press as a clockmaker, to the man who made all the parts of the works and face, did the required engraving, and fitted his product in a case made by a local cabinetmaker. Few clockmakers are known to have made their cases.

The most important source of information about an American craftsman who made clocks is the records of Daniel Burnap, published by the Connecticut Historical Society in a fascinating book, *Shop Records of Daniel Burnap, Clockmaker*, by Penrose R. Hoopes.

The following excerpt from that book gives insight into the working of brass into the various parts needed to produce an eight-day clock movement:

> After the brass parts were cast they were hammered to harden them and the plates were filed flat and square, the wheels were filed flat, the center holes drilled and each wheel blank was mounted on a lathe arbor and its outside diameter turned true. The arms were

Rough castings and partially finished wheels found in Daniel Burnap's shop. A great deal of work was required to make a clock in America before more refined methods of production were devised.

courtesy Connecticut Historical Society

filed out by hand and the teeth cut in the clockmaker's engine. The holes in the plates were laid out and drilled and pillars riveted in place, thus completing the brass parts of the movement. Pinions were forged, turned, slit, and rounded off with files, tempered, straughtened, and the wheels riveted in place on the arbors. The small steel parts were then made, the brass face was cut out, hammered, filed flat, polished, the holes for the dial feet, center arbor and barrel arbors were drilled, the dial feet fitted into place, the dial was engraved, and the movement assembled. Complete directions are given in the notebook for proportioning the parts, performing each of the individual operations on them and for proportioning the Roman numerals on the dial. . . .

Some of his tools were clearly homemade. Wire drawing dies were reworked from old worn out files. The brass templates used for outlining clock hands, plates and escapements were finished just well enough to serve their intended purposes but show none of the refinements to be expected on commercial tools. Lathes were unquestionably of his own construction, the original wood pattern used in casting the head and tailstock of his clockmaker's lathe being among the remnants of his shop, as is the lathe itself. . . .

On pages 109 to 115 in that book are more detailed instructions about the meticulous work involved in the making of a clockworks of brass. They are too tedious for inclusion here. However, one paragraph, concerned with the silvering of a face, is given below because of the wide use made of this process on other objects, particularly the faces of surveyors' compasses, which were often attractively silvered.

> A receipt for silvering. Take an equal quantity of alum, saltpetre & sal ammoniac crude. Pound them together. Then take silver lace or silver filings & put a laying of the powder before mentioned & a laying of the silver until you have mixed the quantity of silver to be dissolved with the powder. Then put it to a moderate fire and heat it 'till it ceases to smoke. Then pour it off & pound it fine & apply it to the brass. To be washed with clean water.

Back view of "moon's age" clock made by Daniel Burnap.

courtesy Philip H. Hammerslough

Beautifully engraved clock dial by Daniel Burnap of East Windsor, Conn. This dial was for Burnap's own chime clock. It has a calendar device for telling the date of days, a second hand, and, on the top, a hand to select one of six tunes the mechanism played. Burnap's engraved dials are not comparable to the finest imported products but by American standards he was an expert, and he engraved dials for other clockmakers.

courtesy Wadsworth Atheneum, Hartford, Conn.

Tall case clock with "moon's age" movement by
Daniel Burnap.

courtesy Philip H. Hammerslough

Among other directions which Burnap provided are those for making the pendulum rod of straight-grained mahogany, for case-hardening and tempering tools, and for proportioning the size of the figures on a clock face to the overall size of the face. He gives directions for making gold beads, for constructing chime clocks, and for making gum arabic fit for use. A number of his chime clocks have survived and are in working condition today.

This record of Daniel Burnap's is unquestionably one of the great surviving documents of an outstanding American craftsman. He made many objects in addition to clocks, all of which show a sensitivity to design and a dedication to fine ideals of workmanship. His designs were not the most extravagant of those produced by American craftsmen, but he was a good solid craftsman who left an outstanding record of his craft, an artisan of whom Americans can be justly proud.

There were a great many other clockmakers working in America from 1700 until 1850. Some of them made clocks with wooden works which were cheap, efficient, and produced in large quantities. They were exported to Europe and were one of the first American commodities to impress Europeans with Yankee mechanical ingenuity and business acumen. Clockworks of cast brass continue, however, to be the pride of American clock collectors.

Door Locks

Brass door locks, like most other brass objects of the seventeenth and eighteenth centuries were seldom signed by their makers. So little is known of them that they are an almost anonymous entity in the field of Americana, but any survey of objects made of brass, or partially made of brass, in America would be incomplete without some comment on these mechanical devices.

The first locks used on American doors were made of wood; they were attractive and ingenious devices, but certainly not very long lasting. On the other hand, the later locks made of iron served the needs of man for many years, but were not particularly attractive appendages in the elegant houses of eighteenth-century America. The dilemma between function and appearance was resolved by the locksmiths of the period by making the functioning parts of the locks of iron and encasing them in the more attractive metal, brass.

Brass lock on inside of first-floor hallway of Pingree House, 128 Essex Street, Salem, Mass. This lock is typical in size and shape of most brass-cased locks used in America in the eighteenth century.

courtesy Essex Institute

Iron-cased door lock with internal mechanism made of cast brass. The lock bolt is stamped "Green & Broad/ New York."

Kauffman Collection

Three views of door lock with iron case; lock bolt stamped, or possibly engraved, "H Wray/Pokeepsie" (Poughkeepsie, N.Y.); original brass knobs; bright portions evident in the back of the lock are brass, the retaining plate is iron; brass nuts show provincial craftsmanship.

Kauffman Collection

The appearance of the door lock was particularly significant for, unlike present-day locks which are inserted within the door, the earlier type were mounted on the surface of the door. They were usually rectangular in shape with pleasing proportions, and possibly an inch thick. They were generally called rim locks. The interior parts were fabricated of iron and fitted into an iron case, which in turn was fitted into a case made of brass. Covering the iron mechanism with a case of brass was a fortunate procedure, for brass has a rich color and its brightly polished surface made a pleasing contrast with the surface of the door.

In nearly all rim locks a bolt shoots out from the end of the case, usually rectangular in shape, and catches in a half-closed end section, called a "keeper." This bolt moves in a horizontal plane and is activated by the key. This is the part of the lock which actually "locks" the door. In addition, a small sliding bolt was often installed near the bottom of the case which could be moved into the keeper by a small knob. This bolt was known as a "night-bolt" because it could be operated only

Typical lock found on the doors of eighteenth-century houses in the Pennsylvania countryside. The brass covering of the lock is very rare. The Rohrer family were lock makers in Lebanon, Pa.

Treeman Collection

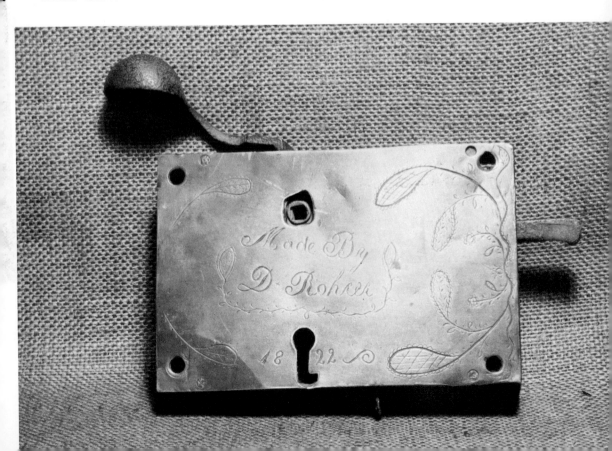

from the inside of the door and was designed for night use. The main bolt of the door could be operated by a key from either side of the door.

In addition to these two locking bolts, there was a latch with a beveled end which slipped into the keeper from the pressure of a spring installed at the opposite end. This part was called a latch because it could not be used to lock the door. It could be moved laterally by brass knobs inside and outside of the door when the door was to be unlatched. Knobs were either round or oval, the oval type being the most popular shape in use today.

Most of the fine houses of the eighteenth century had such brass-cased locks on their front doors. In the nineteenth century the relationship of brass and iron was reversed; the outer cases of later locks were made of iron and the inner working parts were made of cast brass. The earlier brass knobs were continued; however, the oval shape rapidly disappeared and most locks had round knobs.

V. William Bailey—a Craftsman

IT is the object of this book to acquaint the reader as completely as possible with all the facets of coppersmithing and brass founding in the eighteenth and nineteenth centuries in America. In the past, surveys of this type usually supplied the reader with a description of the product, its dimensions, of what it was made, and when it was made. In recent years, by reason of more thoroughly researching into the various sources, the names of the makers have been included in publications dealing with the products of our ancestors. This last procedure has become standard, especially when signed objects, such as those of pewter, copper, silver, and brass, are known.

The age of technology, which seems to be evolving rapidly in the 1960s, has brought two other matters to the attention of authors and readers. The first of these concerns the products themselves—readers want to know how items were made and how they functioned. The second centers on the men who made the products—who they were and how they acquired the skill to enable them to contribute to the development of the craft they practiced.

The impact of technology clearly explains the need for understanding how a highboy was made, or why copper was used to make stills, but the increased interest in the lives of the craftsmen of the past is less easily understood. One might assume that as the importance of machines increases, interest in personalities would lessen, but such is not the case. Some historians suggest that because of the impersonality of machinery, and the public's reluctant acceptance of living in an impersonal world, attention is focused on the people who made the machinery. A similar analogy might be applied to the products of earlier craftsmen. Actually, the analogy is more logical and realistic in the products of our ancestors, for each man's product varied from the products of another, and a knowlege of the maker leads to a more complete understanding of his product.

Some very thorough biographies of craftsmen have been published; among them, *Paul Revere and the World He Lived In*, by Esther Forbes, is outstanding. In it we find, to a remarkable degree, the type of information desired today about craftsmen. In it, too, is a wealth of material pertinent to the study of objects made of copper and brass, for Revere played a major role in the history of both of these metals in America. In choosing one individual craftsman in copper and brass for a short biographical sketch, Revere would appear a logical candidate but, since little could be added to the luster of his name or to the popularity of his products, a more obscure craftsman, William Bailey, has been selected.

While available data on Bailey throws some light on his business ability, facts concerning his personality must be read "between the lines." Such a procedure is a hazardous undertaking, since there is a possibility of creating an untrue image. For this reason most of the emphasis here will be placed on Bailey's business and its products, with little comment about the man. The information about the man may seem fragmentary but, even though he worked a long time ago, his career as a coppersmith has been established, his residences are known, and some of his products have been examined. As full a statement cannot be made of any other coppersmith or brass founder included in this survey, with the exception of Paul Revere.

Mr. Bailey's career started rather early for a craftsman working in the inland city of Lancaster, Pennsylvania, where trading merchandise and the social amenities were not as important as in larger port cities, such as Philadelphia and New York. His advertisement in the *Pennsylvanische Staatsbote*, July 7, 1772, stated that he was opening his shop in York, Pennsylvania, after working ten years in Lancaster for Francis Sanderson. Although this statement immediately calls attention to the earlier coppersmith, Sanderson, little has been learned about him.

The fact that Bailey worked for Sanderson for ten years before opening his shop suggests that he may have been apprenticed to Sanderson. On the other hand, another of his advertisements in the Chambersburg

WILLIAM BAILEY

Coppersmith in Yorktown

Takes this opportunity to report to all, especially his worthy customers, that he now lives right across from the shop, where he carries on coppersmithing as before. As a beginner he has completed with his own hands since last June 27th and sold 47 brew kettles, as well as wash kettles, teakettles, coffee pots, fish kettles, and other similar copperwork. In addition to this, he has worked for ten years at his craft for Francis Sanderson, in Lancaster, and therefore he will vouch for the quality of his work to everyone who wishes to favor him with their business. He will appear on every court day throughout the year in Frederickstown at Samuel Swareingain's; in Carlisle at John Poake's, for he will sell his work as cheaply as anyone in this area or the work that is brought in from Europe. Therefore he hopes to continue to enjoy the pleasure of his customers and others. He repairs all kinds of copper and brass work; he gives the best price for old copper, brass, pewter, and lead; and sells all kinds of brass kettles.   W. Bailey

Advertisement by William Bailey in the *Pennsylvanische Staatsbote,* July 7, 1772, and its English translation.

Weekly Advertiser, May 14, 1794, advised that he was opening a business for himself in Chambersburg "at the Ship, occupied for many years by his father." This statement indicates the possibility that his father was a coppersmith, that he might have been apprenticed to his father, and that later he had gone to work for Sanderson in Lancaster. Though the facts of his apprenticeship will probably remain a mystery, it is known he became a coppersmith, for ample records exist to prove it.

```
WANTED IMMEDIATELY,
      At this BOROUGH,
JOURNEYMEN COPPERSMITHS
WHO are compleat work-
      men at Stills, to whom
      18 dollars per month
will be given by the Subscri-
ber, and provided with meat,
drink, washing and lodging.
None need apply but sober
industrious persons.  Their mo-
ney shall be paid at the end of
each month.
      WILLIAM BAILEY.
York Borough, Aug. 21.
```

William Bailey's advertisement in the *Pennsylvania Herald and York General Advertiser,* Sept. 5, 1792.

His moving from Lancaster to York in 1772 is of interest because about that time Sanderson moved to Baltimore. An advertisement in the *Maryland Journal and Baltimore Advertiser,* August 20, 1773, indicated that "Francis Sanderson, Coppersmith from Lancaster, living in Gay-Street, Baltimore-Town, a few doors above Mr. Andrew Steiger's, Makes and Sells all sorts of COPPER WORK." It would seem that if one of the few coppersmiths, if not the only one, working in Lancaster was moving away, Bailey would have had little competition had he stayed. Maybe business prospects looked better in York at the time, or perhaps even then Bailey was gravitating toward Chambersburg, and York was one step closer, on the same side of the Susquehanna River.

Bailey's 1772 advertisement in the *Staatsbote* calls attention to a number of matters pertinent to coppersmithing. In the first place, the "cut" on the top of the advertisement was a teakettle, emphasizing it as one of his major products. Certainly, a man would never pay for space to show an illustration of an object he did not sell widely in the area.

The shape of the kettle is a hybrid between a European pattern and the Pennsylvania pattern that Bailey is known to have made at a later point in his career.

The second noteworthy point is that Bailey advertised in the German language. Probably other coppersmiths did the same, although none of their advertisements has come to light in making this survey. Southeastern Pennsylvania had a great many first and second generation Germans living there in Bailey's time; and he must have regarded them as prospective customers for his copperware.

This fledgling coppersmith did not advertise a wide range of products. He named only five and, rather surprisingly, he did not include stills for distilling alcohol. Earlier advertisement of other coppersmiths included stills, and Bailey must have later become a big producer of these objects for, in 1792, he placed a "want ad" in the *Pennsylvania Herald and York General Advertiser* for journeymen coppersmiths to make only stills.

For a number of reasons this advertisement is of interest. First, York was a small community in 1792 and one would think that Bailey could have personally inquired about help in making stills. Secondly, offering room and board might have been a way to attract men who had recently

William Bailey's advertisement in the *Pennsylvania Herald and York General Advertiser*, July 1, 1789.

William Bailey,

TAKES this method to inform the public in general, and his old customers in particular, that he carries on the

Copperſmith's Trade,

As uſual, in all its various branches, on as low terms as any workman of that buſineſs in America, at the following places: In the town of *York*, at his Dwelling-houſe; in *Chamberſburg*, Pennſylvania; and in *Hager's-town*, Maryland, adjoining to JACOB HARRY, Hatter, near the Court-houſe. Thoſe three ſhops are ſupplied with the *beſt workmen*, and ſtuff ſuitable for Stills of all ſizes, Brew-kettles, Waſh, Fiſh and Tea ditto; Sauce-pans; Coffee and Chocolate Pots, with ſundry other Copper Work, too tedious to mention.

The higheſt price will be given for old copper, braſs, pewter and lead. Thoſe gentlemen who are pleaſed to favor him with their cuſtom at any of the above mentioned places, may depend on being ſupplied in the beſt manner.

York, Jan. 6, 1789.

been apprentices and were accustomed to such assistance; however, few of such men would have had much experience in the making of stills. The exact connection between sobriety and working on stills is not self-evident, but Bailey made this one of the conditions for working for him.

The image of a craftsman of the eighteenth century always seems improved by the knowledge that he served in the Revolutionary War, and Bailey fits this pattern also. It is recorded in the Adjutant General's Office of the United States that Bailey was a major in Colonel Swope's Regiment, Pennsylvania Flying Camp. An account shows that he was paid for the period from September 23, 1776, to May 8, 1778, and also was allowed for depreciation of his pay the sum of £119, s. 13, d. 9. If he returned immediately to the trade of coppersmithing, that fact is well concealed, for his next advertisment to be found did not appear until 1789.

His 1789 advertisement announced that he was continuing the business of coppersmithing in York and that he had branches in Chambers-

William Bailey, COPPERSMITH, Of the Borough of York,

TAKES this method to inform the public in general, and his numerous customers in particular, that he carries on the Coppersmith business in all its various branches as usual, at his dwelling house opposite to Mr. Andrew Johnston's Tavern, Sign of the Bear and Cub.— at Chambersburgh under the direction of his son William,—at Hager's Town, next door to Mr. Jacob Harry, Hatter, in Partnership with his Son-in-law, Mr. William Reynolds,—and at Frederick Town, near the Poor House, in Partnership with his Brother-in-law, Mr. Robert M'Cully. Notwithstanding the scarcity of Copper, those four shops are completely supplyed with it, suitable for all kinds of Copper work, and in particular Stills of all sizes, Brewing, Coppers, Wash, Fish, and Tea Kettles, Sauce Pans, Coffee and Chocolate Pots. He has complete workmen in each shop, regularly bred to the business, as many of them have been taught by himself. He also carries on the Tin-plate business in all its various branches, in each of the above mentioned places, and will attend on Wednesday and Thursday, in every quarterly Court week, at Mr. Thomas Foster's Tavern, in the Borough of Carlisle, in order to save those of his customers trouble and expence, who wish to agree for Copper or Tin-ware. The highest price will be given for old Copper, Brass, Pewter and Lead at each shop.

He returns his sincere thanks to all his former customers, and hopes the continuance of their favors.

July 24.

William Bailey's advertisement in the *Pennsylvania Herald and York General Advertiser*, July 25, 1792.

burg, Pennsylvania, and Hagerstown, Maryland. He pointed out that his products were as cheap as any made in America and all customers could depend on being supplied in the best manner. It was customary for craftsmen to point with pride to their products, but Bailey seems to have emphasized quality more than most.

His next advertisement appeared in the *Pennsylvania Herald and York General Advertiser* on July 25, 1792. Bailey again mentioned that he was continuing his business of coppersmithing in York, but that he was expanding the "chain-stores," for, in addition to his shops in Chambersburg and Hagerstown, he had started another shop in "Frederick Town" (Maryland). This idea of multiple outlets for his products is probably unique in America in the eighteenth century. They are evidence of Bailey's ability as a craftsman and of his vision and ingenuity in promoting trade.

Another item learned from this last advertisement was the involvement of his family in his various business ventures. Establishing a business was not an easy matter in the eighteenth century and when branches were added, it was only logical to man them with relatives, thereby keeping the profits of the business within the family. Bailey probably continued to manage his shop in York; but at Chambersburg the shop was in charge of his son William; at Hagerstown he was in partnership with his son-in-law, William Reynolds; and in Frederick Town his partner was his brother-in-law, Robert McCully. In addition, Bailey could be found at Mr. Foster's Tavern in Carlisle on "Wednesday and Thursday in every quarterly Court Week."

Possibly the most important announcement in his 1792 advertisement was that he had recently added tinsmithing to his work in copper. This combination was not unique with Bailey for many coppersmiths combined the two trades. Tinplate was cheaper than copper and could be used to fabricate many of the objects previously made of copper. Few, if any, new tools were required to work tinplate and the new combination of Bailey's was a smart move in promoting new business.

In 1793, his roving feet got the best of him, for his advertisement in *The Pennsylvania Herald and York General Advertiser*, June 1 of that year, announced that he had moved to Baltimore. There he operated shops at two locations, while still continuing to transact business in

WILLIAM BAILEY,

COPPER-SMITH AND TIN-PLATE WORKER,

TAKES this method to inform the public and his cuftomers in particular, that he has removed from the Borough of York, in the ftate of Pennfylvania, to Market ftreet in the Town of Baltimore, ftate of Maryland, next door to Mr. George Reinecker's, near Congrefs Hall, where he carries on the Copperfmith and Tin plate bufinefs in all their various branches—alfo, in Calvert's-ftreet near the County wharf: In Hager's Town, Frederick Town and Chamberfburg, as ufual; where any perfon or perfons may be fupplied with the following articles, viz. Stills of all fizes; brewing kettles, fifh and wafhing ditto; fauce pans; coffee and chocolate pots, and all other fort of copper and tin ware too tedious to mention; all of which he will fell on as low terms as any workman on the continent, of equal quality.

He flatters himfelf, from the long experience in bufinefs, that thofe who are not particularly acquainted with his work, and fhould ftand in need of fuch, will find it their intereft to become his cuftomers. He will conftantly keep ftills and wafhing kettles at Mr. Philip Goffler's, in York Town, at the fign of the Buck, the houfe he formerly lived in, on as low terms as any of the fame quality made by workmen, ftamped with his name and warranted to be good. He gives the higheft price for old copper, brafs, pewter and lead, at each of the abovementioned places—and returns his fincere thanks to his cuftomers, and hopes for a continuance of their particular favors, which he has fo long experienced.

Baltimore, June 1.

William Bailey's advertisement in the *Pennsylvania Herald and York General Advertiser,* June 1, 1793.

York, Hagerstown, Frederick Town, and Chambersburg. His advertisement showed maturity and confidence in his business, for he asserted that his workmen were as good as any on the Continent and that he sold his products for as low terms as any man in the trade. His most interesting comment in this advertisement, however, was that he

> will constantly keep stills and washing kettles at Mr. Philip Gossler's, in York Town, at the sign of the Buck, the house he formerly lived in, on as low terms as any of the same quality made by workmen, stamped with his name and warranted to be good.

His mention of products stamped with his name is an uncommon comment to make in an advertisement. It is particularly fortunate that a few of Bailey's products bearing his stamp have been found, confirming his assertion.

In the Hall of Records, Annapolis, Maryland, Book 19, folio 173, dated January 2, 1797, contains an inventory of the senior William Bailey's possessions at the time of his death. Among his possessions were two "Dutch Servants," Isaac Strickler and Samuel Michael, an "Irish Girl," Cath^e Ryan, and one "Male Negro," Joseph Reynolds. Under a separate heading is listed a great deal of copper and tinware.

In looking back over Bailey's life it is easy to see that he was an unusually ambitious businessman. He mentioned in one of his advertisements that "despite the fact sheet copper was a scarce commodity, he had ample supplies at his shops." He proudly stated that his workmen were good, for he had trained them himself.

Partial intestate listing of the "Goods & Chattels" of William Bailey. Most of the household items have been omitted but the "Copper & tin Ware" list is complete. He made many items, such as "cullenders" (colanders), speaking trumpets, and pudding pans.

courtesy Hall of Records, Annapolis, Md.

3 Small ditto —					0 15 0
3 Large Speaking Trumpets —					0 7 6
3 Small ditto —					0 3 9
4 twelve pound Cannisters —					1 10 0
2 Six pound ditto —					0 15 0
1 Eight pound ditto —					0 5 0
2 Gall Measures —					0 7 6
60 Stems of Candle Moles —					0 5 0
4 pudding pans —					0 5 0
1 Doz Tender Boxes —					0 7 6
2 Doz Tin Cups —					0 11 3
4 Sugar Scoops —					0 7 6

Bailey apparently never left his bench to become solely a merchant. After the Revolution, when merchandise was easily available from England, many craftsmen who had been producing coppersmiths turned to importing and engaged only in retail trade. Although such a procedure would not have been particularly easy in York, it certainly would have been in the port city of Baltimore.

Bailey must have been astute in transacting business. His advertisements suggest that he was constantly prospering; that he could operate two shops in Baltimore simultaneously speaks well for his business acumen. His move to Baltimore was probably a smart maneuver because Baltimore was becoming a seaport of importance, and was an unusually good spot to establish a business. Its attraction to a coppersmith might also be that facilities for producing the metal were there, or nearby, and if the metal were not cheaper there, at least it was convenient to get it.

The trend from Pennsylvania to Maryland was marked. Peacock Bigger, a coppersmith in Philadelphia, moved to Charlestown; Philip Syng, a brass founder from Philadelphia, moved to Annapolis; and Francis Sanderson, as noted earlier, moved from Lancaster to Baltimore. There must have been some sound reasons for such migration, and Bailey probably understood all of them. Unfortunately, nothing is known about his son William, who also was a coppersmith. A thorough search of records at Chambersburg might disclose interesting data, not only about his son, but also his father who had lived and worked there.

Only teakettles and one saucepan made and marked by Bailey are known to exist today. It is hoped that other objects "stamped with his name" will be found by people who read this account.

VI. Documented List of Coppersmiths

Name	Residence	Date Working
Adams, David	York, Pa.	1783
Allen, Caleb	Providence, R.I.	1774
Anderson, T.	St. Louis, Mo.	1837
Andrews, T. & W.	Franklin, Mo.	1819
Apple, Jacob	Philadelphia, Pa.	1852
Apple, Philip	West Chester, Pa.	1826
Apple, Philip	Philadelphia, Pa.	1826
Apthorp, Stephen	Boston, Mass.	1742
Arnold, A. H.	Lancaster, Ohio	1826
Attlee, William	Lancaster, Pa.	1795
Audain, H.	New Orleans, La.	1842
Babb, John	Reading, Pa.	1816
Babb, Mathias	Reading, Pa.	1796
Babb, Samuel	Reading, Pa.	1818
Bailey, Robert	Cleveland, Ohio	1837
Bailey, William	York, Pa.	1792
Bailey, William	Baltimore, Md.	1796
Bailey & Clemm	Baltimore, Md.	1784
Baker, John	Boston, Mass.	1685
Baker, John	Brooklyn, N.Y.	1829
Baker, John	New York, N.Y.	1831
Ball, William	Philadelphia, Pa.	1729
Barker, Walter	New York, N.Y.	1831
Barnett, Thos.	St. Louis, Mo.	1831

Name	Residence	Date Working
Barnett & Ivers	St. Louis, Mo.	1832
Bartholomew, Roswell	Hartford, Conn.	1828
Barton, William	Lancaster, Pa.	1830–1843
Bates, John H.	Cincinnati, Ohio	1846
Beader, Henry	Harrisburg, Pa.	1826
Beebe, Martin	New York, N.Y.	1831
Belcher, Joseph	Newport, R.I.	
Benson, Frederick	Baltimore, Md.	1815, 1831
Benson, John	New York, N.Y.	1831
Bentley, John	Philadelphia, Pa.	1852
Bentzell, Frederick	Baltimore, Md.	1831
Bigger, Peacock	Philadelphia, Pa.	1737
Bigger, Peacock	Annapolis, Md.	1752
Billings, William	Providence, R.I.	b. 1763–d. 1813
Bintzel, Daniel	Philadelphia, Pa.	1852
Bintzel, William	Philadelphia, Pa.	1852
Birckhead, E., & Utzman	Easton, Pa.	1824
Black, James	Philadelphia, Pa.	1800
Blanc, Victor	Cincinnati, Ohio	1846
Boardman, William	Baltimore, Md.	1814
Bonner, Hugh	Cincinnati, Ohio	1840
Booth, Henry	Antrim Twp.,	
Bousore, George	Franklin Co., Pa.	1821
	Philadelphia, Pa.	1785
Bradby, Thomas	Philadelphia, Pa.	1800
Bradley, Keighler	Reading, Pa.	1813
Bratzman, Andreas	Salisbury, N.C.	1839
Brillhart, Samuel	Cochoton, Ohio	1820
Bronson, Edward M.	Charlotte, N.C.	1824
Brotherton, E.	Lancaster, Pa.	1806
Brown, Thomas	Philadelphia, Pa.	1852
Bruce, John	Baltimore, Md.	1850
Buchanan, James	Pittsburgh, Pa.	1818
Burd, Tilden & Co.	St. Louis, Mo.	1836
Burker, Henry	Reading, Pa.	1856
Burker, Lewis & Co.	New Orleans, La.	1842
Burkhard, Peter	New York, N.Y.	1841
Busy, John	Baltimore, Md.	1831

Name	Residence	Date Working
Camwrey, S. S.	New Orleans, La.	1842
Carnes, John	Boston, Mass.	b. 1698–d. 1760
Carpenter, Alfred	Boston, Mass.	1848
Carter, John	Boston, Mass.	1848
Cassidy, Hugh	Xenia, Ohio	1830
Cathcart, Whilhelm	Reading, Pa.	1819
Cathcart, William	Lancaster, Pa.	1816
Chandler, Philip	Rutherfordton, N.C.	1836
Chessen, George	Philadelphia, Pa.	1811
Chevalier, Francois	New Orleans, La.	1822
Christ, John	Reading, Pa.	1798
Clark, Forbes	Harrisburg, Pa.	1814–20
Clark, John	Boston, Mass.	1789
Clark, Thomas	Boston, Mass.	1720
Clemm & Bailey	Baltimore, Md.	1784
Clippinger, George	Antrim Twp., Franklin Co., Pa.	1821
Clough, Enoch	Cincinnati, Ohio	1846
Clough, John	Boston, Mass.	1789
Coleman, Henry	St. Louis, Mo.	1829
Collier, Richard	Providence, R.I.	1763
Coltman, J. W.	Boston, Mass.	1848
Compaire, Cladius	S.C.	
Cook, John	Philadelphia, Pa.	1800–1811
Cooke, J.	Cuyahoga Falls, Pa.	1837
Cordwell, William	Boston, Mass.	1789
Corne, Anthony	S.C.	1735
Crabb & Minshall	Baltimore, Md.	1790
Creagh, Patrick	Annapolis, Md.	1752
Cropley, John	Philadelphia, Pa.	1852
Crowell, Peter	Lancaster, Pa.	1816
Cummings, William	Philadelphia, Pa.	1785–1800
Cunningham, William	New York, N.Y.	1831
Curry, James	Philadelphia, Pa.	1795
Darby, Thomas	New York, N.Y.	1831
Darby, William	New York, N.Y.	1841
Dash, John B.	New York, N.Y.	1786

Name	Residence	Date Working
Davis, Edward	New York, N.Y.	1831
Davis & Wiley	Pittsburgh, Pa.	1837
Dawson, R. M.	Pittsburgh, Pa.	1837
Deckebach, Henry	Cincinnati, Ohio	1846
Deemer, Andrew	Chicolothe, Ohio	1816
DeHaven, Abraham	Cannonsburg, Pa.	1796
Dehuff, Abraham	Baltimore, Md.	1814
Dehuff, Henry	Lancaster, Pa.	1816
Delancy, John	Carlisle, Pa.	1796
Delch, John	Philadelphia, Pa.	1840
Deverter, William	Lancaster, Pa.	1869
Dickenbaugh, Henry	Cincinnati, Ohio	1850
Dickey, Isaiah	Pittsburgh, Pa.	1837
Dickey & Co.	Maryland & Pennsylvania	1770–1880
Dickey, Robert	Pittsburgh, Pa.	1837
Dickinson & Stewart	Detroit, Mich.	1837
Diller, S.	Lancaster, Pa.	1848
Diller, Samuel	Lancaster, Pa.	1869
Doffen, John M.	Fayetteville, N.C.	1822
Doughly, Robert	Philadelphia, Pa.	1800
Doughty, Albert	New York, N.Y.	1831
Dove, George	New York, N.Y.	1831
Dowling, John	St. Louis, Mo.	1816
Drowne, Shem	Boston, Mass.	1720
Dubuo, Francois	New Orleans, La.	1822
Dufau, Guillaume	New Orleans, La.	1842
Dunn & John & Sons	New York, N.Y.	1831
Durr, Jacob	Philadelphia, Pa.	1800
Dusenbury, Thomas	New York, N.Y.	1841
Eddy, Orson	Detroit, Mich.	1837
Eggleston & Bass	Fayetteville, N.C.	1807
Eichell, William	New York, N.Y.	1831
Eicholtz, Jacob	Lancaster, Pa.	1821
Eicholtz, George & Jacob	Lancaster, Pa.	1802
Eisenhart, John	Baltimore, Md.	1814
Elder, Francis	Baltimore, Md.	1831

Name	Residence	Date Working
Eisenhut, Andrew	Philadelphia, Pa.	1800
Eisenhut, John	Philadelphia, Pa.	1811
Etter, Jacob	Lancaster, Pa.	1843
Fahs, Tobias	York County, Pa.	1833
Fisher, Charles	York, Pa.	1832
Flagg, David	Boston, Mass.	1748
Flagg, Theodore	Buffalo, N.Y.	1836
Fleming, Robert	Cincinnati, Ohio	1846
Foos, Jacob	Lancaster, Pa.	1869
Fordney, John	Lancaster, Pa.	1843
Forrest, Jacob	Lancaster, Pa.	1869
Foster, Thomas	Boston, Mass.	1739
Frailey, Benjamin	Lancaster, Pa.	1830
Freeston, Robert	Smyrna, Del.	1858
Frettis, Andrew	New Orleans, La.	1842
Gable, ———	Carrolton County, Ohio	1830
Gable, Jacob	Lancaster, Pa.	1843
Gallagher, Miles	Philadelphia, Pa.	1800
Gallagher, P.	Boston, Mass.	1848
Garrigan, John	Cincinnati, Ohio	1846
Gaw, Chambers	York, Pa.	1790
Gaw, Gilbert	Philadelphia, Pa.	1800
Gay, Martin	Boston, Mass.	1800
Geddes, Adam	Washington, D.C.	1827
Geddes, James	Baltimore, Md.	1831
Gemperling, D. D.	Lancaster, Pa.	1848
Genter, John	New York, N.Y.	1750
Gerber, P.	Lancaster, Pa.	1848
Getz, George	Lancaster, Pa.	1843
Getz, John	Lancaster, Pa.	1817
Getz, Peter	Lancaster, Pa.	1843
Gilaspie, Charles	Peters Twp., Franklin Co., Pa.	1807
Gontz, Joseph	New Orleans, La.	1842
Gormly & M'Millin	Pittsburgh, Pa.	1837

Name	Residence	Date Working
Gould, Joseph	Boston, Mass.	1848
Graff, Joseph	Philadelphia, Pa.	1852
Graham, Francis	Philadelphia, Pa.	1800
Graham, ——	New York, N.Y.	1787
Grauel, Daniel	Philadelphia, Pa.	1811
Grauel, Daniel	New Orleans, La.	1822
Greenleaf & Halden	Boston, Mass.	1789
Griggs, Joseph	New York, N.Y.	1765
Grimes, James	Pittsburgh, Pa.	1837
Haffman, Lewis	Cincinnati, Ohio	1846
Haldane, James	Philadelphia, Pa.	1765
Halden, John	New York, N.Y.	1744
Hamlin, Samuel	Providence, R.I.	b. 1746–d. 1801
Hammersly, Thomas	Baltimore, Md.	1796
Hammett, C. Hiles	Philadelphia, Pa.	1840
Hammond, William	Baltimore, Md.	1780
Hamsher, (Widow)	Pittsburgh, Pa.	1812
Hannah & Lawny	New York, N.Y.	1842
Harberger, Henry	Philadelphia, Pa.	1811
Harbeson, Benjamin	Philadelphia, Pa.	1765
Harbeson, Benjamin & Son	Philadelphia, Pa.	1800
Harbeson, Joseph	Philadelphia, Pa.	1800
Harbeson, Joseph	Pittsburgh, Pa.	1807–1810
Harley, Francis	Philadelphia, Pa.	1840
Harley, G. & F.	Philadelphia, Pa.	1811
Harrocks, James R.	Cincinnati, Ohio	1846
Hasler, John	New York, N.Y.	1841
Heisler, B. R.	Wilmington, Del.	1859
Heiss, Goddard	Philadelphia, Pa.	1852
Heiss, William, Jr.	Philadelphia, Pa.	1852
Heller, Henry	Philadelphia, Pa.	1840
Helmuth, Alexander	Philadelphia, Pa.	1800
Hemmenway, B.	Boston, Mass.	1848
Henry, Alexander	Philadelphia, Pa.	1800
Henry, Jack	Pittsburgh, Pa.	1815
Henry, Robert	Lancaster, Pa.	1803
Henry, William	Philadelphia, Pa.	1800
Henshaw & Hamlin	Hartford, Conn.	1767

Name	Residence	Date Working
Heslet, Samuel	Baltimore, Md.	1774
Hey, Aaron	Cincinnati, Ohio	1846
Heyser, Jacob	Peters Twp., Franklin Co., Pa.	1821
Hidel, Frank	Buffalo, N.Y.	1836
Hill & Chamberlain	Boston, Mass.	1848
Hoffman, Jacob	Baltimore, Md.	1789
Holtry, Jeremiah	Cincinnati, Ohio	1846
Hople, Jos.	Cincinnati, Ohio	1846
Horn, John	Lancaster, Pa.	1830
Howard & Rodgers	Pittsburgh, Pa.	1837
Howard & Bartram		1767
Hubley, Fredrick	Lebanon Twp., Lebanon Co., Pa.	1796
Hubley, F.	Crawford Co., Ohio	1830
Hubley, Fredrick	Lancaster, Pa.	1780
Hubley, Samuel	Lancaster, Pa.	1802
Humbert, Andrew	Pittsburgh, Pa.	1819
Hunneman, William C.	Boston, Mass.	1821
Hunneman, William C. & Son	Boston, Mass.	1826
Hunneman, S. & W.	Boston, Mass.	1837
Hunneman & Co.	Boston, Mass.	1848
Ihling, William	Lancaster, Pa.	1843–1848
Ireland, Robert	Cincinnati, Ohio	1846
Isenhoot, Andrew	Philadelphia, Pa.	1785
Jabine & Clayton	New York, N.Y.	1831
Jack, Henry	Chillicothe, Ohio	1816
Jackson, Jonathan	Boston, Mass.	1699
James, Jeffers & Co.	Raleigh, N.C.	1817
Jewell, Charles	New York, N.Y.	1842
Johnson, Hall & Co.	Fayetteville, N.C.	1815
Johnson, John	Cumberland Co., Pa.	1807
Jones, Gershom	Providence, R.I.	1787
Keefer, J. & F.	Pittsburgh, Pa.	1837
Keiffer, C.	Lancaster, Pa.	1848
Keller & Sheriff	Pittsburgh, Pa.	1837

Name	Residence	Date Working
Kellin, Hugh	Buffalo, N.Y.	1836
Kempton, Samuel	New York, N.Y.	1781
Kepner, William	Pittsburgh, Pa.	1819
Kepner & McKnight	Pittsburgh, Pa.	1819
Kidd, John	Reading, Pa.	1796–1800
Kiersted, Jeremiah	Cincinnati, Ohio	1819
Kirck, Henrt T.	Albany, N.Y.	1817
Kirsted, Hezekiah	Cincinnati, Ohio	1846
Knox, Edward	New York, N.Y.	1842
Kower, John	Kutztown, Pa.	1841
Krause, Franklin	Bethlehem, Pa.	1860
Krieder, Daniel	Lancaster, Ohio	1817
Lacker, Joseph	Cincinnati, Ohio	1845
Lackey, Edward	Reading, Pa.	1798
Lawrence, William B.	Cincinnati, Ohio	1846
Lawson, F. & Bro.	Cincinnati, Ohio	1846
Leacock, William	Philadelphia, Pa.	1840
Lechler, F.	New Castle, Del.	1859
Lee, William	Philadelphia, Pa.	1852
LeFrentz, George	York, Pa.	1783–1800
Lehman, B. E.	Pine Grove, Lebanon Co., Pa.	1860
Levan, Jacob	Reading, Pa.	1817
Levibell, J.	New Orleans, La.	1842
Levy & Smithy	New Orleans, La.	1842
Lightbody, Collin	New York, N. Y.	1841
Lindsay, David	Carlisle, Pa.	1792
Long & Smith	New Orleans, La.	1842
Loring, A. B.	Boston, Mass.	1848
Loring, John G.	Boston, Mass.	1848
Lowry, John	Easton, Pa.	1824
Lyne, John	Harrisburg, Pa.	1814
Luckenback, William	Bethlehem, Pa.	1825
Lyne, Robert	Philadelphia, Pa.	1800
McBride, ———	York County, Pa.	1783
McBride, ———	Harrisburg, Pa.	1811
M'calmond, James	York, Pa.	1793

Name	Residence	Date Working
M'Cauley, John	Philadelphia, Pa.	1790–1800
McKim, ———	Baltimore, Md.	1831
McCoy, Neil	York County, Pa.	1784
M'Cullion, John	Hartford, Conn.	1828
Malbreau, Anthony	Philadelphia, Pa.	1800
Maphis, Clement	New Orleans, La.	1842
Maras, J. M.	New Orleans, La.	1842
Martine, James	Cumberland Co., N.C.	1826
Marveau, ———	Philadelphia, Pa.	1800
Mears, John	Cincinnati, Ohio	1819
Mears & Horne	Cincinnati, Ohio	1819
Megee, George	Philadelphia, Pa.	1852
Mengel, S. & Son	Reading, Pa.	1868
Meyers, Ashmore	Philadelphia, Pa.	1785
Miller, August	Cincinnati, Ohio	1846
Miller, Jacob	Harrisburg, Pa.	1820
Miltenberger, George	Pittsburgh, Pa.	1811
Minshall, Thomas	Middletown, Pa.	1802
Minshall, ———	Baltimore, Md.	1782
Morehead, J. M.	Greensboro, N.C.	1829
Morrison, Hugh	Xema, Ohio	1830
Morrison, John	Philadelphia, Pa.	1790
Nailer, John	Philadelphia, Pa.	1785
Neal & Ligett	St. Louis, Mo.	1819
Neal, Reubin	St. Louis, Mo.	1817
Noble, James	Philadelphia, Pa.	1840
Oat, George	Philadelphia, Pa.	1852
Oat, Israel	Philadelphia, Pa.	1852
Oat, Jesse	Philadelphia, Pa.	1800
Oat, Joseph	Philadelphia, Pa.	1840
Oat, Joseph & Son	Philadelphia, Pa.	1852
O'Bryon, Benjamin	Philadelphia, Pa.	1840
O'Neil, Robert	Philadelphia, Pa.	1825
Orr, Robert	Philadelphia, Pa.	1800
Orr, Thomas	Chillicothe, Ohio	1808
Oxland, William	Cincinnati, Ohio	1846

Name	Residence	Date Working
Pascal, Frederick	New Orleans, La.	1822
Patterson, Lewis	Ravena, Ohio	1829
Peterman, John	Lancaster, Pa.	1830
Peters & Co.	Philadelphia, Pa.	1811
Peterson, L. & P. Co.	Pittsburgh, Pa.	1837
Pier, Benjamin	New York, N.Y.	1842
Potter, James	Philadelphia, Pa.	1790
Pratt, George	Buffalo, N.Y.	1836
Prentis, Cyrus	Ravena, Ohio	1841
Price, David	Fayetteville, N.C.	1806
Price, Jacob	Reading, Pa.	1836
Raborg, Christopher	Baltimore, Md.	1785
Raisin, George	Boston, Mass.	1727
Read, W.	Philadelphia, Pa.	1840
Ream, Davis B.	Reading, Pa.	1867
Reed, George	Winchester, Virginia	1796
Reed, Robert	Lancaster, Pa.	1795
Reeder, Francis H.	Raleigh, N. C.	1821
Reich, Br. Chr.	Salem, N. C.	1800
Reich, Jacob	Stokes Co., N. C.	1832
Reifsnyder, Junas	Baumstown, Pa.	1860
Reigart, Henry	Lancaster, Pa.	1803
Reilly, Charles	Philadelphia, Pa.	1800
Resor, Jacob	Cincinnati, Ohio	1819
Reynolds, Joel, & Co.	Hillsboro, N. C.	1823
Reynolds & Turner	Hillsboro, N. C.	1829
Richmond, A. D.	New Bedford, Mass.	1840–60
Rink, Miller H.	Philadelphia, Pa.	1840
Roberts, Israel	Philadelphia, Pa.	1800
Roberts, James	Philadelphia, Pa.	1852
Roberts, John	Orange Co., N. C.	1817
Roberts & Lyne	Philadelphia, Pa.	1800
Roberts & Son	Philadelphia, Pa.	1840
Robson, W. & G. W.	Cincinnati, Ohio	1846
Rogers, G.	Lancaster, Pa.	1848
Rulon, Jane	Philadelphia, Pa.	1852
Rulon, William	Philadelphia, Pa.	1852

Name	*Residence*	*Date Working*
Rutherford, ————	Raleigh, N. C.	1812
Sanderson, Francis	Baltimore, Md.	1773
Sauter, John	Boston, Mass.	1662
Scaife, W. B. & W.	Pittsburgh, Pa.	1837
Schaum, Benjamin	Lancaster, Pa.	1792
Schaum, Peter	Lancaster, Pa.	1790
Schaum, Philip	Lancaster, Pa.	1792
Schlosser, George	York, Pa.	1856
Schlosser, Perry D.	York, Pa.	1856
Schoenfelder, John	Reading, Pa.	1813
Schwing, Jacob	Cincinnati, Ohio	1817
Scott, Horatio	Washington, D.C.	1827
Seffron, George	York, Pa.	1789
Seymour, Friend	Hartford, Conn.	1799
Sharp, William	Cadiz, Ohio	1830
Shaw, John D.	Buffalo, N. Y.	1836
Shenfelder, Asop	Reading, Pa.	1838
Sheppall, H.	Cincinnati, Ohio	1846
Sheriff, Adam & John	Pittsburgh, Pa.	1815
Shrimpton, Henry	Boston, Mass.	1681
Shrimpton, Jonathan	Boston, Mass.	1668
Simmes & Wallace	Baltimore, Md.	1831
Shuler, George	Middletown, Pa.	1803
Shuford, Thos. R.	Lincoln Co., N.C.	1830
Sidler, Jacob	Baltimore, Md.	1814
Simmons, John	Philadelphia, Pa.	1852
Smith, Edward	New York, N.Y.	1793
Smith, John	New York, N.Y.	1769
Smith, P.	Pine Grove, Pa.	1860
Smith & Ream	New Holland, Pa.	1829
Smith, Thomas	Lincoln Co., N.C.	1818
Smull, David	Baltimore, Md.	1831
Smith, Thomas	Boston, Mass.	1725
Snyder, Peter	Swatara Twp., Pa.	1820
Soutier, Anthony	New Orleans, La.	1842
Stafford, Spencer	Albany, N.Y.	1772
Stafford & Whitney	Albany, N.Y.	1816

VII. Documented List of Brass Founders

Name	Residence	Date Working
Addams, Samuel	Cincinnati, Ohio	1846
Aems, Peter	New York, N.Y.	1831
Allen, John	New York, N.Y.	1831
Allison, Samuel	New York, N.Y.	1831
Anderson, Robt.	Baltimore, Md.	1831
Ashford, Stephen	Philadelphia, Pa.	1852
Aspinwall, Lewis	Albany, N.Y.	1816
Auld, Henry	New York, N.Y.	1842
Atches, Robert	Philadelphia, Pa.	1796
Austin, John	Philadelphia, Pa.	1852
Badger, William	Boston, Mass.	1800
Bailey, John	New York, N.Y.	1798
Bailey & Hedderly	New York, N.Y.	1794
Baker, J.	New York, N.Y.	1797
Baragar, John	New York, N.Y.	1831
Bard, James	New York, N.Y.	1842
Batcheleder, James	New York, N.Y.	1831
Beckerton, Thomas	New York, N.Y.	1831
Belden, Amos	New York, N.Y.	1842
Bell, William M.	New Orleans, La.	1842
Betts & Seal	Wilmington, Del.	1860
Bolton & Grew	Boston, Mass.	1796
Booth, Joseph	New York, N.Y.	1832
Bordeaux, Antoine	New Orleans, La.	1822
Bossler, Joseph	Philadelphia, Pa.	1794

274

Name	Residence	Date Working
Bossler, Joseph & John	Philadelphia, Pa.	1797–1799
Boyer, Joseph	Philadelphia, Pa.	1800
Brooks, Thomas	Philadelphia, Pa.	1797–1800
Brown, E. M.	New York, N.Y.	1842
Bruce, John	New York, N.Y.	1831
Buckley, William	New York, N.Y.	1832
Bunce, Jason & Co.	Hartford, Conn.	1828
Burns, Martin	New York, N.Y.	1832
Burns, William	Easton, Pa.	1825
Byers, James	New York, N.Y.	1762
Cahoone, Henry	New York, N.Y.	1832–1842
Callahan & Murfett	New York, N.Y.	1842
Calvert, Edwin	Philadelphia, Pa.	1852
Camet, Pierre	New Orleans, La.	1822
Capron, William	Albany, N.Y.	1793
Carr, Robert	Philadelphia, Pa.	1793–1800
Carr, Robert	New York, N.Y.	1832
Carroll, Jared	Baltimore, Md.	1800
Carter, Thomas	New York, N.Y.	1831
Cater, Thomas	Boston, Mass.	1789
Caustein & Weir	Baltimore, Md.	1785
Champlain, Paris	Hartford, Conn.	1828
Chapman, Nuthill	Baltimore, Md.	1796
Clark, John	Philadelphia, Pa.	1795
Clark, John	Boston, Mass.	1800
Clarke & Co.	Philadelphia, Pa.	1789
Collindridge, William	New York, N.Y.	1831
Comfort, Martin	Philadelphia, Pa.	1795–1797
Craycroft, Samuel	New York, N.Y.	1832
Creogh, Patrick	Annapolis, Md.	1752
Cresson, James	Philadelphia, Pa.	1791
Crocker, Robert	Boston, Mass.	1800
Crover, Nathaniel	Philadelphia, Pa.	1811
Crow, George	Philadelphia, Pa.	1793
Cummings, John	Buffalo, N. Y.	1836
Curtiss, Daniel	Boston, Mass.	1852

Name	Residence	Date Working
Cutler, John	Boston, Mass.	1789
Cutts, Robert	Baltimore, Md.	1814
Davis, John	Philadelphia, Pa.	1795–1800
Davis & Saunders	Philadelphia, Pa.	1792
Davis, Solomon	Detroit, Mich.	1837
Derby, John F.	Pine Grove, Pa.	1860
Dervis & Frickett	Philadelphia, Pa.	1799
Descourdes, Louis	New York, N.Y.	1831
Dodamead, John W.	Camden, N.J.	1852
Donaldson, James	Philadelphia, Pa.	1765
Doolittle, Enos	Hartford, Conn.	1787
Doolittle, James	Hartford, Conn.	1828
Drew, Samuel	Boston, Mass.	1800
Droz, Charles	New York, N.Y.	1831
Dubree, Alexander	Philadelphia, Pa.	1852
Duff & Ivers	New York, N.Y.	1842
Dummond, William	New York, N.Y.	1832
Durand, John M.	New Orleans, La.	1822
Dy———, Timothy	Philadelphia, Pa.	1852
Eachus, Robert	Philadelphia, Pa.	1795–1800
Edwards, Joseph	Philadelphia, Pa.	1811
Edwards, Joseph	Baltimore, Md.	1831
Ehrman & Fordney	Lancaster, Pa.	1819
Ellis, James	Philadelphia, Pa.	1799
Ellis & Burley	Philadelphia, Pa.	1797
Ellsworth, Francis	New York, N.Y.	1832
Emmons, Martin	New York, N.Y.	1842
Etch, Robert	Philadelphia, Pa.	1797
Fagundas, Jacob	Philadelphia, Pa.	1811
Farrand & Gould	Newark, N.J.	1835
Farrell, Richard	Boston, Mass.	1800
Fellows, Henry	Reading, Pa.	1818
Firth, Thomas	Cincinnati, Ohio	1846
Fisher, Peter	Cincinnati, Ohio	1846
Fitzpatrick, John	Philadelphia, Pa.	1781

Name	*Residence*	*Date Working*
Force, Ephraim	New York, N.Y.	1842
Forde, Larence	Philadelphia, Pa.	1795–1799
Frazier, Levin	Baltimore, Md.	1814
Frey, John	Philadelphia, Pa.	1852
Fricke, Michael	Philadelphia, Pa.	1811
Frost, Martin	Philadelphia, Pa.	1794
Gallagher, John	Pittsburgh, Pa.	1837
Ganz, Lewis	Philadelphia, Pa.	1852
Garret & Co.	Cincinnati, Ohio	1840
Gerrish, Samuel	Portsmouth, N.H.	1821
Getz, G. H. & J.	Lancaster, Pa.	1834
Gossler, Henry	Reading, Pa.	1856
Green, Charles	Philadelphia, Pa.	1811
Green, William	Cincinnati, Ohio	1819
Gregory, Thomas	Philadelphia, Pa.	1753
Grey, Robert	Pittsburgh, Pa.	1815
Haldon, John	New York, N.Y.	1765
Hanks, George	Cincinnati, Ohio	1846
Hardenbrook, William	New York, N.Y.	1798
Hatcher, William	Philadelphia, Pa.	1852
Haynes, Henry	Newark, N.J.	1835
Headerly & Riland	Philadelphia, Pa.	1819
Heins, S.	Philadelphia, Pa.	1852
Henry, George	Philadelphia, Pa.	1769
Hent, William	Philadelphia, Pa.	1852
Hinds & W———	Baltimore, Md.	1782
Holmes, Joseph	Boston, Mass.	1841
Holmes, Robert	Boston, Mass.	1796
Homan, Augustus	W. Reading, Pa.	1860
Homes, Robert	Boston, Mass.	1789
Houghton, John	Philadelphia, Pa.	1820, 1852
Hubball, Ebenezer	Baltimore, Md.	1815
Hunt, George	Philadelphia, Pa.	1796
Hunt, John	Baltimore, Md.	1814
Hyatt, John	Philadelphia, Pa.	1723

Name	Residence	Date Working
Irele, Henry	Philadelphia, Pa.	1852
Johnston, Alexander	Pittsburgh, Pa.	1815
Keatley, James	Baltimore, Md.	1831
Keller Peter,	Harrisburg, Pa.	1807
King, Daniel	Philadelphia, Pa.	1767
King, Daniel, Jr.	Philadelphia, Pa.	1811
Kip, James	New York, N.Y.	1782
Kriner, William	Hagerstown, Md.	1828
Lapp, D. C.	Philadelphia, Pa.	1852
Lawton, Jesse	Philadelphia, Pa.	1798
Leach, Thomas	Boston, Mass.	1789
Leavenworth, Hayden, & Scovil	Waterbury, Conn.	
Leaycraft, Richard	New York, N.Y.	1782
Lee, William	Newark, N. J.	1835
Legett, Abram	Savannah, Ga.	1788
Levering, Thomas	Philadelphia, Pa.	1818
Licet, John	Philadelphia, Pa.	1744
Lillie, Thomas	Boston, Mass.	1796
Liner, Jacob & John	Philadelphia, Pa.	1811
Lisemore, John	Philadelphia, Pa.	1852
Little, Charles	Philadelphia, Pa.	1852
Litzenburger, George	Philadelphia, Pa.	1852
Lock & Cordwell	Boston, Mass.	1846
M'ckenna, James	New York, N.Y.	1842
M'Clurg, Wade & Co.	Pittsburgh, Pa.	
M'Ilwhain, Thomas	Philadelphia, Pa.	1811
M'Sherry, D. S.	St. Louis, Mo.	1836
Maxwell, James	Albany, N.Y.	1837–52
Meredith, Daniel	Philadelphia, Pa.	1776
Meredith, Jacob	Philadelphia, Pa.	1796
Mitlenberger, George	Pittsburgh, Pa.	1819
Monie, Jean B.	New Orleans, La.	1842
Montayne, Ab.	New York, N.Y.	1786
Moore, Edward	Pittsburgh, Pa.	1819

Name	*Residence*	*Date Working*
Moore, Joseph	New York, N.Y.	1842
Moore, J. & Co.	Pittsburgh, Pa.	1837
Morse & Fletcher	Boston, Mass.	1846
Moulton & Bradbury	Newburyport, Mass.	1796
Myers, Andrew	Baltimore, Md.	1814
Myers, Isaac	Reading, Pa.	1818
Myers & Fellows	Reading, Pa.	1818
Newey, John F.	Cincinnati, Ohio	1846
Nichols, James	New York, N.Y.	1842
Nisbet, John	Annapolis, Md.	1774
Norman, John	Baltimore, Md.	1814
O'Donell, John & ———	Baltimore, Md.	1791
Orr & Blair	Albany, N.Y.	1852
Overin, George	S.C.	1799
Paglan, Thomas	Philadelphia, Pa.	1717
Paris, Austin	Philadelphia, Pa.	1717
Parke, Charles	Philadelphia, Pa.	1811
Parker, Samuel	Philadelphia, Pa.	1785
Parsons, Hiram	Baltimore, Md.	1831
Powell, Samuel	Philadelphia, Pa.	1743
Proby, Jacob & Solomon	S.C.	1764
Pugh, Thomas	New York, N.Y.	1768
Raborg, Christ & Sons	Baltimore, Md.	1814
Raborg, Christ, Jr.	Baltimore, Md.	1815
Randall, John	Albany, N.Y.	1816
Rankin, William	Detroit, Mich.	1837
Redfer, Samuel	Philadelphia, Pa.	1852
Remshard, Fredrick	Philadelphia, Pa.	1852
Revere Copper Co.	Boston, Mass.	1847
Revere, Paul	Boston, Mass.	1800
Revere, Paul & Son	Boston, Mass.	1806–09
Revere, Paul & Son (Joseph)	Boston, Mass.	1813
Richard, Auguste	New Orleans, La.	1822
Richmond, George	New Bedford, Mass.	1839

Name	Residence	Date Working
Riffert, C. M.	Wilmington, Del.	1859
Robertson, John	S.C.	1760
Robinson, G. W.	Boston, Mass.	1847
Robinson, James	Philadelphia, Pa.	1795
Rodger, Thomas	Philadelphia, Pa.	1800
Rogers, Thomas	Philadelphia, Pa.	1791–1800
Row, Edward	Philadelphia, Pa.	1797
Rufus & Hopkins	New York, N.Y.	1798
Russel, James	Baltimore, Md.	1831
Scandrett, William	New York, N.Y.	1764
Sheriff, John	Pittsburgh, Pa.	1837
Sheriff & Tate	Pittsburgh, Pa.	1837
Siner, William	Philadelphia, Pa.	1852
Skellhorne, Richard	Philadelphia, Pa.	1785
Smith, James	Philadelphia, Pa.	1753
Sommerton, William	Philadelphia, Pa.	1785
Sparhawk, John	Philadelphia, Pa.	1784
Stanley, Charles	Cincinnati, Ohio	1864
Stewart & Clark	Wilmington, Del.	1859
Stotsenburg, E. C. & Son	Wilmington, Del.	1860
Stow, John	Philadelphia, Pa.	1749
Syng, Philip	Annapolis, Md.	1759
Taylor, John	New York, N.Y.	1773
Thiac, Maignan & Durand	New Orleans, La.	1822
Trickett, William	Philadelphia, Pa.	1793
Tucker, John	Cincinnati, Ohio	1864
Turner, Robert	Philadelphia, Pa.	1852
Tustion, William	Philadelphia, Pa.	1811
Van ——, Schuyler	Philadelphia, Pa.	1852
Walker, P. H.	Boston, Mass.	
Wallace & Burns	New York, N.Y.	1842
Wardell, James	Philadelphia, Pa.	1852
Warner, Benjamin	Easton, Pa.	1825
Warner, Herinemus	Philadelphia, Pa.	1791–1800

Name	Residence	Date Working
Warner, Jacob	Harrisburg, Pa.	1820
Warner, Jacob	Philadelphia, Pa.	1811
Warner, Jacob F.	New Orleans, La.	1822
Weckerly, George	Philadelphia, Pa.	1791
Wells, F. M.	South Easton, Pa.	1860
Weir, Charles	Baltimore, Md.	1788
White, Charles	New York, N.Y.	1780
Wickerly, George	Philadelphia, Pa.	1785
Wien, John, Jr.	Philadelphia, Pa.	1811
Wilkins, Jacob	New York, N.Y.	1771
Wilkinson, Peter & Co.	Baltimore, Md.	1794
Willes, William	Williamsburg, Va.	1772
Wistar, Caspar	Philadelphia, Pa.	1762
Witeman, Henry	New York, N.Y.	1750–60
Wittingham, Richard	New York, N.Y.	1795–1808
Wolf, William	Baltimore, Md.	1831
Yates, Thomas	New York, N.Y.	1759
Zweiebel, Michael	Pottsville, Pa.	1860

Bibliography

BISHOP, J. LEANDER: *A History of American Manufactures from 1608 to 1860*. Edward Young and Company; Philadelphia, 1864.

BRAND, WILLIAM FRANCIS: *Life of William Rollinson Wittingham*. E. & J. B. Young & Co.; New York, N.Y., 1886.

Brass Roots. The Scovil Manufacturing Company, 1952.

BRIGHAM, CLARENCE S.: *Paul Revere's Engravings*. American Antiquarian Society; Worcester, Mass., 1954.

CHAMBERS, E.: *Cyclopedia or, an Universal Dictionary of Arts and Sciences*. Printed for W. Innys, J. & P. Knapton, D. Browne, T. Longman, R. Hett, C. Hitch, and L. Hawes, J. Hodges, J. Shuckbruck, A. Millar, J. and J. Rivington, J. Ward, M. Senex, and the Executors of J. Darby; London, 1751.

———. *A Supplement to Chambers' Cyclopedia or Universal Dictionary of Arts and Sciences*. London, 1753.

COTTER, JOHN L. and HUDSON, J. PAUL: *New Discoveries at Jamestown*. U.S. Government Printing Office; Washington, D.C., 1957.

Encyclopedia; or, a Dictionary of Arts and Sciences, and Miscellaneous Literature. Printed by Thomas Dobson; Philadelphia, Pa., 1798.

Encyclopedia Perthensis, or Dictionary of Knowledge. Printed for C. Mitchell & Co.; Perth, Scotland, no date.

FORBES, ESTHER: *Paul Revere and the World He Lived In*. The Houghton Mifflin Company; Boston, Mass., 1942.

FULLER, CHARLES: *The Art of Coppersmithing*. David Williams; New York, 1894.

HARTE, RUFUS: *Connecticut's Iron and Copper*. New Haven, Conn., 1944. Reprinted from the 60th report of The Connecticut Society of Civil Engineers, Incorporated.

KAUFFMAN, HENRY J.: *Early American Copper, Tin, and Brass*. Medill McBride Company; New York, N.Y., 1950.

———. *The Pennsylvania-Kentucky Rifle*. The Stackpole Company; Harrisburg, Pa., 1960.

LARDNER, REV. DIONYSIUS: *The Cabinet Cyclopedia; Useful Arts—A Treatise on the Progressive Improvement and Present State of the Manufactures in Metal*. Printed for Longman, Rees, Orme, Brown, Green & Longman; and John Taylor; London, 1834.

MARTIN, THOMAS: *The Circle of the Mechanical Arts; containing Practical Treatises on the Various Manual Arts, Trades and Manufactures*. Printed for Richard Rees; London, 1813.

MOORE, RICHARD D. and HAWLEY, CYRIL H.: "The Higley Coppers, 1737-1739," in *Bulletin of the Connecticut Historical Society*, July 1955.

Newgate. The Newgate Historical Corporation.

NISBET, CLARA: "Wearing of the Bells," in *The Spinning Wheel*. Hanover, Pa., March 1965.

Pictorial Gallery of the Arts, The. The London Printing and Publishing Company, Ltd.; London and New York.

URE, ANDREW, M.D.: *A Dictionary of Arts, Manufactures, and Mines*. D. Appleton & Company; New York, N.Y., 1886.

WILLICH, A. F. M., M.D.: *The Domestic Encyclopedia; or Dictionary of Facts and Useful Knowledge*. Printed by Abram Small; Philadelphia, 1821.

YOUMAN, A. E.: *A Dictionary of Every Day Wants*. Frank M. Reed; New York, 1872.

Index

(Italic numbers refer to pages on which there are illustrations)